# REPOSITIONING
# FEMINISM
### AND
# EDUCATION

**CRITICAL STUDIES IN EDUCATION AND CULTURE SERIES**

Toward a Critical Politics of Teacher Thinking: Mapping the Postmodern
*Joe L. Kincheloe*

Building Communities of Difference: Higher Education in the Twenty-First Century
*William G. Tierney*

The Problem of Freedom in Postmodern Education
*Tomasz Szkudlarek*

Education Still under Siege: Second Edition
*Stanley Aronowitz and Henry A. Giroux*

Media Education and the (Re)Production of Culture
*David Sholle and Stan Denski*

Critical Pedagogy: An Introduction
*Barry Kanpol*

Coming Out in College: The Struggle for a Queer Identity
*Robert A. Rhoads*

Education and the Postmodern Condition
*Michael Peters, editor*

Critical Multiculturalism: Uncommon Voices in a Common Struggle
*Barry Kanpol and Peter McLaren, editors*

Beyond Liberation and Excellence: Reconstructing the Public Discourse on Education
*David E. Purpel and Svi Shapiro*

Schooling in the "Total Institution": Critical Perspectives on Prison Education
*Howard S. Davidson, editor*

Simulation, Spectacle, and the Ironies of Education Reform
*Guy Senese with Ralph Page*

# REPOSITIONING FEMINISM
# AND
# EDUCATION

## Perspectives on Educating for Social Change

*JANICE JIPSON, PETRA MUNRO,
SUSAN VICTOR, KAREN FROUDE JONES,
AND GRETCHEN FREED-ROWLAND*

*Foreword by Kathleen Weiler*

Critical Studies in Education and Culture Series
*Edited By Henry A. Giroux And Paulo Freire*

BERGIN & GARVEY
Westport, Connecticut • London

Library of Congress Cataloging-in-Publication Data

Repositioning feminism and education : perspectives on educating for
  social change / Janice Jipson ... [et al.] ; foreword by Kathleen
  Weiler.
      p.    cm.—(Critical studies in education and culture series,
  ISSN 1064–8615)
    Includes bibliographical references and index.
    ISBN 0–89789–436–7 (alk. paper).—ISBN 0–89789–437–5 (pbk. :
  alk. paper)
    1. Feminism and education.  2. Women—Education—Philosophy.
  3. Women educators.  4. Critical pedagogy.  I. Jipson, Janice.
  II. Series.
  LC197.R47  1995
  370.19′345—dc20      95–2083

British Library Cataloguing in Publication Data is available.

Library of Congress Catalog Card Number:   95–2083
ISBN: 0–89789–436–7
         0–89789–437–5 (pbk.)
ISSN:  1064–8615

First published in 1995

Bergin & Garvey, 88 Post Road West, Westport, CT 06881
An imprint of Greenwood Publishing Group, Inc.

Printed in the United States of America

The paper used in this book complies with the
Permanent Paper Standard issued by the National
Information Standards Organization (Z39.48–1984).

10  9  8  7  6  5  4  3  2  1

Copyright Acknowledgments

Chapter 5, "Speculation: Negotiating a Feminist Supervision Identity," by Petra
Munro, is a substantially revised version of a 1991 article (by Munro) entitled
"Supervision: What's Imposition Got to Do with It?" *Journal of Curriculum and
Supervision,* 7(1), 77–89.

Chapter 6, "Multiple 'I's': Dilemmas of Life-History Research," by Petra Munro,
is a revised version of a 1993 chapter (by Munro) entitled "Continuing
Dilemmas of Life History Research: A Reflexive Account of Feminist Qualitative
Inquiry." In D. Flinders and G. Mills (Eds.), *Theory and Concepts in Qualitative
Research: Perspectives from the Field* (pp. 163–178). New York: Teachers College
Press.

We offer our experiences
in recognition of the many stories yet to be told.

# CONTENTS

# SERIES FOREWORD

*Henry A. Giroux*

Within the last decade, the debate over the meaning and purpose of education has occupied the center of political and social life in the United States. Dominated largely by an aggressive and ongoing attempt by various sectors of the Right, including "fundamentalists," nationalists, and political conservatives, the debate over educational policy has been organized around a set of values and practices that take as their paradigmatic model the laws and ideology of the marketplace and the imperatives of a newly emerging cultural traditionalism. In the first instance, schooling is being redefined through a corporate ideology which stresses the primacy of choice over community, competition over cooperation, and excellence over equity. At stake here is the imperative to organize public schooling around the related practices of competition, reprivatization, standardization, and individualism.

In the second instance, the New Right has waged a cultural war against schools as part of a wider attempt to contest the emergence of new public cultures and social movements that have begun to demand that schools take seriously the imperatives of living in a multiracial and multicultural democracy. The contours of this cultural offensive are evident in the call by the Right for standardized testing, the rejection of multiculturalism, and the development of curricula around what is euphemistically called a "common culture." In this perspective, the notion of a common culture serves as a referent to denounce any attempt by subordinate groups to challenge the narrow ideological and political parameters by which such a culture both defines and expresses itself. It is not too surprising that the theoretical and political distance between cultural difference as the enemy of democratic life is relatively short indeed.

This debate is important not simply because it makes visible the role that schools play as sites of political and cultural contestation, but because it is within this debate that the notion of the United States as an open and democratic society is being questioned and redefined. Moreover, this debate provides a challenge to progressive educators both in and outside of the United States to address a number of conditions central to a postmodern world. First, public schools cannot be seen as either objective or neutral. As institutions actively involved in constructing political subjects and presupposing a vision of the future, they must be dealt with in terms that are simultaneously historical, critical, and transformative. Second, the relationship between knowledge and power in schools places undue emphasis on disciplinary structures and on individual achievement as the primary unit of value. Critical educators need a language that emphasizes how social identities are constructed within unequal relations of power in the schools and how schooling can be organized through interdisciplinary approaches to learning and cultural differences that address the dialectical and multifaceted experiences of everyday life. Third, the existing cultural transformation of American society into a multiracial and multicultural society structured in multiple relations of domination demands that we address how schools can become sites for cultural democracy rather than channeling colonies that reproduce new forms of nativism and racism. Finally, critical educators need a new language that takes seriously the relationship between democracy and the establishment of those teaching and learning conditions that enable forms of self and social determination in students and teachers. This suggests not only new forms of self-definition for human agency, but it also points to redistributing power within the school and between the school and the larger society.

*Critical Studies in Education and Culture* is intended as both a critique and a positive response to these concerns and the debates from which they emerge. Each volume is intended to address the meaning of schooling as a form of cultural politics, and cultural work as a pedagogical practice that serves to deepen and extend the possibilities of democratic public life. Broadly conceived, some central considerations present themselves as defining concerns of the Series. Within the last decade, a number of new theoretical discourses and vocabularies have emerged which challenge the narrow disciplinary boundaries and theoretical parameters that construct the traditional relationship among knowledge, power, and schooling. The emerging discourses of feminism, postcolonialism, literary studies, cultural studies, and postmodernism have broadened our understanding of how schools work as sites of containment and possibility. No longer content to view schools as objective institutions engaged in the transmission of an unproblematic cultural heritage, the new discourses illuminate how schools function as cultural sites actively engaged in the production of not only knowledge but also social identities. *Critical Studies in Education and Culture* will attempt to encourage this type of analysis by emphasizing how schools might be addressed as border institutions or sites of crossing actively involved in exploring, reworking, and translating the ways in which culture is produced, negotiated, and rewritten.

Emphasizing the centrality of politics, culture, and power, *Critical Studies in Education and Culture* will deal with pedagogical issues that contribute in novel ways to our understanding of how critical knowledge, democratic values, and social practices can provide a basis for teachers, students, and other cultural workers to redefine their role as engaged and public intellectuals.

As part of a broader attempt to rewrite and refigure the relationship between education and culture, *Critical Studies in Education and Culture* is interested in work that is interdisciplinary, critical, and addresses the emergent discourses on gender, race, sexual preference, class, ethnicity, and technology. In this respect, the Series is dedicated to opening up new discursive and public spaces for critical interventions into schools and other pedagogical sites. To accomplish this, each volume will attempt to rethink the relationship between language and experience, pedagogy and human agency, and ethics and social responsibility as part of a larger project for engaging and deepening the prospects of democratic schooling in a multiracial and multicultural society. Concerns central to this Series include addressing the political economy and deconstruction of visual, aural, and printed texts, issues of difference and multiculturalism, relationships between language and power, pedagogy as a form of cultural politics, and historical memory and the construction of identity and subjectivity.

*Critical Studies in Education and Culture* is dedicated to publishing studies that move beyond the boundaries of traditional and existing critical discourses. It is concerned with making public schooling a central expression of democratic culture. In doing so it emphasizes works that combine cultural politics, pedagogical criticism, and social analyses with self-reflective tactics that challenge and transform those configurations of power that characterize the existing system of education and other public cultures.

# FOREWORD

*Kathleen Weiler*

The past two decades have seen the development of exciting work in feminist educational thinking. In the 1970s, the second wave of the women's movement inspired works exploring the nature of sexism in education with the goal of providing equality of opportunity and treatment for girls and women in schools and universities. This work included curriculum revision aimed at redressing the absence of women either as authors or as subjects of study in academic disciplines as well as studies of classroom interactions in primary and secondary schools and universities. Underlying this work was the assumption that if sexist practices and patriarchal beliefs were pointed out, reasonable people—both women and men—would see the destructiveness and inadequacy of their thinking and would move quickly to build a truly nondiscriminatory and equal society.

By the late 1980s, though, the feminist project in education was facing serious challenges from all sides and looking decidedly more complicated. These complications were the result of both the failures and the successes of feminism. One of the strengths of the feminist vision of education, for example, was its challenge to the fundamental assumptions and power arrangements of academic disciplines. When women were made the focus of study, the whole underpinnings of disciplines were shaken. What was valuable knowledge when women's lives and activities were taken as the center, as the starting point? To what extent was the Cartesian division of the world into a dominant rationality and subordinate emotion gendered? Was abstract rationality enough? What about the hidden work done by women: caring, relational thinking, emotional work? Accepting the feminist vision meant more than welcoming women in; it meant the challenge to the unstated privileges men had held simply by virtue of being men. Much of the backlash against feminism as a form of "political correctness" can, in fact, be traced to these disquieting challenges to traditional male privilege.

If the power and strength of the feminist vision of education produced a powerful backlash against it, the weaknesses and narrowness of the original feminist vision have led to criticisms and challenges from different quarters. African American women and lesbians were critical of the assumption of early feminists that all women were white, heterosexual, middle class, and well educated. This question has continued to plague feminism. For women who are not white and middle class, "feminism" seems to present a way of understanding women's lives that does not acknowledge their own experiences. For many women, other aspects of their identities continue to be more powerful than their gender, particularly sexual and ethnic identity. While "race" may be a highly problematic concept, racism continues to be an active and powerful force in shaping society and individual experience, as does homophobia. Working-class women have found the theoretical language of feminist debate alienating, while lesbians have often found that the assumptions and concerns of heterosexual women erase their own desire. This criticism of feminism as assuming a common and unitary identity shared by all women echoes the poststructuralist emphasis on a plurality of meanings and the constant construction of identity through discourse and practices. From these perspectives, feminism itself is in danger of becoming a disciplinary discourse, fixing people in place, demanding a single "true" interpretation of their lives. In the face of these complexities, feminism has fragmented into "feminisms."

Feminist debates over theory are conducted in the important world of ideas. Feminist educators, however, are concerned not only with theory, but also with practice. This book is an account of an attempt to fuse the concerns of feminist theory with political work in the world. It is a multivoiced narrative of the process of collaboration among five women educators who describe their collective and individual attempts to work as educators for social change without imposing a rigid and disciplinary set of values on their students and colleagues. These women met together in a study and research group for over five years in what they call "a political act of coalition-building among women" and "an act of imaginative resistance." This process of coalition building was not smooth: while they shared a commitment to work together, they were also divided by differences—of ethnicity, location in academia (one was a professor, the other four graduate students) and even an understanding of what feminism meant and whether they could embrace the term. Unlike philosophers, these women were engaged in practice; they worked in programs for adolescent mothers, created curricula for multicultural summer programs, taught children whose lives are being stunted by a mean-spirited, racist, and class-divided society. They attempted to mediate the world of abstract theory and the tension-filled classrooms of student teachers who want to become humane teachers in an inhumane world. It is their respect for their own differences and the honesty with which they write that makes this such a rich text. In Parts I and III of the book, each of the five presents a personal narrative of her own research and work in education, particularly around the difficult question of imposition. In Parts II and IV, they reflect upon the process of group collaboration and its impact on their lives and scholarship. The authors speak of this text as "testimony." They write: "We can only offer our interpretations of our work and our willingness to listen." The concept of testimony captures the power and value of this book very well. It is testimony to these women's engagement with issues central to the feminist project in education: the difficulties of collaboration, the dangers of imposition, the power of difference, the need to engage in political struggle, and the meaning of feminism itself.

A major theme throughout these testimonies is the goal of true collaboration, both among themselves in their study/research group and in their own individual research projects. These authors reflect on their initial optimistic assumptions about collaboration and the difficulties of the task they set for themselves. As Petra Munro comments: "I am more cautious about naming the process collaborative or even suggesting that the research process can ever truly be collaborative." Like other authors here, Munro comes to see that "The dilemmas discussed here present no easy resolutions, if, in fact, there are solutions at all. The questions of representation, self-reflexivity, and subjectivity in the collaborative process are ongoing questions." As these accounts document so vividly, it is extremely difficult for people to collaborate in a society that is fundamentally organized to make them compete. Thus, while feminism includes collaboration and equality as important goals, when women attempt to put these ideals into practice, they are faced with their own socially created sense of competition and struggle with the "inherently unequal and potentially exploitative" nature of authority in schools and universities as in other sites. One of the strengths of this book is the honesty with which the authors face this issue. As they comment, "Dissonance, rather than consensus, emerged as being essential to the collaborative process." In struggling with the possibilities of collaboration in a society that so encourages selfishness and competition, they provide testimony of the inevitable difficulties facing any of us if we undertake a utopian project in the best sense.

A second theme running through both sections of this book is a concern with imposition. Each of these women is politically committed (although not always to the label of feminism) and all are concerned about the possibility that their own political or pedagogical beliefs might themselves become disciplinary or silencing of the voices of others. Petra Munro notes the need to negotiate "the contradictions inherent in maintaining a feminist perspective with the goal of social change while at the same time respecting the rights of others to construct their own knowledge." Susan Victor sees this problem in her work with adolescent mothers, trying to work with them around the immediate problems they face without imposing a disciplining conception of what they ought to do and what they ought to feel. Gretchen Freed-Rowland recounts similar experiences in her work with student teachers, "In reality, I cannot be a dispenser of information—only a sharer of my lore, a teller of my stories. From my cultural perspective, it is inappropriate to speak for anyone else, to be an expert, yet this is what the academy, and society at large expect of us." Karen Froude Jones works with these concerns in her collaborative life history and multicultural curriculum with teachers. She points out that "we need to recognize that collaboration and process are about relationships and trust." On the other hand, these authors also explore the possibility that an exaggerated concern with imposition may be condescending to others. Are teachers really so powerful? Are students so impressionable and passive? This is similar to Janice Jipson's critical insight about the maternal metaphor of teaching put forward by some feminist educators: if the teacher is a mother, then are students defined as children, thus "denying them their agency and differences from me."

Connected to the issue of imposition is the powerful issue of difference. This book raises the question of how women can learn to work together while respecting difference. This issue, which has been at the forefront of feminist theory and practice for over twenty years, has produced both dissonance and a creative tension within feminist thought. As these authors caution us, if the question of difference is not addressed, feminism becomes a dead, rigid set of prescriptions that comes to exclude women rather than provide a starting place for the creation of new knowledge and the basis for political action. The problem has been finding a way to work together politically in a patriarchal and class-based educational system intended to silence. Although this group began with a theoretical rejection of the idea of conformity or sameness, nonetheless, differences among these women clearly created tensions. Janice Jipson notes how her "happy illusion" of a shared reality was shattered by the power of difference. The five women responded to these tensions by focusing on a shared political commitment to social and educational change, accepting that this commitment was framed in different ways for each of them. The imagined unitary and fixed identity of "woman" was not enough. These accounts document the significance of other ways of being positioned—as Jewish, as Native American, as middle class, as working class. As Gretchen Freed-Rowland, who identifies herself as an Ojibwa-Winnebago woman, comments: "My life's experience has been one of being in several realities and struggling for some kind of balance." If progressive political change is to occur, these women suggest, we must acknowledge individual identity and difference, while maintaining a commitment to shared political goals and a tolerance of ambiguity and conflict.

A final powerful issue raised by these accounts is the significance of politics and the need to analyze institutional power. In our absorption with the seductive world of theory, it is sometimes hard to keep in mind that we are always engaged in ongoing struggles over resources and meanings. These women were all associated with the Division of Teacher Education at the University of Oregon—Janice Jipson as a professor and the other four women as graduate students. All five were part of a group attempting to establish a teacher education program they describe as "an egalitarian, relational model of collaborative integrated education—no add-ons, no take-aways, no sending children into special places where they will be labeled as trouble, slow, not good enough, or too good for the rest of us." In 1991, in the midst of their experiment in collaboration, the Division of Teacher Education at the University of Oregon was suddenly eliminated, and all the women were faced with the need to find new positions and new intellectual and political homes. Although much of these women's energy went into the self-conscious analysis of their own research and group process, they were also involved in this ongoing political struggle, concerned with "continuing to support and empower each other while confronting external obstacles to our project." The suddenness and finality of the closure of the Division of Teacher Education is a powerful reminder of the vulnerability of social change projects to manipulation and attack from entrenched powers of the status quo.

This book presents testimony of "feminisms" in process. The accounts are filled with tensions, not least an uneasiness with feminism itself, and the question of what exactly it means to be a feminist in education in the contemporary world. All of these women are struggling against a conception of feminism as static and impositional—what Gretchen Freed-Rowland described as "a sense of pressure around the language of feminist theory and pedagogy and what that means, given the languages with which we learned to name our personal and professional experience." Susan Victor points out in her discussion of group work with adolescent mothers that service providers do not have the luxury of abstract theoretical debates. She describes their "visibly present purpose" of working with people on the ground, dealing with their immediate needs for housing, food, uncertainty, and loneliness. What does feminism mean in such contexts, bearing as it does its theoretical complexities and contradictions? Petra Munro, who is perhaps the most committed of these women to a strong definition of feminism, makes the case for feminism as a connecting vision for women working for social change: "We were all trying to survive in an environment which still honored male ways of thinking and being, in which male voices were heard more than female, in which our ideas were more often cutoff, interrupted, or ignored, yet sometimes stolen." While these five women emerge from very different histories and identify themselves in different ways, their narratives share a common theme; they provide testimony to the challenge of continued patriarchal power and the need for women to name their own experiences and goals while respecting the namings of others.

We have written this book as a testament to our collaborative work as five feminist educators working for social change. To write this first sentence is once again to enter contested terrain. Words like "collaboration," "feminist educators," and "social change" represent to us conflicting and contradictory meanings. At the very moment we name these categories, we are unsettled by the illusion of essences and fixed meanings which threaten to impose themselves on us yet again. Our experiences working together over the past five years have taught us that language has little meaning except in relation to cultural, historical, and autobiographical contexts. And yet we can no longer avoid the inevitable—the assuming of a position in relation to this book.

Scattered across the country now in Louisiana, California, Wisconsin, and Oregon, we have spent the past several days talking on the phone confronting the question, What is this book really about? Although we agree on the importance of the project, that is where our consensus ends. Once again the dissonance in our group reminds us of the multiple positions we take in relation to one another, to our life histories, and to our political commitments as teachers working for change. To understand these differences while still working collaboratively for educational transformation is the curricular story we tell. It is an unfinished narrative that resists a neat ending. Instead, we invite our readers to join in a conversation, a conversation which "talks back" to the dominant educational discourses within which we write our lives.

Our work together began at the University of Oregon in the summer of 1989. Abandoning classrooms in California, Illinois, Wisconsin, and Oregon and at U.S. military-based and private international schools in Europe, we were hopeful about the academy as a site for transformation. We left public schools because we wanted to remain teachers, not because we no longer wanted to be teachers. To be a teacher in the 1980s was to risk participating in the imposition of a "New World Order," an order which categorized identity through discourse such as: "at risk," "multicultural," "outcome based," "developmentally appropriate," "back to the basics," and "reflective practice." Despite these new terms, educational discourse continues to be framed by technocratic and behaviorist models. Our alienation from the schools increased, reinforcing our sense of being strangers in a world that we originally had each entered reluctantly (Jan had wanted to be a writer; Petra a lawyer; Susan a psychologist; Karen a weaver; and Gretchen an actor and artist).

And so, in the summer of 1989, as four graduate students and a faculty mentor, we formed a study-research group to help us make sense of our lives as teachers and our commitments to creating alternative approaches to Eurocentric educational practice. We engaged theory, our work experiences, our lives, and our histories as we talked late in the night at our weekly meetings. We quickly learned what is meant by contested, multiple, and partial realities and simultaneously worried about the potential paralysis of naming sites of oppression, racism, anti-Semitism, sexism, classism, and heterosexism in a postmodern culture where meanings are often reduced to mere floating signifiers.

One of the aims of this book is to articulate how our work as educators has been shaped by, and has also shaped, the conversation between critical, feminist, postcolonial, and postmodern theories. To speak of the work of transformative social change is no longer to take for granted the meanings of "empowerment," "liberatory," "dialogue," "collaboration," "feminism," or even "change." Terms like race, ethnicity, class, gender, and sexuality no longer adequately describe the particularities of our experiences. Feminist educators, for example, have urged us to look at how these supposed "universal" terms reproduce gendered relations of power. Postcolonial educators question whose interests are served in the name of liberation or empowerment. Poststructuralists have stopped looking for the subject to empower by asking how we are continually being constructed as subjects through discourse. Postmodernists . . . well, they seem to make no claims except that there are no claims.

Our late-night conversations provided a place in which to articulate how these various master narratives simultaneously spoke to and silenced us. We quickly came to realize that what empowered one of us oppressed another. We continued struggling to find ways in which to avoid imposing meanings on each other. Our process became one of deconstructing the very binaries which imposed themselves on us: theory/practice, culture/nature, teacher/researcher, fact/fiction. Gretchen believed that postmodernism captured the complexity of identity. Petra stood by feminism in the "age of the backlash." Karen suggested that "intellectualism" is itself a "canonized" means of denying the relational because it limits our recognition of the aesthetic, the imaginative, and the

intuitive. Susan insisted that our attempts to grasp the present and to understand it were inseparable from the power of collective memory that merges the
neat categories of past, present, and future. Jan continually reminded us of the
site of privilege from within which we worked.

Our collaboration provided a space for conversation, a place in which to tell
the stories that shaped our lives. And yet we have no illusions that we can
recapture those experiences here. We do not desire to be storytellers in the
traditional sense. In fact, what we share is the shifting relation of our stories to
the multiple positions we take up as women, teachers, mothers, activists,
partners. Aware of the risks of storytelling as reproducing unitary representations of subjectivity, we want to reclaim and rename the way in which
narrative has inscribed itself in our lives: Jan of her immigrant missionary
great-grandmother, Petra of redefining her "fairytale" suburban upbringing,
Susan of the loss of her family in the Holocaust, Karen of her indigenous and
Welsh ancestors, and Gretchen of her Native American community. Rather, our
recollected memories, life experiences, and collective process mirrored the
complex questions we struggled with as educators: How do we come to know?
How can we value the diversity of our experiences? What does it mean to work
for change while honoring the context of others? What would a pedagogy look
like that honored context and situatedness?

Thus, we begin our conversation.

# ACKNOWLEDGMENTS

We would like to thank the women of our extended research group who provided intellectual stimulation and inspiration for this project: Mary Decker, Ellen Givens, Robin Heslip, Kathy Long, Ursi Reynolds, Twila Souers, and Joan Weston. We would also like to acknowledge our colleagues at the University of Oregon from 1989 to 1991, whose work supported and informed us throughout those exciting and challenging years: Carolyn Ames, Chet Bowers, Tony Catalano, Christine Chaillé, Diane Dunlap, David Flinders, Linda Kelm, Cheris Kramerae, Rob Proudfoot, Diane Sheridan, Harry Wolcott, and Linda Zimmerman. Our special appreciation goes to the Center for the Study of Women in Society, which funded many of our projects and offered us our first opportunities for public presentation, and to Lee Ann Bell, Dee Grayson, Renee Martin, and the Research on Women and Education Group, who sponsored our presentations at their own conferences and at the American Educational Research Association (AERA). Finally, we offer our appreciation to Natalie Adams, Shirley Fogleman, Michelle Massé, and Shelley Kies Wells of Louisiana State University and Lynn Flint of Bergin & Garvey for their thoughtful editorial assistance and support during the final preparation of this book.

In addition, we offer our personal recognitions:

∼

JAN: *In many ways, this book has been about relationships. I want to thank family and friends who have contributed to my understanding of the importance of community and mutual respect. I would first like to acknowledge my mother, Jeanette Jipson, my grandmothers, Elsie Jipson and Winnie Mewhorter, and my children, Jenny, Emmie, and Erik, who taught me what nurturance and maternal imposition was all about and who have supported me with their memories, affection, and carefully crafted gifts of love. I would also like to express my appreciation for the encouragement which my father, John Jipson, has provided throughout my career.*

*This book, for me, is also a testament to the importance of partnerships and collective action. The love, intellectual stimulation, and critical reflections of my coauthors and of Bill Bauer, Kathleen Casey, Mary Hauser, Tina Lozano, Nick Paley, Robert Proudfoot, and Herb Van Deventer have been invaluable to me as I struggled with reconstructing my life "after Oregon" and finishing this book.*

∾

**PETRA:** *Because this book truly emerged out of a collaborative endeavor, it is perhaps futile to acknowledge all those who have contributed to its making. However, my first thanks goes to the four other authors. Our work together has inspired me in ways that I could never have anticipated. As always, I owe a tribute to my parents, Bill and Gisela Munro, and my sister, Tina, whose ongoing faith in me means so much. To Andreas, my partner of ten years, I extend my deepest appreciation for sharing my political and intellectual work despite the demands it has taken on our relationship.*

*I thank the following friends and colleagues who support my work by thoughtfully reading endless drafts and whose critique and intellectual engagement I consider a continual honor: Leslie Rebecca Bloom, Mary Ellen Jacobs, Wendy Kohli, Michelle Massé, Elsie Michie, and Ann Trousdale. Central to my survival is the opportunity to work in a larger community of scholars whose own work and support have been essential to my own. I would like to thank the following: William Doll, Madeline Grumet, Cameron McCarthy, Janet Miller, Jo Anne Pagano, and William Pinar.*

∾

**SUSAN:** *Yes, relationships come first. I want to express love and gratitude to my family: to my husband, Rick Lesch, and my daughter, Davita Victor Lesch, for finding me minutes each day to work. To Rick, especially, for telling people about this book, for being proud of me. To my mother, Rena Victor, and my grandmother, Margaret Singer, for being models of women with strength, perseverance, wisdom, and humor. We are now four generations of women, of survivors. To my mother, especially, for being proud of me.*

*My respect, gratitude, and best wishes to the young mothers and staff of Birth to Three in Eugene, Oregon, with whom I worked from 1989 to 1991. Thank you especially to Sheri Gathright, Julia Avatar, Nicole Resenbrink, and Anita Huffman.*

*I so appreciate the willingness of my four coauthors to write through our resistance and finish this project. Thank you especially to Jan, because—even though she doesn't want to be—she is still a mentor/mother to me.*

*Finally, as with everything I finish, I must acknowledge a teacher/mentor of twelve years, Ray Roberts.*

∾

**GRETCHEN:** *First, I want to acknowledge Dr. Janice Jipson, our mentor and friend, and the three other women in our core doctoral student research and writing support group. Your brilliance, passionate integrity, caring, and trust continue to enrich me and my work. When confidence wavers, when I need feedback and editing, you are still there. Second, I need to thank Dr. Robert Proudfoot for his "gifts," and my other "relatives," mentors, and friends who supported me through graduate school and afterward. In particular, I want to thank Diana Kale, Cindy Viles, Cabmen Az, Dr. Deborah La Croix, Dr. Aleta Biesack, Dr. Chet Bowers, Dr. Harry Wolcott, Linda Zimmerman, and Linda Kelm.*

∽

**KAREN:** *I would like to offer recognition to these members of Clergy and Laity Concerned in Eugene, Oregon, and participants in Multicultural Kids Camp for their lifelong dedication to bringing equity and diversity to this region: Paulette Ansari, Nancy Bray, Rich Glauber, Margaret Jacobs, Marion Malcolm, Liliana Navarro, Guadalupe Quinn, and Eric Ward. I would also like to thank the teacher-participants who informed my dissertation and helped me remember that "the work" is for all of our children: Elga Brown, Pat Holland, Alice Kinberg, and Martha Colon-Woody. I would also like to acknowledge my extended-blended-clan-like family for the particular (and peculiar) brand of whimsy, joy, and community they bring to my life. In particular, I would like to thank my mom, Joni (Froude-Jones-) Nelson, for her frequent calls throughout my doctoral program to let me know "we put an extra potato in the oven for you," an offer made with no mention of the fact that she knew I was attempting to live on coffee and bran muffins; my Grandest Grand Chet, Chester W. Froude, for his unconditional support; and my beloved partner, John H. Baldwin, who not only brought three beautiful children into my life, Erin, Ian, and due-in-?, but who is cheerfully attempting to meet the bride price of ten horses requested by my dear grandmothers, Ida Mae Clinton and Rosie B. Francis.*

# REPOSITIONING
# FEMINISM
### AND
# EDUCATION

## IMPOSITION

*Imposition. How to define a term that eludes definition? It is the fluidity, the mutability of the concept that made it such a powerful container for our experience. Theory? We would resist proposing a theory of imposition. Master narratives inevitably impose themselves on us as women and thereby seek to erase us. It is in the multiple positions we take and in our recognition of our positionality that we understand all experience and knowledge as relational. Thus, with this book we speak to those who are concerned with the relations of power and with those processes that privilege one form of knowing and being over another.*

 We begin—and immediately we stumble. Questions plague us: How do we present both our collective experience and the individual experiences that shaped our work together? An impersonal, third-person, authorial voice? Not our style, not us. A unified voice, a joint telling of "our" story? To assume such a unitary perspective would be to "silence our differences."[1] A dialogue? Perhaps, but it has been difficult to sustain dialogue as we have relocated around the country. And even dialogue misrepresents the ongoing tensions, the continued struggles of five diverse women to work across their differences. So we settle, finally, on a *bricolage* of perspectives that seems to jostle and bounce off each other, creating their own positions just as they attempt to capture and tame the issue of imposition itself.

Imposition initially represented to us the prescriptions, restrictions, and prohibitions that exist in the lives of women. It became a thematic lens for clarifying our understanding of the individual challenges we experienced as we encountered the conflicting expectations, rituals, and responsibilities inherent in our positions as women teachers, teacher educators, and community activists. Reflecting on our own experiences as objects of imposition, we were drawn to Kathleen Weiler's (1988) discussion of women's agency in which we moved beyond an understanding of schooling as simply a site of reproduction to one in which we understood our roles as actors and agents in complex social sites. And yet, positioning ourselves as "agents of social change," we engaged in an uneasy relation. We struggled with our desire to empower without disempowering. How could we engage in transforming dominant social relations without reproducing or reimposing the very power relations which we critiqued?

It was imposition within the patriarchal academy which led us to retreat from its halls and seek what we hoped would be refuge in our women's study and research group. Reading the works of other women academics, we now recognize that we were not alone in our struggle to survive in a world where the politics of knowledge and feminine identity are located in sexist, patriarchial, and phallocentric knowledge systems.[2] Our work together was a political act of coalition building among women. It continues to be an act of imaginative resistance. In taking a position relative to our work together, we were able to examine the continual positionings and repositionings of women as they engage with teaching, research, and curriculum. It was because of our diverse theoretical interests and understandings that we were able to attempt to map the issues of imposition through multiple, continually shifting locations.

This book describes several projects, each of which addresses our experiences as women educators in defining our positional perspectives related to our understanding and reconceptualization of teaching and curriculum. Within each project, we faced the dilemma of imposition in our work with student teachers, teenage mothers, children of color, community members, and early childhood educators. Consequently, Part I of this book, "The Location of Politics," presents our reflections as experienced public school teachers and professional educators on the issue of imposition from a variety of personal, ideological, political, and disciplinary perspectives. We share common concerns about education's persistent erasure of issues of race, ethnicity, class, and gender. Threading through our discussions are personal encounters with the imposition of class expectations, cultural perspectives, and gender roles as we have confronted them in our work. Three questions were central to Part I:

1. How do women educators committed to social change deal with issues of imposition?

2. What are the cultural realities of position and imposition in women's lives?

3. What roles do concerns about imposition have in our understandings of curriculum?

In Part III, "Getting Lost," we reflect on our individual experiences in repositioning ourselves as researchers. Our early discussions of imposition had attuned us to the potential inequalities in taking up positions as researchers. Issues of power, authority, truth, and subjectivity resurfaced as we positioned ourselves relative to our research questions and to our participants. Together, Parts I and III reflect on the multiple facets of imposition and positioning which we encountered: as teachers and researchers concerned with our responsibilities for constructing knowledge and shaping the discourse of teacher culture; as women forced to recognize the contradictory manifestations of power within institutions; and as teacher educators committed to sustaining social change.

Placed between our individual reflections on the impact of imposition on our work are our examinations of the role of imposition within our process of collaboration. Unable to clearly separate our autobiographic selves and the relational constructions of our work together, we have written "Appreciating Dissonance: Multiple Perspectives on Collaboration" (Part II) and "Reconstructing Reality: Deconstructing the Collaborative Process" (Part IV) as a way to map an interruption which acknowledges that meaning is never constructed outside of relationships. The structure of this book, the "sandwiching" of reflections on our group process in between our narratives, reveals the complexity of an academic project that has both enriched our understandings of difference and highlighted the challenges of working collaboratively. Thus, in Parts II and IV we address three additional questions:

1. How can a process of collaboration be achieved and maintained by a diverse group of women representing different ideological perspectives and cultural realities?

2. How can individual identity and difference be acknowledged and validated while commitment to shared purposes is maintained?

3. How can women continue to support and empower each other while confronting external obstacles to their projects?

The stories that unfold in this book are multilayered. They speak to the complexities of women's lives: our struggle to become cohesive as a group; our struggle to maintain a vision of transformative education despite current national reforms; our struggle to explore and redefine our understandings of curriculum and what it means to be a teacher; and, perhaps most profoundly, our struggle to define how the concept of imposition seemed to capture the tensions, contradictions, and dilemmas of our everyday lives. To do so while seeking a common voice, one which connects without merging and encircles without binding, has been the challenge of this book and, more important, the challenge of our group.

## POSITIONINGS

> To investigate the politics of identity enables one to reconceive the social relations that are curriculum and instruction.
>
> —Pinar (1994: 244)

> I begin, therefore, with the premise that women's self-representation is largely unmapped, indeed unrecognizable given traditional maps of genre and periodization.
>
> —Gilmore (1994: 5)

∽

In a world which claims to have reached a postmodern state, in which grand theorizing and metanarratives are supposedly no longer valorized, we seek to claim our voices and to make our lives real. Our group initially provided a space in which our voices could be heard. And yet, as we began to speak, it was clear that we did not resonate with one voice. Our exploration of imposition as a construct for meaning-making in our professional lives often resulted in a cacophony of voices as the very process of imposition manifested itself within our group.

From the time we are young girls, we are instructed in how to act and what to think. In constructing an identity for ourselves, we are continually situated within discourse which is not of our own making. Imposed on us are not only the accumulated, and often patriarchal, ideas and histories of our cultures but also the norms of behavior that prescribe what we can and cannot do.[3] The imposition of gender roles obscures what Maxine Greene calls the "lived worlds and perceptual realities of women" (Greene, 1994: 17). Yet to assume that "these roles can be peeled away like layers of an onion to reveal a repressed core, a true self, which has been inhibited, clouded by layers of social conditioning" (Walkerdine, 1994: 57) is also to participate in the imposition of an Enlightenment fiction. In locating ourselves within the complex and contradictory functions of imposition, we have come to understand the irony of postmodernism in which even critique is suspect since it is inevitably embedded in relations of power and domination. Thus, we hope to interrupt the simplistic dichotomy of imposition/resistance (structure/agency) which has been the scaffold for much recent social theory.[4] Central to our work together has been the repositioning of notions like identity, subjectivity, change, and power in ways which disrupt our unitary readings of these concepts by acknowledging the continual negotiation of our understandings as sites of struggle.

Initially, four of us—Jan, Petra, Gretchen, and Karen—began to meet, energized by a desire to better understand how feminist theory and research related to our daily work as teachers. Following Adrienne Rich's (1979) call to "take seriously" our lives as the ground from which to generate and interrogate issues related to curriculum and our work as teacher educators, we questioned, argued, affirmed, and supported each other's ideas and words. Through our talk we situated our struggles as the center of social reality—Jan negotiating her professor/midwife identity, Petra grappling with issues of power and authority in her role as feminist teacher, Gretchen struggling with the cultural implications of working in a Eurocentric educational system, Karen maintaining her commitment to community activism within the limited scripts of the academy, and, later, Susan developing a role in relation to the teenage mothers with whom she worked.

We were all exhilarated by the opportunity to study with women who shared common interests and concerns. We met on Friday afternoons in coffee shops, brew pubs, outdoor cafes—our conversation traversing essentialism, multiculturalism, the heat, the coast, feminist pedagogy, "our" pedagogy, shopping, and returning again and again to a discussion of imposition. Our conversations back then were usually academic but would occasionally develop into passionate arguments about who should or could be called feminist; about whether race, ethnicity, class, or gender most powerfully affected or defined someone; and about why we sometimes hesitated to assert our ideas, looked for outside affirmation, or questioned our abilities and our rights to correct, critique, or evaluate another's work. Our discussions of feminist theory focused on the tension between the need for a "standpoint" (Harding, 1987) which privileged women's experiences as the position from which to critique social relations and our discomfort with the language of many feminists whose universalizing of women's experiences reproduced the gendered and cultural relations of power they were critiquing. Like other feminists (Flax, 1989), we were unsettled by the continued resurfacing of the essentialism/relativism debate. Resonating with cultural feminists' notion of recuperating gendered specificity, we also sought a way to acknowledge multiple perspectives without relinquishing positions from which we could engage in social change. And, like other feminist post-structuralists, we were concerned about taking a position that presumed a unitary, static self or that assumed we could even come to know a "self." [5]

Among the pieces we read first was a selection by Linda Alcoff (1989) in which she talked about the concept of positionality. Reflecting back, we find the essay central to our growing understanding of the issues that faced women students and faculty like ourselves:

> The concept of positionality includes two points: first . . . that the concept of woman is a relational term identifiable only within a (constantly moving) context: but second, that the position that women find themselves in can be actively utilized as a location for the construction of meaning, a place from where meaning is constructed, rather than simply the place where meaning can be discovered. . . . When women become feminists the crucial thing that has occurred is not that they have learned any new facts about the world but that they come to view those facts from a different position, from their own positions as subjects. . . . Seen in this way, being a woman is to take up a position within a moving historical context and

to be able to choose what we make of this position and how we alter this context. (pp. 324–25)

It made sense. In taking up an identity as teachers, were we positioning ourselves actively in resistance to traditional patriarchal impositions or was our concern with being impositional merely one more struggle within the culturally inscribed construction of women in which teachers are positioned as nurturers and facilitators, denying their other roles as active meaning-makers?[6] We asked ourselves, why do we sometimes see teaching as an imposition? Why in positioning ourselves as teachers, did we seem to become "objects," existing in response to other people's needs? In our active construction of ourselves as teachers, we struggled with the contradictions of positioning ourselves as expert, as mother, as therapist, and as other.[7]

Locating positions from which meaning could be constructed rather than discovered allowed us to reconsider imposition as a site of struggle. To view the construction of meaning as resulting only from imposition, Linda Nicholson (1990) suggests, is to neglect that any locale is both a product of imposition (location) and also the site of our desires. Imposition, thus, represents a process of contestation and a negotiation of positionality. Exploring imposition seemed a necessary process through which we could continually discover who we were and who we might become.

We continued reading and moved into critical theory, where an entire new set of questions arose. Gramsci, Habermas, hegemony, hermeneutic rationality? Our heads reeled from the imposition of authority, of alien language, of seemingly impenetrable argument. Perhaps we could agree about the hegemonic nature of our culture but what did those words say about the concrete experiences that we have, as women, assuming a position relative to teaching? How, we asked, could theory's universalizing representations of power, knowledge, change, and agency name the gendered issues inherent, for us, in our construction of these concepts? Was it really "domination" and "submission" that we were concerned with? Was it the imposition of meaning? Or was that, too, a male rendering of the concept? Education as a mode of ideological reproduction, yes—we could each resist the seductiveness of being a high priestess of the cultural canon, but what did that have to do with the chosen role of teacher? Was that an imposition, too?

⁓

PETRA: *During that spring of 1989, I had reluctantly, suspiciously, signed up for the seminar on issues in early childhood education that Jan was teaching— "Women and Children in the Workplace." I could not imagine what I would learn in a seminar which focused on the issues of childhood, child care, and mothering when I was concerned with emancipation, empowerment, and the construction of a new social order through curricular transformation. What, I wondered, did I, a secondary educator and feminist, have in common with an early childhood educa-*

*tor? I didn't really like kids. I had never really expected to be a teacher. Teaching as mothering? No, not me. I was a political activist who happened to be a teacher. Yet Tony, a fellow graduate student, insisted that I had to take the course because Jan was one of the few professors who really modeled collaboration, an emergent curriculum, and alternative pedagogies grounded in a student-centered classroom.*

*Despite my desire to see educational theory in practice, I remember the discomfort, confusion, and ambiguity the first evening of class—sitting in a circle, lengthy personal introductions, and reading the play* Voices *by Susan Griffin. The "voices" in the play created a musical fugue that carried me into spaces that felt like home. The women's voices echoed the complexity of multiple identities and the politics of location. I had learned early the gendered roles expected of me. To be the princess, to want to be saved by the prince—that was to be my suburban destiny. And yet I knew that to be female was to be not valued, not taken seriously. To become a teacher, "women's true profession," was to continually struggle to negotiate a contradictory identity. That semester I learned that to reject the maternal was to participate in patriarchy's devaluation of women; yet to embrace the feminine, the maternal, was paramount to complying in my own oppression. There seemed no way out. I thought back to my years as a high school social studies teacher. I had written in my journal:*

> *What really is the role of the teacher? At times, I feel like a preacher, talking at the students, perhaps trying to convince them or influence their values. Ideally, I see the role of the teacher as facilitator for in effect it is only the students who can decide upon their values and beliefs. Perhaps then it is best only to raise questions, but then it must be determined what questions. Most difficult is getting the students to see the relevance of any question. Ultimately, it should be the students who ask the questions and not the teachers at all. (Evanston, IL, July 26, 1988)*

*As I reflect on this text now as a university professor, I am struck not by how far I have come, but that I am, in fact, still dealing with the same issues. I continue to struggle with what it means to be a teacher and with the discomfort of being in a position of authority. Central to this discomfort is the continual questioning of the process of knowledge construction and legitimization.*

∽

We turned back to Alcoff (1989) who, in attempting to transit the space between cultural feminism and poststructuralism, offers these thoughts:

> The positional definition . . . makes [woman's] identity relative to a constantly shifting context, to a situation that includes a network of elements involving others, the objective economic conditions, cultural and political institutions and ideologies. . . . Through social critique and analysis we can identify women via their position relative to an existing social and

cultural network. . . . I assert that the very subjectivity (or subjective experience of being a woman) and the very identity of women is constituted by women's position. (pp. 323–24)

As questions, turmoil, and tentative reflections surfaced, we realized that through our examination of our positions, we could perhaps also get at the sources of our personal discomfort. Thus, after several weeks of general discussion of imposition as a significant issue in women's work, we refocused our conversations on our lived experiences. But we kept returning to feminist theory, looking for keys to understanding. It was only in retrospect that we were able to identify the ironic imposition of theory on our work together.

∽

JAN: *Theory is the least of the impositions that I worry about. It has been in intellectual arenas, in fact, where I have usually felt most myself.[8] When the criterion was how much you had read or how well you understood, my rural working-class roots did not appear to be the major disadvantage that they were in other, more social environments. Feminism also represented opportunity to me, the possibility of belonging, of naming myself in an affirmative manner despite the ravages of patriarchy experienced throughout my educational life. I found the readings and theory exciting. Rather than imposing on me a master's view, they stimulated and energized me. I felt liberated and alive during our group's long discussions about feminist theory and postmodern analysis, as if I were transcending the daily limitations of my role as daughter, wife, mother, early childhood teacher educator. We read and talked. New ideas stimulated still other new ideas and understandings—it was what I had always believed an academic should do.*

*I thought back to my early religious training in a fundamentalist Baptist church, remembering being told I was doomed unless I could accept the redemptive powers of a demanding Higher Being. I remember believing I had no choice but to heed the restrictions of that religious practice and conform, at least in appearance, to its restrictive norms. School was not much different. The teachers in my rural, Midwestern community "knew" what was legitimate for us to learn and how we were to do it. They effectively transmitted a curriculum of working hard and making do, of great male achievements and certain truths, of "correct" ways to spell, read, compute, and think, of always being ready for whatever comes next. It was, in sum, a curriculum of survival for children who were not expected to ever move beyond that place. Again, I was obedient, earning my grades with no sense that any of it had anything to do with me, personally, other than ensuring my own survival through compliance. Early on I had named the roles inherent in the folktales of my childhood: the good mother, the strong father, the competent child.*

*Resurrecting buried beliefs from my early fundamentalist religious background and from my experiences growing up with people who labored long hours in fields, barns, and warehouses, I insisted, mostly to myself, that "fun" was not a legitimate part of academic life; that work was the only truly worthwhile activity (and the scholarly work of thinking, reading, writing, and rewriting was actually rather suspect); that wasting money or time and being unproductive was unacceptable, immoral almost; and that one must have something to show for one's work. Work came first and work included my responsibilities to others as a teacher. Perhaps overly conscious of my faculty role, I refrained from "getting too close" to students. We never met at my house—I secretly believed that they would be appalled at the chaos of children, pets, dirty dishes, books, and papers everywhere. I suppose I held myself to an idealized image of the "gute hausfrau" as well as the "good professor" and feared exposing my uncertainties and lapses to them.*

∾

We had read discussions by Ellsworth (1989), Alcoff (1989), Miller (1987), and others about the positions that educators assume relative to each other, their students, the curriculum, and the world of ideas and ideologies. We sought to understand the role of imposition in our professional lives and in a change-enhancing process (Shrewsbury, 1987; Weiler, 1988) that would allow us to transform our work activities into more relational, less impositional interactions. We were well aware that educators concerned with bringing about transformative social action have repeatedly faced the dilemma of how to do so without violating the rights of others to construct their own knowledge (Casey, 1993; Lather, 1986; Luke & Gore, 1992).

We read Elizabeth Ellsworth (1989: 306), who suggests that strategies central to a critical perspective, such as "empowerment" and "dialogue," give the illusion of equality while in fact leaving intact the authoritarian nature of the relationship. The hierarchy, according to Ellsworth, is maintained through "conventional notions of dialogue and democracy which assume rationalized, individualized subjects capable of agreeing on universal fundamental moral principles and the quality of human life" (Ellsworth, 1989: 316). Implicit in the notion of empowerment is the assumption that someone needs to be empowered. The process of determining who is in need of being empowered, defining how that process will occur, and assessing whether or not someone has become empowered raised important questions, for all of us, about a critical perspective and its impositional nature. As Ellsworth points out, what might be empowering to one student could at the same time be oppressive to another. Although a critical perspective was attractive to us, we questioned who determines, and thus imposes, the knowledge and action necessary to empower.

∾

GRETCHEN: *As a Native American Indian woman, I do not want to be emancipated or liberated from my peoples and culture. I want respect for the positions we hold within them. Although I name myself as an Ojibwa-Winnebago educator and researcher, I, too, am confronted by the academic epistemologies of legitimized Euro-American theories and methodologies. And, as a Native American woman, I am also uncomfortable with many mainstream educators' lack of concern for context and with their denial of community as holistic, aesthetic, and ecologically interdependent.*

*My concern is with how mainstream feminism portrays itself in the professional literature as embedded in the Eurocentric, Cartesian world view that frames most research and language. The continued privileging of a single theoretical and methodological perspective, which is decontextualized from the real world of real people, creates an illusion of superiority and purity in an abstracted form. We all negotiate and interpret meaning and experience through our own personal and cultural lenses. Many of us are silenced by the power of those who are allowed to name, use, and impose meaning and knowledge. I am attracted to postmodern feminist discourse as an opening up of that liminal space in which the plurality of world views and concerns can be shared. It holds out the promise of a fuller understanding of community and responsibility .*

*Finally, as a Native American woman, I have difficulty with feminists' call to reclaim one's voice as separate from community. It seems to me that class and age and religious and political and sexual preference are all a part of cultural identity. There is a different phenomenological reality in our understanding of our lives as becoming informed by the past within each present context, in our knowing that the future is prepared for by paying attention to the lessons of the past. The issues for women of color seem broader than the present oppression of women in the Western patriarchal paradigm. We cannot begin to address the issues of asymmetry and inequality in people's lives as issues of gender, class, and cultural difference unless we understand how knowledge is tied to power and oppression and how our schools support them. Unless we are willing to accept that knowledge and language are not neutral but culturally, socially, and institutionally constructed and imposed, and until we understand the "historicity" of our embeddedness in language and culture, we will be no closer to solving the problems that face us now.*

∼

Through our discussions, we all came to understand more clearly the culturally bound nature of both critical and feminist discourse. How could any theoretical position, with its inherent metanarrative, ever explain the complexity of any and every person's experiences? We talked of how the feminist critique of critical discourse highlighted its tendency to remain grounded in a liberal, humanist tradition which assumes that there is a "truth" or common experience that can emerge from rational and reasoned thought. We were concerned that by ignoring differences of race, class, and gender, many theorists potentially reinvoked relations of oppression.

Each of our "positionings" forced us to look with greater scrutiny at the multiple forms of feminism. We found within the work of writers such as Aptheker (1989), hooks (1990), Lorde (1985), Minh-ha (1987), Moraga and Anzaldua (1983), and Spivak (1987) challenges that resonated with our discomfort at the imposition of a universal "womanhood."[9] The refusal of these authors to validate women's univocal interpretations of experience generated for us a new appreciation of plurality and stimulated our thinking about ways to value difference and decenter imposition (Hawkesworth, 1989).

**KAREN:** *I do not define my femaleness through feminist theoretical perspectives or my economic level by class or way-of-being-in-the-world solely by culture. I believe that race, class, culture, ethnicity, and gender are interconnected and intertwined with language, community, and spirituality and that our world view emerges out of this relational interaction. While categories can be necessary beginnings for exploring our ways of knowing and being in the world, I find the tendency of academic structures to define themselves through boundaried labels an act of imposition. I hear my voice echoed through the literature of Trin Minh-ha and bell hooks; I find "truths" through the "theoretically" fictionalized works of Rolf Edberg, Zora Neal Hurston, Par Lagerkvist, Aldo Leopold, Naguib Mahfouz, Fatima Mernissi, Octavio Paz, Leslie Marmon Silko, J. R. R. Tolkien, and Elie Wiesel; and I gain strength through my work with a few men and many other women.*

*Nor can I offer a neat label with regard to cultural identity. When I hear Gretchen talk of her family's three generations of commitment to issues for indigenous women and hear Susan's struggle as the daughter of Holocaust survivors, again, I listen and say nothing. I am hearing my father's father speak of poverty, abuse, and racism in the hills somewhere near Raleigh, North Carolina—his pride as he names 14 generations of farmers and coal miners. I listen as he apologizes for raising my father, rootless, in Los Angeles—land of immediate gratification and transient autobiography—and as he tells me of his youth: "We were poor but we were never trash." My heart breaks with compassion—and loss, because he is dying and it is too late to ask my great-grandmother for her stories or even for her real last name. I listen as my mother's father tells me about growing up in Oregon and about his family—the Froudes, who have lived at Dartington Hall in Totnes, Devonshire, since the fifteenth century. I am five generations removed from the Froude ancestor who was sent to the United States and posted a living income to ensure that he would not return to England. "What," I ask my grandfather, "did he do?" "Who did he marry?" "Why did he abandon his wife and young son to return to die and be buried at Dartington Hall?" "Not abandoned," states my grandfather, not answering my other questions. "He went home. WE do not abandon our own." "Let's talk about 'we,' " I say.*

*In reflecting on my experiences and family's life stories, I think about survival strategies and how society encourages categorization by race, class, culture, gender, and language by demanding certain skills for passage into privileged and financially rewarding positions. I seek to understand my colleagues and their feminist orientation(s) because I know the struggle as a woman. For women, passage is often granted if we meet mainstream expectations—attractive yet not intimidating, assertive yet never aggressive. As women in the academy, women who have gained access, we are caught in a paradoxical situation. To **not** acquire the knowledge considered legitimate by U.S. society is often an extremely self-destructive act. Yet to acquire it can be equally self-destructive.*

ᕫ

As we continued our exploration of feminist and other literature, we were drawn to postmodern theories.[10] As Jane Flax (1989) suggests, the goal of a feminist/postmodern discourse is "deconstructive" in the sense that poststructuralists "seek to distance us from and make us skeptical about beliefs concerning truth, knowledge, power, the self, and language that are often taken for granted within and serve as legitimization for contemporary Western culture" (p. 54). In their deconstructions of humanist discourse, postmodernists highlight its implicit assumptions: its reliance on reason, its search for absolutes, and its assumptions of universal experience. By making problematic the notions of subjectivity, gender, power, and knowledge, poststructuralists seek to dislodge the Cartesian grip on what is considered real and legitimate ways of knowing and being.

Susan joined us. Her work with adolescent mothers in a community support/education program brought questions to our discussion of class and gender and imposition in our double lives as practitioners (teachers, service providers, mothers) and academics (scholars, researchers). Our weekly discussions in each other's homes during the fall and winter of 1989–90 became the site for articulating, negotiating, and coming to terms with the various perspectives we embraced as teachers-scholars-practitioners. Did we all have to be feminists? Could we share common political commitments if we didn't have the same theoretical base? What was theory anyway?

Our questions and our discussions mirrored feminist postmodern/poststructuralist debates which maintain the situatedness of knowledge and acknowledge "partial truths" while striving to avoid the trap of relativism. Ironically, discussion of the issues of imposition required that we each take a position. In exploring the implications of curriculum, we raised questions about who can be a knower, about what tests beliefs must pass in order to be legitimated as knowledge, and about what kinds of things can be known (Apple & Beyer, 1988; Giroux, 1986; Miller, 1987).

∽

SUSAN: *I drive to the homes of teenage mothers in nearby rural towns, anxious to care, to mend, to protect. Informed by the gnawing remembrance that no one spoke up for my family during the Holocaust, I have always taken the role of advocate. Now, I feel consumed with an urgency to speak to the emotional struggles of adolescent girls and more, to the societal oppression of young women who become mothers. But then . . . I hear one of the girls use the word "Jew" as a verb or I see a sign in a church describing Jews as "nonbelievers" or listen as one of the young mothers asks, "Hanukkah is just like Christmas, right?" And being Jewish is forced to the forefront of my existence and my work. Like Gretchen, who must consider culture before gender, I must consider what it means to be a woman and a feminist in a patriarchal world only after I consider what it means to be Jewish in a community of Christian values and Christian prejudice.*

*I gained affirmation recently by reading **Deborah, Golda and Me** by Letty Cottin Pogrebin (1991), specifically her description of the struggle to reconcile the two identities: Jewish woman and feminist. I understand my life as an opportunity for service, my role as a teacher and counselor as a "mitzvot," a deed. My feminist head warned of self-sacrifice as I spent my first year as a professor with students waiting in line to see me, my home phone number written in bold on every student's syllabus. Writing? Publishing? Political networking? Not real work to me. Real work is to do for others. Like Jan, I do not see my colleagues, both male and female, experiencing this struggle of priorities, of serving the other first. To do so, however, reflects the core of what being a Jewish woman and being a feminist means to me.*

*Within this book, the label of feminist and the theories of feminism impose themselves on me. I am certainly a feminist, but I am a Jewish woman who is a feminist, not the other way around. The experience of my family, that my father endured 2 years in labor camps before he was 20, that my mother and her mother lost 53 relatives, that my brother and I, the "second generation," the children of survivors, carry the unspoken pain into our adulthood—that is the most salient experience. To be a Jew and to not take daily survival for granted is far more crucial to me than any oppression I experience as a woman or as a feminist. I cannot relinquish those characteristics of my female ancestors which have allowed them to endure wars, pogroms, and never-ending work. I have to find real room within feminism for being a nurturer, a caretaker, someone who puts relationships and sometimes the needs of others first. I must define myself in terms of my relationships with others. I am a teacher of teachers, a counselor of adolescents, a daughter of Holocaust survivors, a wife, a mother, a friend, a colleague, a Jewish woman.*

~

Winter came to Eugene and with it the rain. We struggled with the collegial process—the roles each of us began to assume in relation to each other as we attempted to complete our first American Educational Research Association (AERA) conference presentation. Our discussions of pedagogy mirrored the same issues that emerged in our group process—how to respect different ways of being, working, speaking, and caring. We questioned the positivist ideal of objective and value-free knowledge and considered the implications of a "feminist pedagogy" that includes multiple voices and diverse points of view rather than provides (imposes) *the* truth, *the* answers, or *the* absolute knowledge.[11] We debated how to create a context where students are confirmed as knowers, schools are viewed as a community of learners, personal knowledge is legitimated, and multiple ways of knowing are acknowledged. The questions went on: What would a curriculum that valued caring, connectedness, and collaboration look like? How were our understandings of curriculum influenced by our experiences within relations of domination? How did we position ourselves to resist dominant curricular ideologies?

Although these questions provided an even deeper understanding of the various ways in which women's experiences are delegitimized through the imposition of dominant discourses, some members of the group experienced a familiar discomfort. By basing their critiques of current curricular practices on women's experiences as mothers and nurturers and constructing a discourse of "feminist pedagogy," they seemed to potentially essentialize and distort aspects of womanhood. Was there a danger of reinvoking essentialist claims which suggest that there is such a thing as a "true" feminist pedagogue?[12] Was imposition of an "essential" female pedagogy just a reconstruction of patriarchal discourse?[13]

Through this group and our interactions we each came to realize that only by acknowledging and deconstructing our embeddedness in a cultural and historic framework could we create a space for the beginning of real dialogue with other women across cultures, ethnicities, and national boundaries (Anzaldua, 1990; Narayan, 1988; Spelman, 1988; Spivak, 1987; Tokarczyk & Fay, 1993). Thus, as we thought our way through critical, feminist, and postmodern theories, each of us believed we were finding confirmation of our voices but in different ways. Issues of positionality had become the thread which both connected and encircled our distinct voices and diverse experiences. Yet as we continued to try to understand imposition, new forms of imposition arose in the group itself and understandings, on any level, seemed difficult to achieve. We circled back and around again, interrogating each other from slightly changed positions, and embraced each other from our shared concerns.

## REPOSITIONING

On January 29, 1991, the University of Oregon announced the elimination of its teacher preparation graduate education programs. With foreclosure imminent, we scrambled to finish degrees, find new jobs, relocate families. The disruption was total and the tension, at times, unbearable. Our group, at first, served as a refuge, but as the stress of uncertainty permeated and the deadlines drew closer, arguments turned into battles and we seemed to forget each other in our own struggles to survive. We pulled back, focused on our separate work, and waited, caught in the limbo of the present. The institutional impositions we faced in the past seemed minor compared to being told that our work as teacher educators and scholars and, by extension, we ourselves were no longer valued. We were informed that we were part of the limb which must be pruned to save the tree—dead wood. Thus named, we fell away.

We were repositioned, once again confronted with the inevitable task of taking up new positions. Our collaborative work had attuned us to the complex ways in which imposition functions and, thus, the inevitability of positioning ourselves in what Leigh Gilmore has called "temporary homes of meaning" (1994). These places we call home are no longer just one place. bell hooks (1990) reminds us that "home is that place which enables and promotes varied and ever-changing perspectives, a place where one discovers new ways of seeing reality, frontiers of difference" (p. 148). For each of us, our work together has made tangible the many ways in which we make sense of our worlds. We carry these new understandings into our classrooms, community work, and families, where they enrich our ability to appreciate the complexities of human nature. This is not to say that we do not still confront painful memories of our work together. And yet, despite the still unresolved issues, we have chosen to once again take up this project, to write this book, to begin again to share our experiences and stories so that we might support and learn from others.

## NOTES

1. We draw here on the work of other collaborative groups such as Berman, Hultgren, Lee, Rivkin, and Roderick (1991), Hollingsworth (1994), and Miller (1990). In particular, we maintain, like Lugones and Spelman (1983), that the focus of feminist theory and method on recuperating women's voices should not obscure the examination of how differences are silenced, thus excluding a diversity of voices, in particular those of women of color.

2. See especially Aisenberg and Harrison (1988), Bannerji, Carty, Dehli, Heald, and McKenna (1991), Lewis (1993), and Luke and Gore (1992).

3. Madeline Grumet (1988) in "Where the line is drawn," from *Bitter Milk: Women and Teaching* explores the construction of how women's domestic (private) lives are absent from their professional lives and the implications of this for curriculum.

4. Like Bat-Ami Bar On (1993), Lather (1991), and Whitson (1991), we are suspicious of reproducing binaries which reduce positions to either oppressed or oppressor (Marxism), or actor or acted upon (feminism), since these dichotomies function to reproduce the insidious hegemony of binary modernist discourse. Sandra Harding (1989) suggests that analytical categories should be "unstable" and that we should see our theorizing projects as "riffing" between and over the beats of patriarchal theories rather than as rewriting the tunes of any particular one.

5. See Britzman (1991) and Butler (1990) for a discussion of how notions of subjectivity as unitary, as opposed to non-unitary and culturally situated, privilege patriarchal understandings of the epistemological relation of the knower to the known.

6. We were particularly drawn to the work of Grumet (1988) and Pagano (1990), who explore women's relationship to teaching from the perspective that women teachers are either absent or represented as the objects of knowledge, rarely its subjects.

7. The feminist interpretations of object relations theory by Hirsch (1989), Johnson (1988), and Chodorow (1978) added to our conceptualization of object/subject by pointing out the dismissal of the mother as "subject" and the absence of a discussion of the female child.

8. In *Teaching to Transgress*, bell hooks (1994) writes about theory as liberatory practice.

9. The contributions of feminists writing from their experiences as lesbians and women of color enriched our understandings of the complex issues involved in positioning, in working across and through the borders of identity without giving what Bat-Ami Bar On (1993) calls "epistemic privilege" to any position.

10. We read Benhabib (1990), Flax (1990), and Huyssen (1990).

11. Belenky et al. (1986), Berlak and Berlak (1981), Gilligan (1982), and Gross (1986) were particularly pivotal in shaping our understandings of how knowledge is gendered and is thus always implicated in power relations.

12. Gore (1993), drawing on the work of Foucault, suggests that feminist pedagogy is another "regime of truth."

13. Martin (1994) suggests that the concept of essentialism not only reifies masculinist notions of identity and subjectivity but is not a useful category for feminists since it potentially undermines feminists' ability to make any claims at all.

## REFERENCES

Aisenberg, N., & Harrison, M. (1988). *Women of academe: Outsiders in the sacred grove.* Amherst: University of Massachusetts Press.

Alcoff, L. (1989). Cultural feminism versus poststructuralism: The identity crisis in feminist theory. In M. R. Malson, J. F. O'Barr, S. Westphal-Wihl, & M. Wyer, (Eds.), *Feminist theory in practice and process* (pp. 295–327). Chicago: University of Chicago Press.

Anzaldua, G. (1990). *Making face, making soul.* San Francisco: An Aunt Lute Foundation Book.

Apple, M., & Beyer, L. (1988). *The curriculum: Problems, politics and possibilities.* Albany: State University of New York Press.

Aptheker, B. (1989). *Tapestries of life.* Amherst: University of Massachusetts Press.

Bannerji, H., Carty, L., Dehli, K., Heald, S., & McKenna, K. (1991). *Unsettling relations: The university as a site of feminist struggles.* Toronto: Women's Press.

Belenky, M. F., Clinchy, B. M., Goldberger, N. R., & Tarule, J. M. (1986). *Women's ways of knowing.* New York: Basic Books.

Benhabib, S. (1990). Epistemologies of postmodernism: A rejoinder to Jean-Francois Lyotard. In L. Nicholson (Ed.), *Feminism/postmodernism* (pp. 107–132). New York: Routledge.

Berlak, A., & Berlak, H. (1981). *Dilemmas of schooling: Teaching and social change.* New York: Methuen.

Berman, L., Hultgren, F., Lee, D., Rivkin, M., & Roderick, J. (1991). *Toward a curriculum for being.* Albany: State University of New York Press.

Britzman, D. (1991). *Practice makes practice.* Albany: State University of New York Press.

Butler, J. (1990). *Gender trouble: Feminism and the subversion of identity.* London: Routledge.

Casey, K. (1993). *I answer with my life: Life histories of women teachers working for social change.* New York: Routledge.

Chodorow, N. (1978). *The reproduction of mothering.* Berkeley: University of California Press.

Ellsworth, E. (1989). Why doesn't this feel empowering?: Working through the repressive myths of critical pedagogy. *Harvard Educational Review, 59*(3), 297–324.

Flax, J. (1989). Postmodernism and gender relations in feminist theory. In M. R. Malson, J. F. O'Barr, S. Westphal-Wihl, & M. Wyer (Eds.), *Feminist theory in practice and process* (pp. 51–74). Chicago: University of Chicago Press.

Flax, J. (1990). *Thinking fragments: Psychoanalysis, feminism and postmodernism in the contemporary west.* Berkeley: University of California Press.

Gilligan, C. (1982). *In a different voice: Psychological theory and women's development.* Cambridge, MA: Harvard University Press.

Gilmore, L. (1994). *Autobiographics: A feminist theory of women's self-representation.* Ithaca, NY: Cornell University Press.

Giroux, H. (1986). Curriculum, teaching and the resisting intellectual. *Curriculum & Teaching, 1*(1 & 2), 33–42.

Gore, J. (1993). *The struggle for pedagogies.* New York: Routledge.

Greene, M. (1994). The lived world. In L. Stone (Ed.), *The education feminism reader* (pp. 17–25). New York: Routledge.

Gross, E. (1986). What is feminist theory? In C. Pateman and E. Gross (Eds.), *Feminist challenges: Social and political theory* (pp. 190–204). Boston: Northeastern University Press.

Grumet, M. (1988). *Bitter milk: Women and teaching.* Amherst: University of Massachusetts Press.

Harding, S. (1987). Introduction: Is there a feminist method? In S. Harding (Ed.), *Feminism and methodology* (pp. 1–14). Bloomington: Indiana University Press.

Harding, S. (1989). The instability of the analytical categories of feminist theory. In M. R. Malson, J. F. O'Barr, S. Westphal-Wihl, & M. Wyer (Eds.), *Feminist theory in practice and process* (pp.15–34). Chicago: University of Chicago Press.

Hawkesworth, M. (1989). Knowers, knowing, know: Feminist theory and claims or truth. In M. R. Malson, J. F. O'Barr, S. Westphal-Wihl, & M. Wyer (Eds.), *Feminist theory in practice and process* (pp. 327–353). Chicago: University of Chicago Press.

Hirsch, M. (1989). *The mother/daughter plot: Narrative, psychoanalysis, feminism.* Bloomington: Indiana University Press.

Hollingsworth, S. (1994). *Teacher research and urban literacy education.* New York: Teachers College Press.

hooks, b. (1990). *Yearning: Race, gender and cultural politics.* Boston: South End Press.

hooks, b. (1994). *Teaching to transgress: Education as the practice of freedom.* New York: Routledge.

Huyssen, A. (1990). Mapping the postmodern. In L. Nicholson (Ed.), *Feminism/postmodernism* (pp. 234–280). New York: Routledge.

Johnson, M. (1988). *Strong mothers, weak wives.* Berkeley: University of California Press.

Lather, P. (1986). Research as praxis. *Harvard Educational Review, 56*(3), 257–277.

Lather, P. (1991). *Getting smart: Feminist research and pedagogy with/in the postmodern.* New York: Routledge.

Lewis, M. (1993). *Without a word: Teaching beyond women's silence.* New York: Routledge.

Lorde, A. (1985). *I am your sister: Black women organizing across sexualities.* New York: Kitchen Table, Women of Color Press.

Lugones, M., & Spelman, E. (1983). Have we got a theory for you!: Feminist theory, cultural imperialism and the demand for "the woman's voice." *Women's Studies International Forum, 6*(6), 573–581.

Luke, C., & Gore, J. (1992). Women in the academy: Strategy, struggle, survival. In C. Luke & J. Gore (Eds.), *Feminism and critical pedagogy* (pp.192–210). New York: Routledge.

Martin, J. R. (1994). Methodological essentialism, false difference, and other dangerous traps. *Signs: Journal of Women in Culture and Society, 19*(3), 630–657.

Miller, J. (1987). Women as teachers/researchers: Gaining a sense of ourselves. *Teaching Education Quarterly, 14*, 52–58.

Miller, J. (1990). *Creating spaces and finding voices.* Albany: State University of New York Press.

Minh-ha, T. (1987). Difference: A special third world women issue. *Feminist Review, 25*(1), 5–22.

Moraga, C., & Anzaldua, G. (1983). *This bridge called my back: Writings by radical women of color.* New York: Kitchen Table, Women of Color Press.

Narayan, U. (1988). Working together across difference: Some considerations on emotions and political practice. *Hypatia, 3*, 31–47.

Nicholson, L. (1990). *Feminism/postmodernism.* New York: Routledge.

On, B.-A. B. (1993). Marginality and epistemic privilege. In L. Alcoff & E. Potter (Eds.), *Feminist epistemologies* (pp. 83–100). New York: Routledge.

Pagano, J. (1990). *Exiles and communities: Teaching in the patriarchal wilderness.* Albany: State University of New York Press.

Pinar, W. F. (1994). *Autobiography, politics and sexuality: Essays in curriculum theory, 1972–1992.* New York: Peter Lang.

Pogrebin, L. C. (1991). *Deborah, Golda and me: Being female and Jewish in America.* New York: Crown Books.

Rich, A. (1979). *On lies, secrets, and silence.* New York: W. W. Norton.

Shrewsbury, C. (1987). What is feminist pedagogy? *Women's Studies Quarterly, 15*(3/4), 6–14.

Spelman, E. (1988). *Inessential women.* Boston: Beacon Press.

Spivak, G. (1987). *In other worlds: Essays in cultural politics.* New York: Methuen.

Tokarczyk, M., & Fay, E. (1993). *Working-class women in the academy: Laborers in the knowledge factory.* Amherst: University of Massachusetts Press.

Walkerdine, V. (1994). Femininity as performance. In L. Stone (Ed.), *The education feminism reader* (pp. 57–72). New York: Routledge.

Weiler, K. (1988). *Women teaching for change: Gender, class, and power.* South Hadley, MA: Bergin & Garvey.

Whitson, J. A. (1991). Poststructuralist pedagogy as counter-hegemonic discourse. *Education and Society, 9*(1), 73–86.

# PART I

## THE LOCATION OF POLITICS

By repositioning Adrienne Rich's term "the politics of location," we claim our teaching as a political act. In doing so we reclaim our experiences as a site of curricular theorizing. Part I includes five personal narratives which detail the authors' efforts to position themselves in their own teaching. Written from critical, feminist, and postmodern perspectives, the chapters introduce questions concerning the role of imposition in curriculum and supervision. Questions are addressed concerning how curriculum is constructed, whose values and knowledge are represented, whose voices and needs are acknowledged, and whose cultural contexts are represented. Questions are also raised about how curriculum is enacted and experienced, about whose ways of knowing are privileged, and about whose definitions of what it means to teach are privileged.

Janice Jipson, in "Teacher-Mother: An Imposition of Identity," reflects on her attempts to resolve personal concerns about imposition by adopting the model of connected teaching, thereby focusing on the role of the teacher educator in encouraging, and sometimes imposing, multiple forms of knowledge, multiple ways of knowing, and active personal and social constructions of knowledge. Recognition of and respect for difference form the foundation for her analysis and provide another lens for the illumination of the imposition inherent in the act of teaching. While the multiple relationships that exist between students and teachers in classrooms are acknowledged and the appropriate nurturing of these relationships is explored, she also examines the social construction of "mother" and its metaphorical possibilities for characterizing teachers' work.

Susan Victor, in "Becoming the Good Mother: The Emergent Curriculum of Adolescent Mothers," describes the process of developing and implementing a curriculum for teenage mothers in a psychoeducational/support group setting. The focus is on the experience of an educated, middle-class Jewish-American teacher working with working-class adolescent mothers. The analysis points to the unintentional imposition of the author's life experiences and formal education in the form of agency-imposed curriculum on the cultural realities of the adolescent participants in the program.

In "Multicultural Curriculum Development in a Multiple-Cultural Context," Karen Froude Jones analyzes the development of multicultural curriculum for teachers and children from diverse cultural backgrounds. Her critical reflections are grounded in the belief that the values institutionalized within American public school systems are based on predominantly Euro-American beliefs which emphasize the objectivity of knowledge. The author critiques the assumption that it is the responsibility of educators to authoritatively transmit or impose a mainstream "cultural literacy" on their students.

In "Here I Go Again: Supervision, Defining a Cultural Role," Gretchen Freed-Rowland examines the problems of imposition as they are based in contradictory cultural expectations. As she describes her experiences supervising in an elementary education program, comparing these with her personal/professional life as a teacher and supervisor working in several European countries, she recounts her struggle with the expectation of universities and public schools that supervisors intervene in their students' classrooms in order to evaluate competency. This expectation contradicted her cultural belief that as a Native American woman, she had no right to engage in such intervention. Nevertheless, she recognizes the unintended imposition of her values and needs when supervising student teachers.

In "Speculations: Negotiating a Feminist Supervision Identity," Petra Munro explores the process of providing field support to preservice secondary social studies teachers and, specifically, recognizing the dilemma in her desire to support student teachers' right to construct their own knowledge with the desire to foster social change. The struggle to be impositional versus being the "neutral observer" is highlighted, as she negotiates her belief in student-centered teaching with her commitment as a feminist to promoting necessary changes in public school instruction.

# CHAPTER 1

# Teacher-Mother: An Imposition of Identity

*Janice Jipson*

It is with a sense of amazement that I look back over this chapter, many months after I first drafted it. I recognize, for perhaps the first time, the irony and inevitability of my beginning a book on imposition with a reflection on the meanings of teaching and mothering, interactions which represent, for many, a true imposition. As an educator and sometimes curriculum theorist, I project onto the subject of imposition both my own educational definitions and my childhood experiences. While I am well aware of the broad academic discussions of issues of cultural and social imposition, this essay details my expanding personal awareness of the impositions in my own life and of my position and impositions as a teacher

It all began in 1989 in San Francisco. I was listening to a discussion of feminist teaching and the building of community. Janet Miller stood at the front of the room, suggesting that we think of curriculum in terms of collaboration, context, the personal construction of knowledge (Miller, 1989). I was soothed by her words, a lullaby as comforting and familiar to me as the Sunday school songs my grandmother sang when I was little, a cozy spot as safe as home should be; her words seemed to suggest the "happy ending" of my childhood stories, of universal love, almost achieved.

But just at the point when I was feeling affirmed and assured that I was a "good" teacher, who did do the "right" things, Janet referred to how we, as women teachers, often worried about "imposition." I was startled. Her words had a dramatic effect. "That's it!" I said to myself. "Imposition, that's what I struggle with each time I teach." The script unfolded in my mind, the dialogue familiar:

Should I lecture? Who am I to assume to be the expert? Certainly the students have a lot to offer on this topic, too. Assignment? Of course you can turn it in tomorrow. Who am I to say that my seminar paper is more important than your trip to Denver/mother's birthday/statistics course/child's band concert? And besides, what right do I have to be the validator of your work? Appointment? Well, Friday is my writing day, but your needs are important to me—so let's meet!

I returned home, imposition entrenched in my thoughts. I acknowledged my growing discomfort with being positioned, because of my faculty role, my education, my Euro-American identity, as some kind of authority and considered my desire to be seen, instead, as a partner, an informed companion. What was imposition? I asked myself. And why did I seem to resist so intensely imposing on others? For me, the notion of imposition seemed to represent my long history of being told what to do, think, and be and my desire not to reproduce that history with others. I sometimes thought of my teaching self as the "mother of multitudes" and dreaded the thought of being the controlling, manipulative, bad mother-mentor-monitor of my students.

Active resistance to what I saw as the impositional demands of teaching emerged when I extended the role of being a "good mother" to one whereby I conspired to help students avoid any perceived imposition on their learning by presenting, always, alternative ways of looking at the curriculum or of meeting institutional requirements. Fiction as curricular text (Jipson & Munro, 1992), autobiography as research (Jipson, 1992a), reflective journals as substitutes for formal evaluation (Jipson, 1992b), action research projects—as I incorporated them all into my teaching I continued to ask, "Am I also passively avoiding patriarchal impositions myself?"

## POSITIONING: LEARNING TO BE

We learn of the imposition of another's will literally at our mothers' knees. The recognition of the more public imposition of power and patriarchy comes much later. My first memories of my own positioning relate to knowing that I was to be a "good girl." Strict reminders in my family admonished me to look out for my sister, to change into play clothes before going outdoors, and to do things the right way, whether it be dusting furniture, pulling weeds, or plucking chickens. Sunday school songs taught me about achieving salvation, that my cup would run over with joy if I observed the appropriate religious conventions. Too young to recognize the imposition of a particular cultural way of being in the world, I tried to be that good girl and, in the process, learned the culturally sanctioned behaviors for women of my generation: compliance, domesticity, and nurturance.

As I look back on my childhood I can identify intermittent and usually abortive acts of resistance, circumvented attempts to insert myself into the adult-imposed experiences of my daily life. I was fortunate in my childhood not to be subjected to the violence and abuse that many children experience daily. The social and cultural impositions I faced were more about appropriate behavior, the local rural work ethic, my position in my community. My early memories of school, perhaps like those of many children, focus on the unpleasant, the embarrassing, the misunderstood attempts to allow the real self to be part of the classroom.

I remember first grade. Daydreaming about riding a white horse during oral reading, I was appalled when Mrs. Wise called on me to read and I had no idea where to start. I still recall the shame I felt and the vows I made never to be caught off task again. In fourth grade, bored with required revisions to an assigned thank you note to my aunt, I explained to the teacher that I had already done it at home and mailed it. Her anger when my lie was exposed was exceeded only by that of my mother, which reinforced my earlier acquired lessons about never offending adults. Later still, "normal" adolescent rebellion took the form of skipping classes, sneaking home late, and trying out lipstick, nail polish, and dance steps at my friends' houses in defiance of the rules of my religion. I avoided trouble at all costs.

With lessons learned about obedience and "truth" and recognitions established about authority and power, I left home for college desperate to be independent from adult control. While I identified the impositions of my family, church, school, and community as primarily oppressive and while I affiliated with the student resistance movements of the 1960s and 1970s, I retained a personally inhibiting fear of authority figures, a disabling passivity and avoidance of conflict, and a sometimes self-disruptive need to take care of others. I had learned well the socially imposed female role and in some ways had internalized what Sue Middleton (1993) calls "the dominant image of the feminine woman, which demanded their intellectual, sexual, and personal subordination" (p. 86).

## BECOMING THE TEACHER-MOTHER

Acknowledging the impositional nature of nurturance and the risks of positioning myself in a nurturant role continues to be very difficult for me. My identification of teaching with mothering extends back almost as far as I can remember. I come from a family where the women were traditionally teachers as well as mothers. My maternal great-grandmother came to the United States as a Swedish teacher-missionary in North Dakota. On both my mother's and father's sides of the family, great-aunts taught in one-room country schools. When my mother finished high school she, too, began to teach in those same country schools and attended a county normal school to get her teaching license.

My mother taught throughout my childhood, often in the classroom next to the one I attended or just down the hall. I remember, in particular, seventh grade, when my mother was my teacher. To a young adolescent, the distinctions between mother and teacher were blurred and confusing. Unsure of who she was supposed to be in relationship to me, I could not determine who I was either. Later, when my mother attended a state teacher's college to obtain her bachelor's degree in education, I was given the responsibility for caring for my younger brother and sisters, becoming the mother so she could continue to be the teacher. "Mother" and "teacher" seemed to be roles which could be interchangeably assumed by the women in my family. They also, therefore, seemed to be implicit in female identity and survival. While as a young girl I had actively rejected the idea of becoming a teacher, I had never doubted that I would be a mother.

Later, when I did become a teacher, the metaphor of teacher as mother seemed unquestionable for me—particularly since the beginning of my teaching career coincided with the birth of my two daughters. I wanted to take care of everyone. I wanted everyone to be happy. As I reflect back on those days, I now see the limitations of the metaphor and how an essentialized role of myself as mother had been imposed upon me and how I had extended that role into my teaching—it was something I was well prepared to do. I liked the image of myself as mother-sugar, the nurturer and caretaker of my own children, my friends and family, and even my students. I did not ask myself if mothering was what my students wanted or consider my complicity in continuing to impose traditional and essentialized ways of being.

Marianne Hirsch's (1989) book, *The Mother/Daughter Plot,* has been central to my reconceptualization of teacher as mother, to my understanding of the processes of imposition, and to my reflections on the dynamics of my work. I often wondered why my favorite book from childhood was *The Box Car Children* (Warner, 1950), a story of four orphans who find shelter and create a home in a deserted boxcar in the woods. Reading Hirsch recently, I recognized that my ongoing fascination with the reconstructed family life of the boxcar children was based on my understanding of myself as a teacher as well as on my relationships to my birth family.

Marianne Hirsch describes Freud's "Familienroman," the familiar story in which the "developing individual liberates himself from the constraints of family by imagining himself to be an orphan or bastard and his 'real' parents to be more noble than the foster family in which he is growing up . . . the imaginative act of replacing the parent with another, superior figure." She goes on to reframe Freud's definition, characterizing it as "the story we tell ourselves about the social and psychological reality of the family in which we find ourselves and about the patterns of desire which motivate the interaction among its members" (p. 9).

While I am still attempting to fully understand the significance of *The Box Car Children* in my life, I believe my fascination with the story anticipated my attempts to create a revision of my birth family through the establishment of alternative communities of nurture with students, with professional colleagues, and with the doctoral student research group—each of which has turned out to be transitory, a fragile shanty located in what Joanne Pagano (1990) terms the "patriarchal wilderness." By repositioning myself as the mother, I sensed that I could "protect" my newly formed families from the impositions that had troubled my early life; I could allow them to be themselves in my classroom, to create their own meanings. Marianne Hirsch's metaphor of the family romance thus provided a useful window into my developing role as teacher-nurturer during the twenty-odd years of my teaching career.

As I engaged in the process of reconceptualizing my role as an early childhood teacher educator, I continued to struggle with issues of authority, power, and control. As a mother and a teacher who is the daughter and granddaughter of teachers, I had, for most of my life, assumed without question that mothering and teaching were the nurturant work of women. While this relationship was undoubtedly imposed upon my thinking by traditional cultural expectations and by my own familial experience, I resisted examining it critically. Its functionality in scripting my life was too comfortable.

At the same time, however, I experienced dissonance between my romanticized role of teacher-nurturer and the institutionally imposed expectations that I be the expert, the disciplinarian, the giver of grades. Not at that time recognizing the potentially impositional nature of my nurturance, I resented and ultimately resisted what I saw as oppressive and impositional institutional behaviors toward my students.

Connections among mothering, teaching, imposition, and feminism became clearer to me several years ago. I was in Portland at a women's research conference, looking at the displays of books, when I discovered a special issue of *Women's Studies Quarterly* (1987) on feminist pedagogy. The essays in the journal offered a sympathetic way to think about my teaching and the dilemmas I was facing over issues of authority and control. As I read the discussions of teaching by Carolyn Shrewsbury, Nancy Schniedewind, and Ellen Berry and Elizabeth Black, I felt my own style of teaching acknowledged and validated in a manner very different from that which typically came with student course evaluations and peer reviews.

I felt particularly affirmed by Carolyn Shrewsbury (1987), who wrote of the need of women to build and maintain connections as the web of existence and who supported Carol Gilligan's (1982) contrast between "a self defined through separation and a self delineated through connection, between a self measured against an abstract ideal of perfection and a self assessed through the particular activities of care" (p. 10). Her words confirmed for me my attempts to avoid the oppressive relationships common in academic settings. By rightly focusing my energy on the relational aspects of my classroom, I believed, I could dilute the impositional effects of my power as a teacher.

I was teaching, at that time, a seminar on language development and was very excited by the high level of participation and enthusiasm of the students in the class, which included Petra, Susan, Gretchen, and Karen. As I reflected on the class and on the articles I had been reading, I faced, in a new way, the problem of reconciling my rather informal, not overtly impositional, elementary-school style of teaching (small-group, cooperative learning projects; drama and art activities; snacks; and "show and tell" of favorite books, experiences, and ideas) with what I perceived to be the norms of my profession—the distant, formal, rigorous approach to graduate education that positioned the teacher as the conveyor of expert knowledge and the determiner of the adequacy of others.

My colleagues and I at the University of Oregon had spent quite a bit of time during that quarter talking about the masks and alternative personas we all assumed to facilitate our academic work when we feared that being ourselves was not going to be legitimate. Unaware of Lee Ann Bell's (1989) ideas about the impostor syndrome, we puzzled over the conflicting feelings we had about "faking our way" through institutional rituals while, at the same time, realizing that our service to our communities, our mentorship of our students, and our involvement in scholarly activities were substantial and meaningful to us, at least.

As I had reflected on these discussions in terms of my personal experiences, it had seemed that they spoke to my inability to "fit into" the academic community of my institution. The journal articles on feminist pedagogy which I had discovered referred to those same issues but in a way that seemed to preclude apology and defeat. They appeared to valorize that way of teaching and being with which I identified so strongly. I found that I, too, still needed the approval of an outside expert.

In the excitement and infatuation of seeing myself legitimized as one who practiced her own form of feminist teaching rather than as a teacher who failed to accurately reproduce the traditional ritual behaviors of my profession, I began to imagine the multiple ways in which I could enact my now revalidated practices. I reread *Women's Ways of Knowing* (Belenky, Clinchy, Goldberger, & Tarule, 1986), *Maternal Thinking* (Ruddick, 1989), *In a Different Voice* (Gilligan, 1982), and *Caring* (Noddings, 1984) with a new sensitivity to how they defined me as a woman teacher and in doing so, reaffirmed feminist and relational conceptions of knowing and teaching as alternatives to traditional models of education.

At this point, mothering, nurturance, teaching, and feminism still seemed marvelously compatible to me. Belenky, Clinchy, Goldberger, and Tarule's (1986) model of "connected teaching," based on the metaphor of midwife and mother, particularly appealed to me as a way of conceptualizing my work as a teacher. Nel Noddings, in her book *Caring* (1984), augments their perspective on nurturance with her description of the "one-caring teacher" (p. 9) who is reactive, responsive, and receptive. I particularly liked how she describes the caring teacher valuing the feelings and ideas of each student and receiving them "for the interval of caring, completely and non-selectively" (p. 176). She writes, "Whatever she does for the cared for is embedded in a relationship that reveals itself as engrossment and in an attitude that warms and comforts the cared for" (p. 19). It was a perfect description of what I wanted to be as a teacher.

I also resonated with Paula Roy and Molly Schen's (1987) idea of being able to provide a safe place in the classroom that honored all voices and silences; nurtured the wholeness of learning rather than its fragmentation; emphasized process over product; and honored the private, personal, and subjective. The idea of creating a classroom where all participants could be themselves was very attractive. I determined that I would undertake a reanalysis of my teaching and explore just what feminist pedagogy might look like in my own classroom.

During the first part of the self-study process, I analyzed how my teaching corresponded to what Belenky, Clinchy, Goldberger, and Tarule (1986) call connected teaching and reflected on my role as a teacher in terms of their metaphor of midwife and mother. I sought in the model of connected teaching a legitimate escape from the impositions of the traditional teacher role. And, in my self-directed course of study, I literally "fell in love" with my self-imposed role of teacher-mother.

My background has made it almost inevitable that I would enthusiastically embrace the idea of teacher as midwife. The oldest of four children, I was given major responsibility for my younger brother and sisters after school and while my mother went to summer school. Fifteen years later, I found myself in a similar situation, as a single parent of two toddler daughters and one of two teacher education faculty at a small private college, taking care of my own children but also teaching 10 or 12 young women to become elementary school teachers. Nine years ago, with a new baby and my own doctoral program completed, I once again became a teacher-mother, struggling to maintain that dual identity which seemed so inevitable, yet so difficult.

Madeline Grumet (1988) was a very strong influence on my thinking about myself as a teacher-mother, her writings describing so clearly my own thoughts about teaching. In *Bitter Milk* she considers what teaching means to women and discusses our essential bonds, as women teachers, to first our own mothers and then to our children. She anticipates my recurring desire to contextualize my own work, even here, through stories about my mother, my grandmothers, and my children. She looks at the meaning of these relationships to our relations with other people's children, pointing out the contradictions between our experiences of childhood and mothering and the curriculum we offer, her words hinting at the unavoidably impositional nature of teaching. Grumet also speaks to the "mothering" process of teaching itself:

> Fluid and ubiquitous, housework and children have required women to
> accept patterns of work and time that have no boundaries . . . it is women

who compensate for the highly rationalized and fragmented arrangements of school time and space with our own labor and effort. For those who sustain the emotional and physical lives of others, there is no time out, no short week, no sabbatical, no layoff. The incredibly time-consuming work of consulting with students and of responding sensitively and helpfully to their work is too often ignored when the teaching schedule is drawn up, when class size is determined, when salaries are negotiated. . . . And so, even though we secretly respect this maternal pedagogy of ours, it seems personal to us, not quite defensible in this public place, and we provide this nurturant labor without demanding the recompense it deserves. (pp. 86–87)

I was immediately attracted to her discussion of maternal pedagogy, and my courtship with her ideas was intense. She was writing about the difficult position I found myself in, also facing work that never seemed to end, knowing that the nurturant work with my students was essential to me and was even what defined me as a teacher, but also realizing that these efforts were not valued in the salaried, merit and tenure-based system of education in which I was employed. The imposing standards of the institution and its expectations that I present an expert and authoritative persona to the students seemed to conflict directly with my need to relate to them on an interpersonal level and share in the process of co-constructing knowledge. Grumet's writings helped crystallize the dilemma for me. I began to understand better that there were inherent conflicts between being the nurturant teacher and performing the contracted job of teaching but that teachers, like mothers, were positioned by our society to serve.

My desire to understand how the teacher-nurturer functions in academic institutions led me to explore my self-assigned role as teacher-nurturer directly. Long-distance discussions with my colleague Kathleen Casey, who had also recently discovered Marianne Hirsch's (1989) *Mother/Daughter Plot*, helped clarify the personal meaning the metaphor held for me. As she shared the stories she was collecting for her life-history study of women teachers (Casey, 1993), I became even more committed to studying the enactment of teacher-nurturer in my own classroom. I applied for and received a curriculum grant from the University of Oregon Center for the Study of Women in Society to develop a course on "Women and Children in the Workplace" in which I consciously experimented with feminist pedagogy. The next term, I conducted a seminar analyzing issues in feminist research and formed the research support group with Petra, Susan, Gretchen, and Karen to promote our mutual socialization into academic rituals and environments while, I hoped, allowing each of us to reexamine our roles as teacher educators and the problems we faced with issues of imposition. My whirlwind romance with being mother/midwife climaxed a year later, in the development of a course on "Teacher as Mother," a seminar which turned out to be critical to my reconceptualization of these issues.

The "Teacher as Mother" seminar was cotaught with Petra. We spent an intense month creating a syllabus that incorporated the reading of fiction, selections from feminist theory and teachers' biographies, and life histories constructed by participants in the seminar. Petra and I agreed that the seminar was going to be "perfect," uniting theory, fiction, and personal life experience in a way that validated participants and empowered them to become active agents in changing their own teaching and that of their schools.

Susan, Gretchen, and Karen registered for the class along with 15 other women. On the first day we told the class that we hoped to explore metaphors of mothering and nurturing through the use of literature and life history and to establish a mutually supportive context for our learning. The fictions about mothering—Buchi Emecheta's (1979) *Joys of Motherhood*, Doris Lessing's (1988) *The Fifth Child*, Toni Morrison's (1987) *Beloved*, Tillie Olsen's (1980) "As I Stand There Ironing," and a selection from Louise Erdrich's (1985) "Beet Queen"—were assigned as the primary curricular texts, thus fulfilling another of my long-suppressed fantasies—to sit around with a group of thoughtful colleagues and discuss novels and poetry. Petra was interested in promoting understanding of the readings about feminist theory. I wanted to encourage the use of fiction as curricular text.

I began the seminar by articulating my desire to examine my own personal questions about the relationships between mothering, nurturance, and teaching. In exploring the metaphor of teacher as mother, I hoped to analyze my own chosen role as teacher-nurturer and my attempts to develop a relational educational context that supported the personal knowledge construction of the students. As I later examined these attempts to respect and validate difference and to honor the needs of the students, I found that my romanticized role of teacher-mother somehow was not received by the students in quite the way that I had intended.

## THE IMPOSITION OF NURTURANCE

As I look back, I recognize that I had been seduced by the notion of being the good mother, creating an alternate family in the classroom, caring for the students in the belief that they, like good children, would sustain me and care for me, too. My previous struggles to be the "good university professor"—objective, rational, and distant—had been extremely painful. The notion of connected teaching, with its emphasis on the nurturing of relationships based upon commitment and caring, had affirmed, for me, the interconnectedness of people, ideas, and experiences and had intuitively guided my teaching for the past 20 years. But in this class it was not working right. Not all of my students understood mothering to be synonymous with nurturing or caring. Some found my "connected" teaching style impositional.

In enacting my aims as a feminist teacher, I had valued interpersonal involvement highly and thus tried to facilitate it during the class meetings. What became problematic, however, was the process of selecting issues and experiences for inclusion. Whose issues? Whose experiences? By leading the discussions, Petra and I invariably made the decisions. I had positioned myself as a participant in the seminar with personal experience to share as a woman, a teacher, and a mother, but I also carried the often contradictory official responsibilities of monitoring the seminar, reading journals, grading papers, and providing instructional leadership.

Petra faced the added burden of being both the graduate student colleague of the other students in the class and also their instructor. The intricacies of the relationships among participants were made more complex by the presence of several students from the early childhood master's degree program, the education department secretary, and the other members of the women's research group, all of whom, at times, claimed special status or had unique instructional needs. In our anticipated classroom of collaboration and connection these complications should have enriched the multiplicity of perspectives. In the reality of the seminar, differing needs and expectations contributed to a mood of frustration and discontent. Multiple perspectives often seemed disruptive rather than enriching.

The participants' concern with collaboration, trust, oppression, and resistance was apparent during the seminar. Concerns arose over "accuracy," representation, and privacy in the life-history assignments. The fiction was dismissed by some as irrelevant or offensive. Debates ensued about whether it was appropriate to critique each other's work. One student commented that "you're not oppressed unless you feel oppressed," provoking strong disagreement and even anger in the class. These issues became central themes both in the construction of meaning around the formal curriculum and in the understanding of the ongoing interaction within the seminar context. As participants critiqued the meaning of mothering, teaching, and nurturance in terms of the content of the course, they found themselves also analyzing them in their ongoing interactions and experiences with each other. As they identified the mothering in the fiction they were reading, they faced the reproduction of these relationships with each other, with me, and with Petra—but in some cases the "mothers" were not always perceived as "good."

Arguments broke out during class. While Petra and I reminded seminar participants of the importance of accepting everyone's voice and examining each position openly, control issues within the seminar were of prominent concern to all. It was not the congenial family gathering we had planned. Despite our desire for an egalitarian and collaborative classroom, the issues of power and position would not go away. Issues of mothering and teaching were emotionally intense for most of the women in the class and they held clear and often contradictory expectations about how they should be handled. I rationalized that the repeated disagreements during the seminar were related to Petra's and my privileged positions in the group and to my inability to always be "on" as the good teacher-mother. I suspected that the problems with group process were the result of my lingering needs for control and of my absence from class during two critical weeks at the beginning of the term. I sometimes missed the cues and thus the opportunities offered by the discomfort of the class and had focused on myself, on my inability to enact the perfect seminar that Petra and I had envisioned.

As I reflected later on our experiences in the seminar, the plot began to make sense. I had imposed my metaphor of teacher as mother on the class. I had wanted to provide my students with opportunities to explore feminist theories but also to focus on their own experiences as they related to being women, teachers, and mothers. Many of the students had no interest in the theory and expected the course to emphasize their personal roles as the mothers and teachers of young children. For some, mothering was irrelevant to their understanding of teaching. For others, theory was not given a central enough place in the curriculum. I had wanted us to connect with each other around our experiences as mothers and teachers, but I had also wanted to make clear the interconnections between our own experiences and the lives of women in other situations, as represented in the novels and in the biographic selections. For some of the students, the mothers of the novels and their life experiences were too strange to relate to, too far from the reality of daily life in Eugene. Identifying with mothering was the last thing some of the others wanted to do.

As our imposed curriculum was questioned from all sides, I retreated further from directly teaching the class. Strategies once taken for granted, such as formally explicating the text or asking questions about reading assignments, became the impetus for my agonizing reflection and self-criticism. Was I doing connected teaching right? How impositional could I be in a class where I had vowed to have collaboration and connection? In retrospect, my certainty about what they should do, my desire for them to reenact my practice of using literature to understand my own experience, seemed inappropriate, an unpardonable imposition. I began to recognize that in even simple interactions with the students, the imposition of my ideas, my values, and my stories would occur. The power I carried as a teacher and as a member of their thesis and dissertation committees could not be denied.

I struggled with what Maher and Tetreault (1994) term the "use of authority" (p. 20). By simply being in the classroom, I was still "in control." It seemed at the time necessary for me to relinquish that control if the romanticized relationships of the seminar were to work. Conflict and pain over issues of responsibility welled up in me, and I realized that I could not simultaneously be the mother of all of them, nor did they want me to be. Their needs and expectations were so different, some seeking intense analytical discussions of theory or critical deconstruction of the fictional texts; some seeming to say, as Saundra Gardner's (1989) student commented, "You need to act more like a teacher and less like one of us" (p. 66); others just wanting to be there and enjoy their relationships with me and with others in the group; and a few seeking an interpersonal connection that frightened me with its intensity and need. I became paralyzed, enmeshed in preserving the illusion of the happy family, unsure of what my role as teacher should be.

## RETHINKING THE TEACHER-MOTHER ROLE

I had begun to fully construct the family romance in the surrogate family of our classroom—wedded through the syllabus to theory and representing myself as the safe, nurturant caretaker of my students, I had succumbed to a conventional and essentialist definition of "mother" as a child-centered and self-blaming martyr, protecting her "children" from the outrages of "male devised educational strategies" (Hirsch, 1989: 14). I had positioned myself to be the social idea of motherliness, what Hirsch calls the "object of idealization and nostalgia," but found myself to be the mother whose children-students seemed to "reject and surpass [her] in favor of allegiance to a morally and intellectually superior male world" (p. 14).

Consistent with what frequently happens in families, my response to the perceived failure of my maternal-nurture fantasy was to become the fictional wicked stepmother, blaming students for not reading the texts, criticizing them for not doing their group projects "right," chiding them for not getting along with each other. Frustrated with having their needs and expectations imposed on me, I accused them, in my mind, of betraying me for the security of the familiar world of patriarchal power and institutions, where, as Hirsch (1989) describes, "mothers have little control over their children's paths to maturity . . . where children betray their mothers and abandon them, or are forcibly abducted, and where husbands act as enemies, [and where] maternal anger is depicted as . . . threatening" (p. 39). I suppose it was inevitable that eventually I psychologically abandoned the class for the safety of my solitary office and writing projects; I truly became the silenced mother, my anger creating for me a space of separation (Hirsch, 1989).

It has taken me several years to gain insight into my romantic attraction to the idea of being the teacher-mother, to understand the impositional nature of that role, and to identify the dysfunctional nature of the family I tried to create. The class focused my awareness on issues of attachment and separation, my romanticization of the teacher–student relationship, and the reality of the "family plot." As I examined the social construction of mother, I recognized that to be the mother meant to acknowledge an imposed "patriarchal construction" (Hirsch, 1989: 167), whereby the paternal is elevated to a position of superior power and, as mother, I am placed in opposition to him. By naming myself as teacher-mother, I felt I had given up my direct authority as teacher-expert, relinquishing it to some unnamed patriarchal standard of the university which some of my students still espoused. I saw that my being the mother defined the students as children, thus denying them their agency and their difference from me and denying myself my separate identity from them. I realized that this, then, was the imposition of nurturance. Recognizing that my impositions on the students were clearly as significant as the institutional and cultural impositions under which I worked, I acknowledged, again, the multisided issues, the impositional nature of all relationships between students and teachers, and the very real difficulties inherent in the teacher-as-mother position.

I take very seriously Elizabeth Ellsworth's (1989) suggestion to reflect on the "desire for unity in a community of opposition." I have become more aware of the complexity of the relationships between me and my students and of the potential for the negotiation of position and power in the classroom. By analyzing the continually interrupted and reinitiated dialogue in the "Teacher as Mother" seminar, I am able to appreciate more completely the tentative and shifting balance between theory, fiction, and life experience and the reoccurring tension between curriculum and the emergence of personal relationships and meaning.

I have also reconstructed my metaphoric definition of teacher-mother, recognizing, with Petra's prompting, that my enactment of teacher-as-mother was as much about social change, about making people's lives better, as about caretaking; that teaching, for me, is a political act. I recognize how I had been swept up with the essentialized definition of mothering and teaching as a facilitative, nurturant, caretaking role, as "women's true profession." But it can be more than that. As I struggled to make sense of this teaching experience, I reread Kathleen Weiler (1988), whose words powerfully reminded me that women do teach for change. My deep attachments to my female ancestors, I realize, are firmly rooted in their determination to reshape the public spheres of their times through missionary work, teaching in one-room country schools, and nursing—to work, like the teachers in Kathleen Casey's (1993) study, for social change. Understanding this has helped me to realize that my own teaching practice encompasses political activism and social change as well as nurturance—I am doing the missionary work of the 1990s, impositional perhaps, but engaged with the same passion and hope as that of my great-grandmother. I've decided that mothering can be an epistemological standpoint after all.

And still I have questions. As I reflect back on my experience with the class, I ask: Can we even hope to reach a common metaphor for our relationships with each other and for our work as teachers, or must we learn to link our different stories across what Elizabeth Ellsworth calls our "irreducible differences"? How are we constructed as women teachers and how best can we open ourselves to a critical and feminist pedagogy? I still wonder: What are the impositions inherent in the connected teaching role? In what ways do dissent and resistance allow participants to become separate and maintain autonomous values and identities? Can our transformations of the curriculum ever be achieved outside the active participation-through-resistance of our students?

How can we acknowledge student voices, with our own, as the source for reconceptualizing our work? And finally I ask: Are the impositions which separate us essential to our roles as teachers? Are they inescapable realities of which we must constantly be aware? Are we each always both the imposer and the imposed on?

## REFERENCES

Belenky, M. F., Clinchy, B. M., Goldberger, N. R., & Tarule, J. M. (1986). *Women's ways of knowing: The development of self, voice and mind.* New York: Basic Books.

Bell, L. (1989). Something's wrong here and it's not me: Challenging the dilemmas that block girls' success. *Journal for the Education of the Gifted, 12*(2), 118–130.

Berry, E., & Black, E. (1987). The integrative learning journal. *Women's Studies Quarterly, 15*(3 & 4), 59–64.

Casey, K. (1993). *I answer with my life: Life histories of women teachers working for social change.* New York: Routledge.

Ellsworth, E. (1989). Why doesn't this feel empowering?: Working through the repressive myths of critical pedagogy. *Harvard Educational Review, 59*(3), 297–324.

Emecheta, B. (1979). *The joys of motherhood.* New York: George Braziller.

Erdrich, L. (1985). Beet queen. In S. Walker (Ed.), *The Graywolf annual two: Short stories by women* (pp. 15–31). St. Paul, MN: Graywolf Press.

Gardner, S. (1989). Responding to differences in the classroom: The politics of knowledge, class, and sexuality. *Sociology of Education, 62*(1), 64–74.

Gilligan, C. (1982). *In a different voice: Psychological theory and women's development.* Cambridge, MA: Harvard University Press.

Grumet, M. (1988). *Bitter milk: Women and teaching.* Amherst: University of Massachusetts Press.

Hirsch, M. (1989). *The mother/daughter plot: Narrative, psychoanalysis, feminism.* Bloomington: Indiana University Press.

Jipson, J. (1992a). Midwife and mother: Multiple reflections on curriculum, connections, and change. *Journal of Curriculum Theorizing, 10*(1), 89–116.

Jipson, J. (1992b). What's feminist pedagogy got to do with early childhood practice? In S. Kessler & B. Swadener (Eds.), *Reconceptualizing early childhood education* (pp. 149–161). New York: Teachers College Press.

Jipson, J., & Munro, P. (1992). What's real: Fictions of the maternal. *Journal of Curriculum Theorizing, 10*(2), 7–28.

Lessing, D. (1988). *The fifth child.* New York: Random House.

Maher, F., & Tetreault, M. (1994). *The feminist classroom.* New York: Basic Books.

Middleton, S. (1993). *Educating feminists: Life histories and pedagogy.* New York: Teachers College Press.

Miller, J. (1989, April). *Critical issues in curriculum.* Paper presented at the annual meeting of the American Educational Research Association, San Francisco, CA.

Morrison, T. (1987). *Beloved.* New York: New American Library.

Noddings, N. (1984). *Caring: A feminist approach to ethics and moral education.* Berkeley: University of California Press.

Olsen, T. (1980). As I stand there ironing. In J. Mazow (Ed.), *The woman who lost her names* (pp. 29–37). San Francisco: Harper & Row.

Pagano, J. (1990). *Exiles and communities: Teaching in the patriarchal wilderness.* Albany: State University of New York Press.

Roy, P., & Schen, M. (1987). Feminist pedagogy: Transforming the high school classroom. *Women's Studies Quarterly, 15*(3 & 4), 110–115

Ruddick, S. (1989). *Maternal thinking: Toward a politics of peace.* Boston: Beacon Press.

Schniedewind, N. (1987). Teaching feminist process. *Women's Studies Quarterly, 15*(3 & 4), 15–31.

Shrewsbury, C. (1987). What is feminist pedagogy? *Women's Studies Quarterly, 15*(3 & 4), 6–14.

Warner, G. (1950). *The box car children.* Chicago: Albert Whitman.

Weiler, K. (1988). *Women teaching for change: Gender, class and power.* South Hadley, MA: Bergin & Garvey.

# CHAPTER 2

## Becoming the Good Mother:
## The Emergent Curriculum of Adolescent Mothers

*Susan Victor*

I don't mean to impose . . .

The door was partially opened as I knocked, silently wondering, as loud music streamed through the door, if Cassie had indeed come home from the hospital. Her husband, a prep cook and busboy at a local fish restaurant, had left me an "it's a girl" message the day before. As I mused over the fact that Dave and Cassie have been together since the sixth grade, Cassie opened the door. I walked in, followed by Shira, a 19-year-old mother of two, clearly showing the bulge of a third. "Shame on you," Cassie quipped, glancing at Shira's stomach. "Tell me about it," Shira grimaced.

Cassie pointed to the bassinet where her newborn, Teresa, lay sleeping. Four-year-old Claire, her first, played outside with neighbor children. Cassie picked up the telephone to continue her call with the local newspaper, to place a birth announcement. Although she had known me since the previous April, within the context of her home, she assumed the distance and quiet suspicion of the others in the house. I tried to relax but I was aware that, unlike Shira, I was bothered by the loud music, the smoke, the four friends sitting on the couch, seeming to stare into space or at Dave, who lay shirtless on an opened sofa bed in the middle of the living room. As I walked toward the bassinet, they viewed me guardedly and I felt my skin emanating "agent of social control" (McRobbie, 1978).

It reminded me of many visits to the homes of the adolescent mothers in the program, where everything about me seemed somehow wrong—my clothes, my language, my purpose. Later, I asked Shira if they (Cassie's family) thought I was from CSD, the local child abuse prevention/protection agency. Shira smiled knowingly but said nothing and took another bite of her hamburger. I saw myself in my mind, hugging Cassie as we left, telling her that she looked "wonderful" and the baby was "just beautiful," and I cringed. The artifacts of my European middle-class upbringing brought to light a clash of cultures and class.

Cassie and Shira and 13 other adolescent women participated in a psychoeducational/support group which I facilitated for a period of 19 months. For the purposes of this chapter, the group serves as the context for an examination of the issues facing adolescent mothers as mothers, women, and adolescents and highlights the issues of imposition I faced as teacher-counselor and curriculum developer.

I began working for a parent education and support agency in a town in the Northwest in January 1989 (Victor, 1990). My initial role was that of curriculum consultant; I was asked to create a 3-to-6-month curriculum "package" for the five groups in the teenage parent program (approximately 200 young women aged 12 to 21). At the time, I struggled not only with the concrete tasks of creating a curriculum guide and "lessons" within "units" for the group setting, but more with the question, whose curriculum is this anyway? Any curriculum I develop, from my perspective as a Jewish American high school psychology teacher raised in a European, middle-class family, is not their curriculum. Curriculum based on what I think is important cannot reflect their experiences as a culture; rather, it is an imposition of my life experiences and formal education (and perhaps my desire to promote social and psychological change) on the 15 adolescent mothers in the group.

My attempts to develop and implement curriculum in the program presented a conflict of agendas. How do I, as curriculum developer and later as a group facilitator, negotiate the needs of the agency (above which hovered a board of directors anxious to secure more funding), the views of the academic "experts," and the emerging curriculum of the women in the group? In the struggle to find compromises, I had to face the prevailing societal beliefs and expectations of this population held by representatives of the agency, the majority of the academic experts (for example, Elkes & Crocitto, 1987; Elkind, 1984; and Furstenberg, Brooks-Gunn, & Lansdale 1989), and me.

In April 1989, I was hired by the agency to be a "teen parent educator." The title does not connote the myriad roles I assumed in relation to my group: facilitator/group leader, therapist, teacher, social worker, counselor, chauffeur, mother figure, friend, and advocate. As facilitator, I tried to foster exploration of the many issues the members face as women, mothers, and adolescents: relationships, effects of sexual abuse, the expression of feelings, the expectations of parenting and domestic tasks as "women's work," second pregnancies, the pain of separation, sex, the desire to be a good parent—and the constant fears of making a mistake—healing high school experiences, and coping with discrimination (Victor, 1992). This last topic infused many discussions and, perhaps more than any other, raised the question of imposition.

An example: I pointed to a large chart with the children's names, asking questions about their social/physical/cognitive development in the last 3 months. The girls seemed bored and annoyed. "Did you see *Geraldo* yesterday?" one asked. They all spoke at once, words and anger tumbling out. They were pissed off. Geraldo had had three teenage mothers on the show and apparently presented (with the help of a provocative expert and, as usual, an enthusiastic audience) their experience as dismal and shameful. "They said our lives were over," Laura said, looking at me with a "Can-you-believe-this-bullshit?" face. We discussed society's stereotypes and how they were clearly just that, and certainly did not fit the experiences of this group. They said we should write a letter. We did. I stopped myself from taking their words, which I had written on the back of my "development lesson," and forming them into a "correct-sounding" essay. Instead, I handed the sheet to Laura to write. They decided a letter to the television station was not enough and that it should be printed in the agency's column in the local newspaper. Seven weeks later, I brought them copies of their column (although the editor demanded I add "800 to 1,000 words"). The pride was in their faces for weeks, and it made me realize how much they had to say about their experience. The transformation of my lesson into an opportunity to have their voices heard promoted their growth and self-esteem (and ultimately awareness of their children's needs) more than the study of a chart of the children's development would have.

This chapter is about the experiences of adolescent mothers—as reflected in the discussions of 15 women over a 19-month period—and about the points at which I, their teacher-counselor, confronted several impositional impasses in relation to them and to their learning. I analyzed the 70 sessions with the group in attempts to address three dilemmas. First, how have prevailing stereotypes forced us to neglect the concerns of adolescent mothers as adolescents, women, and mothers? "Experts" lack a true understanding of how adolescent mothers respond to the needs of a child while coping with adverse social and economic circumstances and resolving issues of their own development. This is reflected in my struggle to decide throughout what to call them. I get chastised by my feminist colleagues for referring to them as "girls." They grimaced when I addressed them as "women," and the phrase "teen moms" seems to reinforce stereotypes.

Second, whose knowledge should serve as foundation for curriculum? By insisting that the group members adapt to a curriculum imposed by bureaucratic decisions about funding and infused by societal discomfort with adolescent sexuality and adolescent parenting, we facilitate their dependency and deny their participation in the social construction of their own knowledge (Belenky, Clinchy, Goldberger, & Tarule, 1986). Moreover, their curriculum may not fit my labels. What *do* adolescent mothers say about their experiences as adolescents, women, and mothers?

Third, how did the cultural, psychological, and educational baggage I brought to this process affect the content and processes of the group? My interpretations of and reactions to the women's words and actions, in reflecting artifacts of my 30 years, confounded and enhanced their education. In addition, my belief that they must understand the dynamics of past family relationships and their effects on the present self infused any curricular decision I made. As Jan did, I must also reconceptualize teaching as mothering and mothering as learning. In this context, to be the teacher-mother has multiple meanings and poses multiple problems.

I begin by contextualizing this project within the, at times, patriarchal restrictions of the agency, raising challenges to the agency's philosophy. My journals of the 19 months supply the "data" for a summary and analysis of the group's content and process(es). My attempts at resolving the conflicting agendas of the agency, the facilitator, and the members as well as other areas of impositional conflict are questioned anew in the conclusion.

## THE IMPOSING FIGURE

The primary agenda of the agency is the prevention of child abuse and neglect. The following are the agency's statements of philosophy and objectives and my initial reactions:

1. We are dedicated to promoting good parenting skills and positive attitudes toward parenting.
   *What are "good parenting skills"? Their definition must be age-, class- and culture-specific.*

2. The agency is open to all parents regardless of race, religion, lifestyle, level of education, or economic status.
   *What problems arise when the agency attempts to address the needs of two disparate economic groups, and what is the meaning of having separate curricula?*

3. We do not advocate any particular political or theoretical orientation toward child rearing, with the exception of "encouraging parents to find ways to promote the physical and emotional health, safety and well-being of their children."
   *Is it possible to do this, to teach without a political and/or theoretical position?*

4. Support groups should aid to strengthen family relationships by providing an outlet for the expression of concerns, as well as modeling nurturing behavior.
   *For whom? If adolescent mothers are really still children, was I not valid in the tremendous urge I felt to mother the mothers?*

5. Parenting is an extremely valuable occupation.
   *Could it be a contradiction to emphasize that and getting a job, going back to school, and so on?*

6. Support groups should be noncompetitive.
*Yet competition may be a natural reaction to feelings of self-doubt in adolescents.*

7. Group facilitators should have some knowledge of child development, parenting approaches, child abuse, and communication skills. *But what kind of knowledge? Women learn in connection with others, according to Belenky and others (Belenky et al., 1986), and teenage mothers especially value experiential knowledge. The degrees I hold or the books I have read are not valid indicators of true knowledge in these areas of parenting.*

8. Groups should not be therapy groups; parents needing extensive emotional assistance are referred to mental health professionals. The group instead should be a forum for support and education.
*It will become clear as I describe the group and my role in it that it served all three functions: support, education, and therapy. Hence, my role shifted from facilitator to teacher to therapist; the formal role was not defined and had no limitations.*

The program for adolescent parents began in 1983 to address the special needs of adolescent mothers. In 1987, close to 500 women under 19 gave birth in the county, according to Planned Parenthood (1988). There is an intense focus in the teenage parent program on practical as well as emotional support and the fostering of the healthy development of parent and child. The three components of the program are psychoeducational/peer support groups, social activities, and home visits. The group, as the primary function of the program, is to be a nurturing and nonthreatening environment in which to discuss personal concerns. The members must perceive the group as a nurturing and safe place in order to risk exposing themselves. The five groups are divided by age (14–17, 17–21, 21–24/graduate) and geographical area. The teen parent program's goals, besides fostering healthy development, include the following:

1. To prevent future unwanted pregnancies.
*Unwanted by whom? The teens want them, sometimes less than consciously. They express logical reasons for wanting a second child, reasons we may not like but with which we may not be able to argue.*

2. To encourage continuing education and/or job preparation.
*Does this not conflict with the statement that "parenting is an extremely valuable occupation"? By encouraging another occupation, are we not devaluing motherhood as not "doing something"?*

3. To develop healthy interpersonal relationships.
*This is probably the core of the curriculum, from my perspective.*

Whereas most such programs are aimed at prevention, this program responds to the need of this population for social support (Scales, 1987).

## THE GROUP: A CONTEXT FOR DEVELOPMENT

The 15 women[1] who came to my group were aged 17 to 20. Five were living with a partner and one was a single mother who lived with her mother and daughter. There were 22 children in the group: 10 boys and 12 girls, ranging in age from 3 weeks to 3½ years. Five women had two children; two were pregnant with a second; and one had three. The youngest age at first pregnancy was 14; the remainder first became pregnant at 15 or 16.

Ten women relied on their partner's income from manual labor jobs (mostly within the lumber industry); eight received some form of federal assistance (Aid to Families with Dependent Children [AFDC] and/or low-income housing, food stamps, or Women, Infants, and Children [WIC]—a federal program which provides infant formula and food); six had part-time jobs (in retail, fast food, or child care). Eleven finished high school or its equivalent; three left high school in the first or second year, and one was completing her high school requirements at a teen parent school—a self-contained classroom housed in a church which several had attended. Four were attending college and two had recently finished degrees at a business college.

A brief family survey was given to the 186 women in the program. Although the exercise was initially one for funding purposes, the numbers provided some concrete validation of the staff's beliefs about this population and confirmed findings in the literature (Landy, Schubert, Cleland, Camillia, & Montgomery, 1983). Of the women in my group who responded to the survey, 7 were sexually abused, 5 were emotionally abused, and 2 were physically abused as children. Eleven grew up in a family where a member was alcoholic or used illegal drugs, and an additional 4 described their families as having "a lot of fighting." Only 4 grew up with both parents. Four admitted to having been in a relationship in which they were battered by the partner. Three noted they had a "problem" with alcohol or drugs.

## TEEN MOTHERS ARE TALKING: AN ANALYSIS OF THE GROUP CONTENT

The content reflects recurring topics which were not necessarily part of my formal curriculum but were reflective of the participants' emerging curriculum. They are issues the group participants faced as women, mothers, and adolescents, issues that serve as a reflection of their developmental as well as their class position, their participation in the culture of late adolescence, and their experience as an oppressed class, gender, and population. (The factor often missing in the academic literature is the compounding class and gender struggles these young women face before pregnancy.) As I weave through these topics, pausing to reflect on their meaning for the group and for the curriculum, I begin to see the participants' creation of a new personal identity, as individuals and as a collective.

## The Body, Delivery, and Birth Control

They lamented loudly the changes to their bodies and longed for the 105-pound body of sophomore year. On a home visit to Judy, she showed me a picture of herself as a cheerleader; "See, see, I was thinnnn," she asserted as though, looking at her body now, I'd never believe her. At a visit to the hospital after Sally gave birth to her second daughter, she insisted, "I brought my jeans to wear home. They're size 3!"

I heard these comments at times as "typically adolescent" but more often as premature concerns of young women who have become older before their time. They sounded like older women who mourn the loss of the young body they had before childbirth. They were also young women who felt the pressure to fit an image perpetrated by glamour magazines and diet soda commercials. For adolescents who are just getting comfortable with a changing body, pregnancy and delivery prompt sudden and dramatic physical changes, compounding anxiety around physical appearance (Schneider, 1987).

The pregnancy is a touchstone; its discovery and, later, the delivery found their way into many discussions. Sharing delivery stories appeared to be a way to initiate or welcome a new member into the group. They described hospital delivery rooms and procedures in detail: who was present, the length of labor, the comments of doctors and nurses. They gave advice to expectant mothers in the group.

One third of the women in the group had two children. The rest struggled with the desire to have another and often decided to do so for what seemed to them to be logical reasons: Siblings should be "close together." "They'll be teenagers and I'll be in my 30s and have my whole life." Besides, "you don't want to be an old grandparent." But what about education? What about careers? I asked but restrained myself from imposing the results of my upbringing, and felt guilty that I appeared to devalue motherhood as not "doing something." It was a clash of traditions. All agreed that "motherhood is the most important job." For many, it resulted in feeling competent and significant for the first time in their lives (Dash, 1989; Fine, 1988; Williams, 1994).

Concerns about birth control echoed those of most women. They mistrusted and disliked every form. "I have a friend whose sister-in-law got pregnant on the pill and her baby was deformed." Martha got two periods a month while Rachel got two a year. Shira claimed she conceived while on the pill, but after some prodding, she revealed she had taken two weeks off because "I'm allergic." Shaina, a prenursing student, tried to explain the fertility cycle but after several minutes was reminded (by me) that the rhythm method only works if the cycle is regular. I suggested alternatives such as the diaphragm, and Patti looked at me with a grimace: "That's so old-fashioned." The group fell into a sort of "ooh, gross" discussion about diaphragms and tampons. I was struck by the shift in tone, from women to adolescents, from confusion and concern to generalized fears bordering on the paranoid. I made a note to bring in a speaker from Planned Parenthood later that month. Another imposition?

### Relationships, Men, and the Promise of Romance

Fantasies of romance and the ideal partner pervaded the discussion, as did frustrations with inequity in child care and domestic responsibilities, sexual demands, and lack of communication and trust. As one of the members reflected, the discussion always "goes back to sex" and men. They talked, as women, about the difficulty in knowing what men are feeling, about knowing when you love someone. "You don't. Everyone told me I'd know, but I still don't," Carly said, at her one-year anniversary with Jeff. They talked about knowing if you can trust.

They were frustrated as women that child care is "women's work" and that they often felt like they "have two kids to clean up after." Adolescent mothers may experience more conflict and stress in relationships with partners (Garcia-Coll, Hoffman, & Oh, 1987). Husbands or boyfriends may be, on the one hand, the primary source of support and on another, an additional source of stress (Levenson, Atkinson, Hale, & Hollier, 1978).

The importance of relationships and the desire for a man were reflected in comments like "I'd die if Jeff left me" and repeated memories of first encounters and weddings. Sullivan (1953) believes the adolescent needs to achieve crucial relationships with others in order to "secure her own interpersonal needs" and reduce the anxiety caused by isolation. McRobbie (1978) speaks of the social pressure adolescent girls experience to find the "ideal romance." Denisa, the only "single" mother in the group, became engaged to a man after knowing him only one month. On some less than conscious level, she responded to the feelings of missing something whenever we talked about partners. The group gave her a shower; one month later, the wedding was called off after Doug abused her. Many expressed painful disillusionment in their relationships.

They vacillated between the obstinacy of adolescents and the passivity of women forced to assume subservient roles. In their attempts, perhaps, to resolve the discrepancy in demands to become an adult and be feminine, the young women fell into stereotypic definitions of femininity rather than embracing their experience and knowledge as women, as suggested by McRobbie (1978) and Fine (1988). Wise and Grossman (1980) assert that teenage girls become pregnant in an attempt to confirm their femininity. Should they fulfill society's expectations of a maturing young adult versus those of a maturing young woman in a particular social context, they get chastised for not being "feminine" (Hudson, 1984).

Coping with unpredictable anger—both their own and that of their partners—and expression of other emotions was a multigenerational struggle. They recognized with insight the effects of "my father's temper" and shared ways of releasing anger. "It's never okay for a man to hit you," I said once in the group. "Oh, yes it is," Heidi retorted, "if you hit first." Talking with their partners "like we do here" seemed an impossible task. They wondered aloud why men don't talk. Although our last meeting of each month was open to partners, none came.

### Abuse and the Sexual Self

The topic of abuse surfaced in some form or context at almost every session. In contrast, it was not discussed in the more than 30 studies I reviewed. Close to 50% of the young mothers in the program had been sexually molested. Sex and their own sexuality had, for many, been an intrusive, at times violent, experience. They were victims of a perception of sexuality as violence not desire (Fine, 1988). A "discourse of desire" as suggested by Fine (1988) is empowering, in contrast, as it fosters a recognition of their needs and removes much of the stigma attached to their identity as sexually active adolescent women. It does not take psychological expertise to recognize the connection between forced premature sexuality and early pregnancy. As Rachel, who disclosed that she had been molested by her grandfather for several years, hypothesized, "Maybe that's why I had sex so young."

Butler and Burton (1990) suggest five reasons why child/adolescent sexual abuse may be linked to adolescent pregnancy. First, an adolescent girl may become pregnant by the perpetrator. Second, similarities in family dynamics exist in families of incest victims and those of adolescent mothers. Such similar characteristics may include a physically or psychologically absent mother, one whose absence may propel the daughter into a "motherly" role for younger siblings. Third, a sexually abused girl may learn that she is valued only to the extent that she fulfills the sexual desires of others, and thus, she becomes promiscuous. Fourth, low self-esteem, the need for comfort, and the desire to forget the abuse may together foster the creation of an "instant family." Fifth, for an adolescent girl who has been sexually abused, pregnancy may be a way to escape, an opportunity for independence.

Indeed, that a period of "youth" exists between and distinct from childhood and womanhood is a premise of developmental theory that does not fit these women's experience (Hudson, 1984). The boundaries between being a girl and becoming a woman are much less accentuated; the social oppression of females, the forced subordination, is the thread throughout the transition. When young women rebel against the oppression, it is in a form which still conforms to social expectations, in that it is often an expression of sexuality, that is, pregnancy and early motherhood. Thus, "girls' most common form of rebellion serves only to bind them more tightly to their subordination as women" (Nava, 1984: 15). Being a mother may serve to keep them oppressed but, at the same time, save them from the oppression of their adolescence.

The trauma of pregnancy appears, however, to trigger repressed memories of early sexual abuse.

> I was sitting on the bus and I just remembered. It was so weird. I was seven and a bunch of us kids were outside. There was this guy living next door who'd talk to us. This one day, he told them to go home and picked me up. (I was really small for seven.) The last thing I remember is him holding me like this . . . you know like a baby. That's the last thing I remember.          —Laura

In addition, the sexuality of pregnancy and giving birth often leads to an aversion to sex afterward. The tragedy of the victimization is compounded by their belief, typical of troubled adolescents, that they are "the only one" to whom this has happened or who has had these feelings. The self-blaming is prevalent. Rachel agonized before telling me about her own molestation experience because she feared "what you would think of me." My attempts to console her with statistics and my own experiences were not nearly as effective as a home visit with Sally, when she told Rachel and me quite openly about being molested by her stepfather over a period of 10 years. The abuse resulted in two pregnancies. On the drive home, Rachel interrupted her silence only once to say, "I'm blown away."

### Becoming the Good Adolescent Mother: Discrimination and Being a "Watched Woman"

> You're in a grocery store and your kid is crying. Everyone is staring and thinking, "teen mom."          —Rachel

If we recognize teenage mothers as a "culture," perhaps we will recognize that they are victims of discrimination. The women complained of frustrating encounters with members of the medical profession and representatives of social service agencies who treat them with condescension and disrespect. I recall sitting in a fast-food restaurant with two of the mothers and their children; while several customers stared with evident disapproval, the words of Sharon Olds's poem "Young Mothers IV" (1980: 42) kept going through my head:

> Suddenly I think she will scream, this watched woman, this marked woman stared at like the women with shaved heads in Germany in '44.

One of my objectives as a teen parent educator was to encourage the women to use community resources, to ask questions of "experts" when they were not sure. Many lacked a close relationship with their own mothers or other female relatives and thus often depended on other experts for guidance. They were adamant in their beliefs that no one could know how to parent unless she has done so. They did not believe they could be "taught" parenting skills any more than a parent of any other age could. They did not see themselves operating at a disadvantage due to their age. The absence of parenting questions directed at me probably reflected their belief that I did not possess true knowledge of motherhood. Indeed, whenever I asked questions about child development or child care, in order to facilitate discussion, they treated these like display questions and emphatically gave *me* the answers.

The belief among women that true knowledge can be gained only in relationships with others is discussed by Belenky et al. (1986); they write, "Valued lessons learned did not necessarily grow out of their academic work but in relationships with friends and teachers, life crises and community involvements" (p. 4). In this context as well, the women came to know themselves and to gain knowledge through relationships with others and life events.

Teenage mothers are rarely presented positively in the academic or popular literature. They are perceived in society at large as incompetent and irresponsible. They are viewed as lacking adequate parenting skills or the educational background to prepare their offspring for school (Furstenberg, Brooks-Gunn, & Lansdale, 1989). The perception of society as an "unsupportive ecology" (Lamb, 1988) is pervasive; they feel "like everyone is watching" and judging. This fear got projected by new members onto me and the other group participants. The anecdote about Cassie that began the chapter is an example.

They tested me silently; my adherence to confidentiality and my expressions of solidarity and care usually led to trust. The letter to Geraldo taught them two valuable lessons: first, someone in a position of "control" can be an advocate, and second, their voices can be heard. Each time a new mother joined the group, however, the struggle began anew. Learning to accept me as a support person meant taking some risks. Becoming their advocate meant my taking some risks. The Geraldo letter brought criticism from within the agency that perhaps I had "made them sound too good."

My cultural and class background was thrown in my face often. Visiting Cassie at home was one of many times when I faced the awkwardness of my European middle-class background. The agency insisted we provide the women with "material support," yet each time I brought a bag of donated clothes or tubes of toothpaste to the group, I felt the shame of my own privilege and the disrespect of assuming they wanted charity, as well as the disturbing realization that we were not doing enough to empower them.

### High School Memories

Adolescence and the high school years trigger emotional memories for most of us. For these teen mothers, high school seemed at once very distant and, from an emotional stance, very close. They could no longer explore different identities because the demands of parenting placed limitations on their exploration (Catrone & Sadler, 1984). Returning to school was often difficult because the role of mother changed the role of peer. Attempts to fall completely into the mother role could be thwarted by peer pressure to be sociable and by grandmothers who wanted to assume child care responsibilities (Levenson et al., 1978).

They recalled the blatant condemnation: Peers ridiculed, friends turned away, and teachers rejected. The awkward interactions and the covert message that they were a "bad example" forced many to leave school. Leaving is a reaction to the discomfort, but it can alter their educational and economic futures. Some completed their high school education in an alternative teen parent class housed off campus in a nearby church, the redemption quality of which was also discussed by Lesko (1990). To enter the class, a student must be pregnant (not parenting) and thus labeled by the district as "handicapped." The isolation does not represent the "least restrictive environment" discussed by Payne-Smith (1982), and it reinforces messages of incompetence and shame. Students had to complete their high school education by the time the child was 18 months old or return to the regular high school.

Shaina felt resentment at the pressure to leave, as she described the atmosphere at Millton High:

> The teachers stopped calling on me when I started showing, but I stayed.
> I wanted to walk with my class.

Carly, whose 3.97 grade point average made her salutatorian, gave birth to Amy during the summer between sophomore and junior years:

> I had to stay in school. I had to do it for me and Amy. I was determined not to go on welfare.

Melanie, Mariah, Rachel, and Kay had the opposite reaction. They felt "more comfortable" in the teen parent class because "everyone was going through the same thing." The lives they led in high school before the pregnancy seemed distant and foreign. Rachel described the experience of trying to resume her life as a high school student:

> After Jacob was born, I tried to go to a basketball game. It was like people thought I was there to get drunk again. In maturity level, it was me up here

and my friends down here. I couldn't believe I used to act like this. I was kind of glad I wasn't involved in that anymore.

Perhaps adolescent parenthood can reverse a path of self-destructive behavior, the presence of a baby prompting necessary maturity (Lesko, 1990; McRobbie, 1991).

Several participants knew each other in high school or knew of each other. Remnants of shifting alliances, rumors, and cliques surfaced slowly and suddenly in the group. Forms of "peer shock" (Elkind, 1984)—betrayal, exclusion, and disillusionment—present new challenges in adolescent social relationships. After a month or two without the intrusion of new members, the group seemed to solidify, allowing members to explore old conflicts and loyalties within a newly established solidarity. Rachel suddenly blurted out to Carly, "I didn't think you liked me." Shaina, whose friend Erica planned to join the group the following week, asked Melanie, in a concerned voice, if "you guys are still mad at each other." "Oh, God, no," Melanie responded. "That was years ago."

### Children's Development: Whose Is More Normal?

During early adolescence, children's cognitive processes begin to move from an egocentric perspective, where understanding of events is achieved only through personal experience (I, me, my), to a larger sociocentric view. This parallels an adolescent's ability to think in more global, abstract terms, reflective of the stage known as formal operations (Elkind, 1984). These shifts seem to be interrupted when a young adolescent becomes a parent (Wise & Grossman, 1980). Although she is learning to think and speak in abstract terms and anticipate the future, the teenage mother may regress to concrete, egocentric thinking in response to the immediate need to solve child-rearing problems (Marecek, 1987). In discussions about child development or any issue related to the care of children, for instance, I observed a seeming inability to consider such issues from a broader perspective of social concern.

Their furtive glances at me during many an exchange regarding the children's development seemed like searches for approval. Although they did not view me as an expert on parenting, they projected onto me and each other a need to know they were doing the right thing. The competitive tone of these discussions reminded me again that they are adolescents. At the risk of diminishing their concern for their child's normalcy, I could substitute anything in place of "my child." Their self-doubt, or what I interpret as self-doubt, was often soothed with comparisons. Their children's developmental milestones (crawling, standing, walking, getting a tooth, sitting on the toilet, saying a new word) were presented as their (the mothers') accomplishments. It was as though they wanted to say, "See what a good job I'm doing."

The direct instruction of child development and parenting skills is emphasized in most curricula or educational programs for teenage parents (Payne-
Smith, 1982). My attempts in the 19 months to impart such information directly
were unsuccessful and, I believe now, unnecessary. It was clear that they listened
to each other and to other mothers regarding issues of child rearing. I could not
impose my nonmother status via book knowledge. As Jan described, I did not
possess mothering knowledge, and my mothering of them was perhaps imposition enough. Moreover, the topics did not need to be compartmentalized into
"units" or "lessons." We talked about parenting and development whenever we
talked. The best I could do was to encourage reflection: How might that affect
Lacey? What's it like for Joshua to see you two fight? What might happen if
Damon is not ready for toilet training?

### "Sperm Donors" and New Fathers

The former is a term Rachel coined for the father of the (first) child who has
not been seen or heard from since the pregnancy. Typically, the first father leaves
the relationship and denies any responsibility (financial or otherwise) for parenting (Lamb, 1986). Often his physical disappearance is supported by his parents.
Rachel's resentment that her son's biological grandparents ignored his existence
was echoed by others. Carly, whose boyfriend left her when she became pregnant
and was later killed in a car accident, described how his parents were paying Amy's
doctor bills for a while and then suddenly stopped without explanation.

As much as the women resented the biological father's neglect, they feared
his return at least as much. Laura, who was interviewed on a local radio station,
did not want her name or the baby's name revealed, in case the biological father
heard it. (She had married and her husband had taken on the father role.)
Melanie shared with relief that her husband was allowed to adopt her first child
because the biological father had neglected to respond to the court. Denisa,
pregnant with her second and alone, received threatening calls from her former
fiance who claimed he would take the baby.

Those women who married the father of the second child faced additional
questions. Their concerns revolved around telling the child, providing equal
love and attention for both, and dealing with feelings of emotional inadequacy
and social ridicule in the older child.

> I worry so much about Jacob. We go to Jeff's parents' house, and they are
> all over Jeremy [the baby] and hardly pay any attention to Jacob. The last
> time, the two little cousins told Jacob he could not play with them because
> he wasn't "a real Brown."

Contrary to the literature (Marecek, 1987), these young mothers did seem
able to see the future, to predict psychological consequences, and to express

concern about the effects of the child's early identity on the child's later emotional well-being. They did worry. We spent several sessions discussing the issue of whose last name the child of a different father should have. The intense need for a resolution seemed a reflection of the fervent need in adolescence for an identity; within the last name lay, somehow, all that the child was or would become. (Giving the child the maternal last name was a possibility most did not consider.)

### Jobs Versus Careers—Economics

"It's a setback, that's all. My life isn't over." Carly's comment is in direct response to the prevailing preoccupation with teen pregnancy as a socioeconomic problem. The eight women in the group who received a form of federal assistance felt simultaneously dependent on and frustrated with a system which fosters both dependency and frustration. The decision to marry and the decision to find a job were complicated by the system; it was clear to me that the women in the group stayed on welfare because the costs of child care and medical insurance far exceeded the amount of money they could earn at traditionally low-paying jobs in the community.

Surviving financially meant being able to negotiate the welfare system effectively. They became skillful at knowing what to say when, and learned that receiving needed funds often depended on the mood of the caseworker. It may be a lesson in social awareness, but the system also perpetuated their tendency to focus control of their lives outside of themselves. I provided information in the form of community resources but did not engage in any moral discussion about honesty. They could express their frustration but it would have felt wrong for me to moralize. (How could I encourage financial planning if my checkbook balance was frequently negative?) What appeared, again, to be an inability to see the larger picture of their future and instead to focus on juggling each bill as it came,was a response to the experience that one's economic (and personal) decisions are out of one's control.

Those who relied on their partner's income from manual labor jobs were rarely more secure. Salaries, schedules, and benefits within the lumber industry are inconsistent. Most of the partners worked graveyard shifts, leaving the mothers alone, feeling unsafe at home. As facilitator, I felt the pressure to encourage educational and occupational development, yet it often felt impositional. I spoke in the language of "careers" while they, out of immediate necessity, spoke of "jobs."

Carly, who attended college full time and aspired to be an elementary school teacher, worked part time at a fabric store and lived with her mother, who operated an in-home day care. Shaina and Terri attended the community college and succeeded financially only because both husbands were in a union. Three women were finishing degrees at a business college; fortunately, the college worked with the local welfare office to support these students with deferred tuition, child care (until they find a job), and a clothing allowance.

University students, however, receive no such help. The federal government will only provide this assistance to students who are in short-term vocational programs. For many, a college degree seemed unattainable. On several visits with me to the university, they reacted to the environment as though it were a foreign culture. This, I firmly believe, was the result of their low self-perceptions of their intellectual abilities; I feel certain many could succeed in college. Their beliefs about higher education reflected the success of the social and governmental perpetuation of a class system, as well as the internalization of societal messages regarding their capabilities as girls/women and young mothers.

These are issues of economic class, issues faced by parents of all ages who are oppressed. These are not exclusively adolescent issues, but they are added burdens to young mothers. If adolescents are struggling to create a personal identity (Elkind, 1984; Erikson, 1968), they are amenable to external messages of worth and competence. Where, then, is the locus of blame?

### Families of Origin: Separation or Reconnection?

We were discussing mothers, and Shaina, whose generosity and sweet nature make the neglect of her mother painful to hear, told us:

> Rick and I met when I was a freshman. I didn't get pregnant until the middle of my senior year, but my mother kept saying I was pregnant. When I finally was, she kicked me out.

She waited for her mother's call or visit and was disappointed both when it came and when it didn't. She had the ability to look insightfully at the impact her mother's lack of interest had on her and how it possibly prompted her pregnancy.

> I wanted someone to love. Now, I want to be close to Damon because my mom and I were never close.

If any one thing provided me with clues as to who these teenage mothers were, it was the overwhelming pull I felt to mother them. My experiences in this regard with Shaina were the most salient. The fondness we felt for each other was not expressed directly; she tried to please me, to be the model group member. I think about her often and how I wanted to become the internalized good mother (Chodorow, 1979) I perceive she never had. On a psychological level, I believe Shaina's and my relationship was an example of a reciprocal desire for connection, in order to resolve or regain something. The words of Klein and Riviere (1964) perhaps best describe this "something":

Ultimately, in making sacrifices for somebody we love, and in identifying ourselves with the loved person, we play the part of a good parent, and behave towards this person as we felt at times the parents did to us, or as we wanted them to do. . . . In acting towards another person as a good parent, in fantasy we re-create and enjoy the wished-for love and goodness of our parents . . . by playing at the same time, the parts of loving parents and loving children. (pp. 66–67)

The numbers on the sociological survey provide some quantitative validation for my perception that these women were survivors of very disruptive family systems. They lacked an internalized sense of "parent" who cares unconditionally. Many struggled, as did Shaina, with mothers who were uninterested and uninvolved.

They needed their mothers but felt the simultaneous pull to distance from them. Shira's third pregnancy brought up longing for the mother who disappeared when her second child was 3 months old. Shira wrote her a letter every week for several weeks and in my weekly telephone call said angrily, "No, I haven't heard anything." I told her on her birthday that I felt that she needed a mother and that I wanted to take care of her sometimes; she got tears in her eyes.

Being in relationships with families of origin and coping with remnants of the family's dysfunction are tasks at all ages. For adolescents, this means beginning to separate and establishing a sense of one's own identity. For adolescent daughters, it perhaps means separating and reconnecting with mother (Salzman, 1990). For adolescent mothers, the separation-individuation process prompts complicated questions: How do these adolescent women continue the physical and psychological separation from their families while coping with separation from toddlers? In a psychoanalytic framework, the adolescent must disengage from "internalized love (and hate) objects," that is, parents or parent figures, in order to create intimate relationships with others (Blos, 1979). Adolescence is a recapitulation of the infancy and toddler years, in that the attachment/separation process repeats itself. The toddler years, according to Kaplan (1984), are a preview of the desire for autonomy in adolescence, and adolescence is an active revision of infancy and childhood. Does the sudden desire for independence in a toddler trigger the adolescent mother's own unresolved separation? Are their difficulties in separating from their own children a reflection of fears of an adolescent or fears of a new parent or both?

Perhaps we need to speak about adolescent pregnancy as "desperate actions, desperate efforts at connection" (Gilligan, 1990: 9). Adolescence was a period during which these girls searched for connection, not only in response to feelings of loss, but to the realization that they were physically and/or emotionally abandoned by a parent. The baby represents a logical (unconsciously logical?) resolution to the dilemma of adolescence, as suggested by Stern (1990) and Salzman (1990). The baby not only allows simultaneously for connection and self-determination, but also facilitates a renewed connection with the mother.

As adult women, they were beginning to explore the effects of their family experience on current relationships, self-concept, and parenting styles. My belief that the group content should focus on understanding dynamic issues of family informed the development of my curriculum. I believe it is all about parenting and we have to start with the self. They needed to understand how they might reconstruct their own unsatisfactory experience with their mothers through the relationship with the baby. The baby may hold the promise of emotional gratification (Sidel, 1990) yet force a recapitulation of abandonment.

An additional area of focus in this regard was the expression of feelings and affection. In one session, Rachel and Melanie described an inability to show affection.

> I can hug the boys but to tell Jeff, "I love you," would just about kill me.

> I don't remember my mother ever hugging me, so now it feels weird.

Learning to experience feelings is in some ways the opposite task of what one would expect of adolescents, for whom unpredictable expressions of emotion and sudden mood changes are the norm. These women rarely cried; they stiffened against my hugs and looked away with quick "thanks" or "hmm hmm's" when I complimented them. I do not think they knew what to do with my imposed caring. My personal cultural background encourages overt expressions of affect and affection, yet I frequently responded to their discomfort by distancing myself. I understood their reactions as defenses and sometimes could see their moist eyes become dry and distant, as they responded to the threat of feelings. Rachel did cry in talking about her sick father, and Stephanie broke down in disclosing the molestation of her daughter. At these times, a collective silence fell on the group until someone said, "Let's talk about something else."

Perhaps they had too much to feel. At a home visit with Sally, she described how she was molested by her stepfather, how her parents fled the country, how her grandparents kidnapped her daughter, and how she was placed in a home for "unwed mothers." She talked rapidly and with big eyes which asked for no sympathy but simply belief. Judy tried to please her alcoholic mother by cleaning her house every week, and Denisa struggled with separating from her emotionally disturbed mother. It was a goal of my work to help them regain some lost childhood and adolescence because I saw them mourn the loss of childhood. I overheard another facilitator say to a member of her group who observed sadly that her childhood ended at age 12, "You'll get some back by playing with your child."

It's not that simple. Erikson (1968) and Elkind (1984) speak of the need for adolescents to have a time to grow, a time to integrate new social and sexual roles, in order to develop a "personal identity." Gilligan and her colleagues highlight the "problem of connection" and the need for girls to negotiate the needs for intimacy and individuality. I see them, as reflected in this context, as children, adolescents, young women, and mothers needing to face the "tasks" of all these roles. The struggles of this generation—the number of teenage pregnancies, the depression and suicide rates, the ever increasing community violence, the loss of lives to substance abuse, and diminishing hopes for economic (and planetary) survival—speak to the needs of today's adolescents to be listened and responded to.

## GROUP PROCESSES: REVEALING RECIPROCAL IMPOSITION

> They start arriving at ten to three, pulling babies out of carseats and waiting quietly at the door. One or two help me carry things into the church while the rest set the children in the nursery. By the time I distribute snacks and instructions to the child care providers and return to our meeting room, they are sitting silently in hard folding chairs, waiting. The first hour of our discussion feels like wading through honey and I can't tell if their anxiety is decreasing or mine is increasing. By 4 or 4:15, the room and the people in it have warmed up. Pauses between contributions become nonexistent; one person's words flow into another's. They stand for emphasis, move their chairs closer into a circle and look at their watches, hoping to slow down the time they wanted to speed up an hour ago. (Journal entry, November 1989)

The nonverbal actions in the group provided another layer, at times more revealing, of clues to the reactions of these adolescent-adult-girls-women-mothers to the content and context of the group. The arrival of late members, the presence of new ones, and the disappearance and return of others became group issues. Most of the time, my attempts to "process" these, that is, facilitate a discussion of their reactions to such events, were met with shrugs. They did have reactions, however, and often these emerged suddenly: "So, what happened to so-and-so?" or "I hate it when we miss a week."

My needs to have the discussion focused, to bring personal stories to a sociocentric level and yet to speak in the immediate sense of their relationships with each other were, I thought, remnants of my teacher and counselor behaviors. We had to achieve something, and getting through a "plan" calmed my need to do that. What revealed itself was the need I had to re-create my family, to be the caretaking child again or to be the "mother" who makes everyone happy. Group was "good" when the members were happy and close and time was used effectively; the success of my performance as group facilitator was somehow measured by their affect.

I understand the world and my relationships with people through a psychodynamic, object relations framework. My conflicts with people are a reflection of patterns I learned in order to cope as a child. Thus, I interpret the processes in the group in the language of a clinician—defenses, anxiety, separation. The silence in the group during the first hour I was quick to label as resistance, but was I imposing my abstract neuroses on their real developmental concerns? The heating in the church did take an hour to kick in, and they were shy adolescents, and new people did enter the group frequently. Moreover, their silence must be considered in the context of girls' development; Gilligan and Brown (1993), Bell (1989), and others point to the impasse faced by girls as they move from late childhood into adolescence, a time when conflicting messages and internalized beliefs force them to "go underground," to become silent. To have a voice is to potentially risk relationship; girls learn early that approval of significant others (teachers, for example) is often contingent upon their silence.

Concerns which did spark considerable discussion were those revolving around child care and group commitment and agreements. Rachel sat down at the start of one session and said, "We need to talk about confidentiality again," in response to "someone telling someone at work I was pregnant." It is a serious issue and I repeated the group's definition of confidentiality frequently. I know and the literature validates (Carrera & Demsey, 1988) that teenage mothers need a safe, supportive environment in which to share concerns, but the girls knew about gossip and rumors and trust. They had to see confidentiality before they believed in it.

The solidarity of best friends and cliques in the group was reminiscent of high school years with fears related to confidentiality and trust. Two women in the group remained in silent conflict over an outside issue for 4 months, despite my attempts to achieve resolution. One made the choice to end the conflict by leaving the group; I agonized over her decision and my discomfort in leaving something unresolved. Many had concerns about not being liked but could not express these to each other. Instead, they told me, pulling me into the role of friend or confidant. There were many moments, though, when they were able to express their concern for each other. Denisa mentioned shyly that she would deliver her baby "alone" (without family or partner); several women immediately insisted on being with her, and eventually everyone teased her about moving the group to the hospital on her delivery day.

Besides such touching messages, attendance also conveyed commitment to the group and its members. "It's not fair that some girls just show up for parties or stuff like that," I heard several protest before our agreement (on paper and signed by each member) that members had to attend three out of four sessions for three months to remain in the group. They worried about their place and carefully calculated how many sessions they had missed or checked in with me. They did not like missing a week nor did they like "wasting time" planning social events, with the interesting exception of Tupperware parties (perhaps a social commentary on traditional roles and new technology). They seemed to want to get planning over with and get back to "the real stuff." Many felt frustrated when talk remained on a superficial level and "we didn't get anything done." I question which came first, their needs or my need to get something done.

Generally, during the two hours, the children remained in the nursery. Child care was an unpredictable, problematic facet of group meetings for quite some time. When we were fortunate enough to have two child care providers, only the nonwalkers stayed with the group. Children were perceived as a real disruption; the members expressed clearly that they needed a break from children and had little patience for the two or three mothers who struggled with separating from their children for this time. The fact that the agency neglected to provide adequate child care conveyed a rather contradictory message, given our goal to foster responsible parenting.

Thus, among the functions the group served, a break from the stress of parenting was a valued one. For any mother on whom the primary responsibility for child care falls, this would be true. The format of the group shifted constantly from support to education to therapy, and as my role shifted, they became participants, students, or clients. They introduced me as "my friend," "my group leader," "a sort of counselor," or "Susan." In a sense, we became a family, and I became accustomed to spending hours on the telephone the evening before the group: one needed a crib; one wanted me to play bingo with her on Saturday night; one was close to tears because it was midnight and the baby wouldn't sleep. The boundaries in our system were not always clear, but I think the interdependence, intimacy, and care were evident.

## THE GESTATION OF A CURRICULUM: A POSTSCRIPT

The dilemma of whose knowledge should be the foundation of curriculum persists. Given the awareness that the concerns relevant to the lives of adolescent mothers reflect issues of adolescence, womanhood, and motherhood, how do I, as curriculum developer, negotiate between their needs and the agendas of the agency and myself? The women's curriculum emerged from group discussions and behavior and from the relationships between the women and between them and me. The agency continues to need a formal curriculum in order to provide printed validation to funding sources and important others in the community and to show that we achieve *something*. I saw my role as making the implicit curriculum explicit.

The foundational purpose of this and similar agencies providing support and education to adolescent parents informs a curriculum focused on the immediate needs related to child care and child rearing. Yet the emergent curriculum of the group encompassed issues of adolescents and women as well as those of mothers. What these young mothers brought to the group context was a need to reflect on the past as well as to consider the present. Do we perpetuate an abandonment of adolescent mothers by focusing only on parenting skills and the needs of the child? Do we neglect the needs of the young mother as "subject"?

An important component of the emergent curriculum was the self-awareness gained within the group context. The hidden curriculum of group process included lessons about interpersonal communication, about perceptions of self and other, and about unmet needs and unresolved conflicts. Uncovering the processes underlying group interactions led to an awareness of self and under-standing of the self and one's identity as a mother. We were ultimately able to "cover" the parenting components of the formal curriculum by surfacing how members responded to each other and to the children within the immediate context of the group. In this way, learning became a process of reflecting on one's needs for empathy and respect vis-à-vis other group members and me.

My attempt at a resolution took the form of a participatory research study. Each week, I introduced "lessons" within each of four "units" (group issues, personal development, parenting/child development, life skills/community re-sources). This outline represented my initial resolution, albeit an inadequate one from the group's standpoint. For 3 months, the group members and I evaluated and redeveloped this curriculum. Although this study relieved me from the discomfort of imposing curriculum by allowing them to direct their education, it presented yet another dilemma: Is the research itself impositional? Imposing the idea of a curriculum on the adolescent mothers in this group surfaced their culture and my biases. It presented them and me with an opportunity to reflect on issues of knowledge, power, connection, and need. Melanie expressed concern once about my age, my nonmother status, and the role I assumed as the "big friend" or mother in the group (Chodorow's [1988] "love object"?). Her comments demonstrate perhaps the group's success in making me the good mother.

## NOTE

1. Over the 19-month period, a total of 38 women participated in this particular group. The size remained constant at 15.

## REFERENCES

Belenky, M. F., Clinchy, B. M., Goldberger, N. R., & Tarule, J. M. (1986). *Women's ways of knowing: The development of self, voice and mind.* New York: Basic Books.

Bell, L. A. (1989). Changing our ideas about ourselves: Group consciousness-raising with elementary school girls as a means to empowerment. In C. Sleeter (Ed.), *Empowerment through multicultural education.* Albany: State University of New York Press.

Blos, P. (1979). *The adolescent passage: Developmental issues.* New York: International Universities Press.

Butler, J. P., & Burton, L. M. (1990). Rethinking teenage childbearing: Is sexual abuse the missing link? *Family Relations, 39*(1), 73–80.

Carrera, M., & Demsey, P. (1988, January). *Restructuring public policy priorities on teen pregnancy.* New York: Sex Information and Education Council of the United States Report.

Catrone C., & Sadler, L. S. (1984). A developmental model for teenage parent education. *Journal of School Health, 54*(2), 63–67.

Chodorow, N. (1979). Feminism and difference: Gender, relation and difference in psychoanalytic perspective. *Socialist Review, 9*(14), 51–70.

Chodorow, N. (1978). *The reproduction of mothering.* Berkeley: University of California Press.

Dash, L. (1989). *When children want children.* New York: Morrow.

Elkes, B. H., & Crocitto, J. A. (1987). Self-concept of pregnant adolescents: A case study. *Journal of Humanistic Education and Development, 25*(3), 123–135.

Elkind, D. (1984). *All grown up and no place to go: Teenagers in crisis.* New York: Addison-Wesley.

Erikson, E. (1968). *Identity, youth and crisis.* New York: W. W. Norton.

Fine, M. (1988). Sexuality, schooling and adolescent females: The missing discourse of desire. *Harvard Educational Review, 58*(1), 29–53.

Furstenberg, F., Brooks-Gunn, J., & Lansdale, L. C. (1989). Teenaged pregnancy and childbearing. *American Psychologist, 44*(2), 313–320.

Garcia-Coll, C. T., Hoffman, J., & Oh, W. (1987). The social ecology and early parenting of caucasian adolescent mothers. *Child Development, 58*, 955–963.

Gilligan, C. (1990). Teaching Shakespeare's sister: Notes from the underground of female adolescence. In C. Gilligan, N. P. Lyons, and T. J. Hamner (Eds.), *Making connections: The relational worlds of adolescent girls at Emma Willard School* (pp. 6–29). Cambridge, MA: Harvard University Press.

Gilligan, C., & Brown, L. M. (1993). *Meeting at the crossroads: Women's psychology and girls' development.* Cambridge, MA: Harvard University Press.

Gilligan, C., Ward, J. V., & Taylor, J. M. (Eds.). (1988). *Mapping the moral domain.* Cambridge, MA: Harvard University Press.

Gordon, L. (1988). *Heroes of their own lives.* New York: Penguin.

Horn, M. E., & Rudolp, L. B. (1987). An investigation of verbal interaction, knowledge of sexual behavior and self-concept in adolescent mothers. *Adolescence, 23*(87), 591–597.

Hudson, B. (1984). Femininity and adolescence. In A. McRobbie & M. Nava (Eds.), *Gender and generation* (pp. 31–53). London: MacMillan.

Jipson, J. (1989, October). *The emergent curriculum: Contextualizing a feminist perspective.* Paper presented at the Bergamo Conference, Dayton, OH.

Kaplan, L. (1984). *Adolescence: The farewell to childhood.* New York: Simon and Schuster.

Klein, M., & Riviere, J. (1964). *Love, hate and reparation.* New York: W. W. Norton.

Lamb, M. E. (1986). Characteristics of married and unmarried adolescent mothers and their parents. *Journal of Youth and Adolescence, 15*(6), 487–495.

Lamb, M. E. (1988). The ecology of adolescent pregnancy and parenthood. In A. Pence (Ed.), *Ecological research with children and families* (pp. 99–121). New York: Teachers College Press.

Landy, S., Schubert, J., Cleland, J. F., Camillia, C., & Montgomery, J. S. (1983). Teenage pregnancy: Family syndrome? *Adolescence, 18*(71), 679–694.

Lesko, N. (1990, April). Social context and the "problem" of teenage pregnancy. Paper presented at the American Educational Research Association, Boston, MA.

Levenson, P., Atkinson, B., Hale, J., & Hollier, M. (1978). Adolescent parent education. *Child Psychiatry and Human Development, 9*(2), 104–117.

Marecek, J. (1987). Counseling adolescents with problem pregnancies. *American Psychologist, 42*(1), 89–93.

McRobbie, A. (1991). The culture of working class girls. In A. McRobbie (Ed.), *Feminism and youth culture: From Jackie to just seventeen* (pp. 35–61). Boston: Unwin Myman.

McRobbie, A., & Nava, M. (Eds.). (1984). *Gender and generation.* London: Macmillan.

Nava, M. (1984). Youth service provision, social order and the question of girls. In A. McRobbie & M. Nava (Eds.), *Gender and generation* (pp. 1–30). London: Macmillan.

Olds, S. (1980). *Satan Says.* Pittsburgh: University of Pittsburgh Press.

Payne-Smith, C. (1982). A needs-based curriculum for teenage mothers. *Education, 102*(3), 254–257.

Planned Parenthood Federation of America. (1988). Planned Parenthood Fact Sheet, Eugene, OR.

Salzman, J. P. (1990). Save the world, save myself: Responses to problematic attachment. In C. Gilligan, N. P. Lyons, & T. J. Hamner, (Eds.), *Making connections: The relational worlds of adolescent girls at Emma Willard School* (pp. 110–146). Cambridge, MA: Harvard University Press.

Scales, P. (1987). How we can prevent teen pregnancy and why it's not the real problem. *Journal of Sex Education Therapy, 13*(1), 12–15.

Schneider, S. (1987). Helping adolescents deal with pregnancy: A psychiatric approach. *Adolescence, 23*(86), 285–291.

Sidel, R. (1990). *On her own: Growing up in the shadow of the American dream.* New York: Penguin.

Stern, L. (1990). Conceptions of separation and connection in female adolescents. In C. Gilligan, N. P. Lyons, & T. J. Hamner, (Eds.), *Making connections: The relational worlds of adolescent girls at Emma Willard School* (pp. 73–87). Cambridge, MA: Harvard University Press.

Sullivan, H. S. (1953). *Interpersonal theory of psychiatry.* New York: W. W. Norton.

Victor, S. (1990). The emerging concerns of adolescent mothers. *Oregon Counseling Association Journal, 12*(2), 25–29.

Victor, S. (1992). Days of their lives: Reflections on adolescent girls and adolescent mothers. *School of Education Review, 4,* 72–81.

Williams, C. W. (1994). *Black teenage mothers: Pregnancy and child rearing from their perspective.* Lexington, MA: Lexington Books.

Wise, S., & Grossman, F. K. (1980). Adolescent mothers and their infants: Psychological factors in early attachment and interaction. *American Journal of Orthopsychiatry, 50*(3), 454–466.

# CHAPTER 3

# Multicultural Curriculum Development in a Multiple-Cultural Context: Whose Voice?

*Karen Froude Jones*

## THE VOICE OF THE AUTHOR

Although I don't identify myself as a teacher, feeling that I really haven't the wisdom or experience to merit that label, most of my professional experiences have been in the field of education. Over the years I have become "teacher" to many. My motivation for working for social change through education is rooted in my experiences with extraordinary teachers—both formal and informal. Informally, we were well educated by my family. My dad spent the first 14 years of my life completing his doctorate in oceanography. We didn't study cultures and environment; we interacted—skin diving with locals off coral reefs, surfing, hunting; living and traveling throughout Mexico, California, and the Hawaiian Islands. My mom had intended to be a biological illustrator; she had me rather than her initial degree. She became a teacher after her divorce so that she would have the time to raise us, with the support of my grandparents Froude and Jones, with whom we often lived.

Our travels focused on coastlines. While I was growing up, I saw southern California change from a place of pristine beauty to its current status as an environmental and potential social disaster. Although the devastation had begun with the Spanish intruders in the 1500s, the pace had so accelerated by the 1950s that many of California's natural resources and its original beauty had been leveled and depleted. The culprits were economically powered bulldozers driven primarily by people (we assumed they were all from the East Coast and all from New York) who had already destroyed their homelands. We watched as Disney filled in a wetland in Anaheim that was vital to flock migration on the

Pacific corridor, while other major corporations dammed, diverted, and chan-
neled rivers, created harbors that greatly upset the natural underwater topog-
raphy (resulting in the loss of protective sandbars), dumped hazardous waste
into the waters, and "fished out" the local areas. We watched until it became
unbearable, and then we took action.

Throughout my childhood, our primary residence was in Laguna Beach,
California, an unusual place. During my formal school years, I never saw a
fistfight or experienced harassment, racism, or sexism; it was a magical, safe
place in which to grow up—even during the '60s, when you could buy (or sell)
anything at Taco Bell for $5.00. My teachers all had advanced degrees and all
were raising their families in the local community (this was back when a family
could live in Laguna on a teacher's annual salary of $7,000—not enough now
to rent a garage). Most of my teachers believed in integrated/exploratory/holis-
tic education.

My memories of the Laguna Beach public elementary schools consist of
painting patios blue and nailing together two-by-fours in a re-creation of Los
Angeles harbors, and writing and performing plays, songs, and dances with Ron
Rodecker (third and sixth grades). During the years from 1967 to 1969, while I
was attending seventh and eighth grade, the junior high was nongraded and
team-taught, and relied on a computer to print out individual daily schedules.
Our field trips (mostly facilitated by our science teacher, Charlie Reich) included
weeks floating down the Colorado on hand-made rafts, exploring tide pools on
the northern California coast, drawing and observing in the local hills, and for
a small group of us, a visitation/participation program with the Navajo/Dine
students at Canyon de Chelly. Our other teachers (specifically the history team
of Tommy Warren, Ron Newman, and George Nettleman) emphasized multiple
perspectives, examination of original documentation, and lots of Marxism. The
invited guest speakers included Huey Newton (from the Black Panthers) and
other activists from the American Indian Movement (AIM) and the Sierra Club.
We were encouraged to be "political," to be aware of and take an active role in
local, national, and international events. We fought for years—and friends are
still fighting—to maintain a "green belt" around the community; we harassed
the young military personnel at Camp Pendleton who were assigned to guard
the installation of the San Onofre Nuclear Power Plant; and we did whatever
we could to stop the installation of oil derricks off the California coastline. It
was made clear to each of us in that school that our voices were important.

Fortunately, for the sake of comparison, this idyllic experience was offset by
an extremely repressive ninth-grade year in an elite girls prep school in La Jolla
(perhaps the "capper" was climbing back over the wall after making out on the
beach with the local minister's son and landing virtually in the arms of the
headmistress) and a few neo-Thomist (desks in rows, rote memorization)
teachers. When I returned to Laguna Beach as a 10th grader, one year after I had
graduated from that dynamic junior high, a newly elected conservative school

board closed down the program. Most of my teachers moved on with my class to the high school; others left teaching for doctoral programs, back-to-the-land farms, or their work as artists and activists. It was a powerful experience. What I learned was a need to hide my intentions, to "smile pretty" on the surface, and to see formalized schooling as a very simple hierarchical game, primarily to be tolerated for the sake of education. I stopped attending classes in the 10th grade, in favor of studying at home. My mom and stepdad (a wonderful man) gave all six of us children the opportunities to make our own decisions. My parents and teachers got together and gave me permission to do this as long as I kept getting straight As. I was informally made an emancipated minor so that I could call in my own absences—which I did for weeks at a time. Instead of attending classes, I worked, read, wrote, dance, drew, wove, and traveled throughout the western states. After graduation, my traveling became more extensive and I lived in many different places and learned things that a textbook (and most of the textbook authors) could never have offered.

Later, as an elementary teacher working in rural Oregon from 1984 to 1987, I tried to bring to my students the joy for lifelong learning that I had experienced in the Laguna Beach public schools and within the context of my family. I was aided in this quest by finding myself in a resident master's program (full-time teacher, full-time graduate student, two-thirds salary) during my second teaching year. I was told that my advisor was a newly hired professor with a just-completed degree in anthropology and education from Oregon State University. Dr. Rob Proudfoot's work (1990) had been with the Vietnamese and Laotian refugee populations. . . . He sounded interesting.

"Interesting" hardly captures the experiences of that year. Rob Proudfoot is also Seneca (Turtle clan), Onandogan, and Welsh, a lifelong teacher-learner and an impassioned activist. He came in like a hurricane, and the University of Oregon has never been the same. What Rob gave me was the space to learn and teach from my heart, as well as some savvy advice, based on his ongoing experiences, for survival in the institution. He was able to remain active in the community while working for change through education. Most important to me was that his personal theoretical orientation was emerging through his own journey as a teacher-learner. He has named this perspective the "relational model." It is a theoretical orientation that really has to be experienced in order to be believed. For Gretchen, it provided a way to interconnect her very disparate worlds of family, community, supervision, and scholarship. For me, it offered additional recognition of the relationships and interconnections that each person brings to an experience. From my perspective, the relational model requires that education be regarded as a synergistic process, reflective of interacting considerations that include race, class, gender, history, culture, community, and language. I can only offer the reader my perspective on this theoretical perspective because it has yet to appear in written form (probably as much a result of Rob's traditional Seneca background with its emphasis on orality as of his zealous respect for process—which the written form usually negates).

Throughout my second and third years as an elementary teacher, Rob worked with me as an advisor, friend/mentor, and colleague. After a rewarding third year teaching sixth grade and continued frustration with the limits of classroom walls, I considered going for a doctoral degree. With Rob's encouragement, I returned to the University of Oregon. My intention was to focus on the impact of Christianity and European intellectualism on traditional oral cultures—the umbrella was to be multicultural education. Rob was to be my background advisor; we both have pretty strong personalities, and in the hierarchical structure of the university, we assumed we would have some uncomfortable power struggles, which we did. I was assigned Dr. Chet Bowers as an advisor, and I learned a great deal from his work. I also took most of Dr. Harry Wolcott's courses on education and anthropology. They are brilliant scholars and gentlemen, and I learned quite a bit from them. However, 1987 and 1988 were very lonely years. I really wanted to work with a female advisor; I had spent years at Berkeley and Stanford being a scholar, and I wanted a blend of conversation and cozy—I wanted the relational.

Jan arrived and Rob suggested that I take her course on language development. For the first time since my master's program, I was in a class where the professor had good "wait time," respected her students, paraphrased only when seeking to provide ties for her students, and was herself an intellectual and an activist. It was with great relief and enthusiasm that I received an invitation to join a small group of doctoral students for an informal research seminar on feminism. I was not too enthused about the topic; however, I was very interested in working with Jan, Gretchen, Susan, and Petra. As revealed in this book, it has been a fascinating journey.

Through Jan's mentorship I was able to blend my scholarly endeavors at the university with my relationships in the community. My frequent trips to the reservation to facilitate a self-sufficiency project with my Navajo grandmothers and my work developing curriculum with environmental groups and in multicultural education were institutionally recognized under independent studies and academically validated through ethnographic work with Dr. Wolcott. In addition, I was discovering that life-history and reflective anthropological approaches were meeting more of my needs than traditional courses in curriculum theory. I started coursework at Oregon State University in anthropological linguistics with Dr. Dorice Tentchoff, and Petra and I explored feminist anthropology at the University of Oregon with Dr. Carol Silverman. These wonderful women both greatly enriched my work, and the materials they offered provided fuel for many exciting discussions with Jan, Gretchen, Petra, and Susan. At this time, our collaborative group was of primary importance to me; it was providing a bridge between the academic and larger communities. It is with this, I hope, somewhat relational approach that I locate myself in my experiences as codirector of a summer camp during the years 1988–1992.

## REFLECTIONS

This chapter is about the experiences of a group working in collaboration to develop and implement multicultural curriculum for a summer camp. Integral to multicultural education is the idea of empowerment: the recognition and validation of the voices of members of society previously kept silent. In the process of developing and implementing this curriculum there were many voices clamoring for recognition. In this chapter, my voice as the camp facilitator/codirector is interwoven with those of the other participants as I reflect on the curricular development and implementation processes and ask: How can we collaboratively develop and implement curriculum that is inclusive of all traditions, that is a celebration of multiple voices, without imposing our own values and expectations?

## THE PARTICIPANTS

Multicultural Kids Camp is a one-week summer camp for children from diverse class, racial, and cultural backgrounds. The camp is a project developed and maintained by members of Clergy and Laity Concerned (CALC). One of the mission statements of CALC is the building of community. They continually work with other nonprofit organizations at the local, national, and international levels in order to "expand awareness and gain collective strength in the global struggle for human dignity." The representatives from CALC involved in this process were Carolyn Kirk, Maria Sol, and Gloria Hughs.

Carolyn Kirk, the founder of the state chapter for this organization, describes the group as an agency "whose staff and volunteers [are] very much a multiracial group" dedicated to "exposing how racism operates in the community" and working globally for peace and justice. She remembers the motivation for forming the first multicultural camp for kids, in 1982, as a chance to:

> inculcate a sense of self-worth for all the kids and on that basis to help them develop a sense of appreciation for cultural diversity; by doing that to interrupt the stereotyping and the negative connotations that people have about each other in the context of this society; and also to empower them to feel that they can do something on issues of peace and justice.

Maria Sol, an active member of her Mexican American community and a longtime CALC volunteer and member of the steering committee, has been involved with Multicultural Kids Camp since the first year, as "a volunteer driver," and in the following 5 years as a codirector. She has also been invited every year to come to the camp as a representative of Latino culture, "to do some sharing of my own culture, to give them another perspective." During these visits, she is usually asked to talk in general terms about "her" Latino culture (although she defines herself as Mexican American, not Latino) and to make crepe-paper flowers with the children, a craft "many people seem to feel is representative of the Latino culture."

Gloria Hughs's position with CALC included public relations, grant writing, and communication between the steering committee and the various projects sponsored by the agency. Throughout this process, she worked at maintaining an objective stance in order to facilitate communication between and among the groups developing and implementing the curriculum. During our periodic meetings to "whine and dine" (that is, the two of us getting together for coffee and shared concerns), she frequently provided me with insights and methods for overcoming seemingly insurmountable obstacles in terms of relationship building among the different members of the group.

For the years 1986–1990, cosponsorship of Multicultural Kids Camp was shared by the Willamalane Parks and Recreation Agency. The people who directed this program for Willamalane were Antoinette Hayward and Kate Kempe. Antoinette and Kate felt that Multicultural Kids Camp, integrated into their summer offerings, broadened the awareness of the local children and "enhanced their experience" through exposure; "just the knowledge that there are people out there" was perceived as beneficial to the local community. As Antoinette said, "A lot of these kids come from Springfield logger back-grounds—'let's go out and get a deer at deer season'—and I think that it gives them an awareness that there are other realities, even in Springfield." The impressions that Kate and Antoinette received during the weeks before camp and at registration were mixed:

> Some of the people signing up for it didn't even know what multicultural week was, what it stood for, what it meant, and I think, if they even asked, they may not have understood after I explained it to them; they just said, "Okay, I'll take that one." . . . And other people called back in April and May asking when multicultural week is happening this year.

Teaching at the camp, and described in their own words, were Paulette Ansari (also the camp codirector), "an African American woman, the librarian at one of the local middle schools, a storyteller, and the mother of four lively, beautiful children"; George Ann Baker, "a member of the Klamath-Paiute nation"; Rich Glauber, "a New York Jew, a musician (and a recent dad)"; Liliana Allende, "a Peruvian woman, a teacher in bilingual education"; Nancy Bray, "a longtime reading teacher in the local public schools, a parent of two children, and a Welsh-American"; and myself. In the following passages, the voices of these participants are interwoven.

## THE VOICE OF THE RESEARCHER/CAMP CODIRECTOR: FACILITATION OR IMPOSITION?

It was my job as camp facilitator/codirector to somehow create an experience that was multicultural and that recognized each of these voices as well as those of the children. I was raised to believe that one looks back to the future—that it is vital to know your roots. As a primarily Welsh woman whose family also retains strong ties to its English ancestors (while barely recognizing our indigenous ancestors), I saw multicultural education as education that is multicultural—an opportunity to expand other people's awareness of the diverse and distinctly different cultures within many "American" backgrounds—rather than as a curriculum *for* culture. I feel that in this time of internationalization and global environmental degradation this is a particularly vital distinction. Educators have the rare opportunity for effecting social change through the next generation of students—from my perspective, the change that needs to be made is respect for humanity as well as for the planet. That change can only come when people have some respect for themselves, and education that is multicultural offers that possibility.

It is my belief that societal change can be created through education by reflecting the many diverse experiences of practitioners and their students. Catherine Cornbleth (1990) suggests that curriculum provide opportunities for critical self-examination, "for domination and for resistance or transformation" (p. 50). Janet Miller (1990), in "Teachers as Curriculum Creators," suggests that educators become their "own sources of authority [and] concurrently invite students to become readers, writers, and revisers of their own stories, their own versions of educational experience" (p. 86). Curriculum should not consist of prepackaged and fabricated units of information but should be redefined as an educational opportunity for recognizing diversity and the strength of "a person's life experience," as suggested by Connelly and Clandinin (1988: 1). The statements of these researcher-scholars support my ideals as well as those of Gretchen, Susan, Jan, and Petra. We all feel that curriculum should emphasize the process of education, the power of developing self-worth, and the strength of no one being in a designated teacher or learner role: The presenters learn from the children, as the children learn through contextual experiences created with the presenters. The original model for Multicultural Kids Camp embodied these ideals and was transformational; it reflected the need to celebrate cultural diversity and to work collectively for cultural understanding. I dreamed of expanding that curriculum to include biodiversity in order to recognize a broader web of relationships.

Taking my ideals for education that is multicultural and forming them into a workable curriculum was a challenging process. I agreed to be the camp facilitator/codirector because I had worked with this program for several years as an instructor and I felt that a relationship of trust and respect had developed among the participants. I felt that we had built a strong foundation for collaboratively developing and implementing a curriculum designed to broaden definitions of multicultural education. In retrospect, I believe that I was moving a little too fast, too soon, imposing my belief in educational and social change on a number of individuals with strong personal and political agendas of their own. As does every member of this collaborative group, Gretchen with supervision, Petra and Jan as teachers, Susan in her work with the teen moms, I worried about the imposition of my well-intentioned "facilitation." This chapter is, in part, an exploration of the pitfalls inherent in the manner with which I approached the process of collaborative multicultural curriculum development and implementation.

While my realization of the ramifications of social change through education were apparent to me by high school, I was not really directly involved as an active change agent until the academic year 1985–86. I was teaching sixth grade in a small, rural community in Oregon. I had just completed my master's program in multicultural education and I was determined to implement more of the theoretical curriculum ideals I had been exploring. I was supported in this project by my principal-administrator, my teaching colleagues (Dr. Proudfoot and his first doctoral student, Dr. Michelle Collay) from the nearby University, and the parents of the 24 children in my class. My goal was to create a classroom environment based on mutual respect and responsibility, in which all issues would be addressed from multiple perspectives and all voices would be recognized as equally "legitimate."

During this year, I tried to work as holistically as possible in order to provide the children with opportunities to learn to see and hear beyond the imposed limitations of language and the emphasis in this society on decontextualized forms of knowledge. I strived to provide an arena in which the children could question the fundamental ideas of a society that is described by Frederick Turner (1986), in *Beyond Geography*, as "a crucial, profound estrangement of the inhabitants from their habitat: a rootless, restless people with a culture of superhighways precluding rest and a furious penchant for tearing up last year's improvements in a ceaseless search for some gaudy ultimate" (p. 5). I supplemented, and eventually scrapped, the required textbooks and we read local and national newspapers and political commentary. I also made available to the children the literature I considered to be important, including *The Phantom Tollbooth* (Juster, 1972), *The Great Tree and the Longhouse: The Culture of the Iroquois* (Hertzberg, 1966), *The Lord of the Rings* (Tolkien, 1966), and *1984* (Orwell, 1949), and created opportunities for them to read (with administrative and parental permission) materials they considered personally relevant.

In addition, we frequently took public transportation into the university town of Eugene (about 45 miles down river) in order to make real the ideals of education that is multicultural. We attended workshops on undoing racism (a program that has since been developed by Bahati Ansari into "The Racism Free

Zone Project" [1992]), learned organizational development (based on the work of Schmuck and Runkel, 1985) from Dr. Michelle Collay, and spent time at the courthouse in order to understand judicial processes. We interacted with members of diverse cultures and communities. Through these processes of exploration, communication, and exposure, the children began to develop teaching-learning relationships with members of the African American, Laotian, Vietnamese, Japanese American, Korean, and Native American Indian communities.

Interwoven throughout all of these experiences were moments of whimsy and fun. One child, Faith, had never been in an elevator. So we went to the highest building on the university campus and, like the character Babar (De Brunhoff, 1933), spent the morning riding "up the elevator and down the elevator" (p. 7). Back at school, we frequently climbed over the back fence and went out into the woods. I facilitated these planned excursions and supported the spontaneous proposals of the children because I wanted them to realize that there are things to be learned from interpersonal and environmental relationships that are wiser and richer than anything touched upon in traditional classroom settings. I also wanted them to take responsibility for their education—to accept learning as a lifelong process.

I tried to offer these children an educational experience that mirrored the values of relationship, community, and respect that I feel should be intrinsic to educational processes, that I had valued during my education. I strived to create a sense of community in which these values could thrive. As a result, when I left that district, the children told me they felt abandoned and isolated. I still receive calls from them. Years later, they are still labeled by the administration as "too assertive"; they want to know the alternative perspectives on any given idea, and they have an "annoying" habit of calling teachers on what they see as classist, sexist, or racist attitudes. Perhaps as a result of our year with each other, most are no longer properly socialized to fit into their rural Oregon school.

In the development of the curriculum for Multicultural Kids Camp, I worked to integrate my belief that education that is multicultural should be inclusive, emergent, and ecologically sensitive with the ideals expressed by the teachers and agency facilitators. I took the position of camp codirector because I believe in collaborative, participatory, and action research and I wanted the opportunity to work with other teachers from a variety of ethnic, racial, and cultural traditions. In light of my last teaching experience, I felt that this opportunity to learn with children and other adults offered a chance for reflection in my development as an educator. Like Gretchen, hoping to take the ideals of the relational model to her student teachers, I wanted to take those ideals to the greater community. I hoped that I would learn how to integrate the best of multicultural education into an educational experience reflective of my holistic and integrated multicultural/relational/ecological ideals in a manner that would celebrate the voices of the children without disrupting their connections to their families and communities.

## THE DEVELOPMENTAL PROCESS: INCLUSION OR IMPOSITION?

In order to work toward a more holistic format, I imposed several changes. To begin with, I chose not to follow the "Sesame Street" format of previous years. I felt that the rapid-fire projection of a variety of cultures through food, crafts, and visitors would only enhance stereotypes: I believe that cultures are also the intangible threads of interaction that weave language, thought, and environment into dynamic patterns that cannot be caught in fabricated displays. To have told the children that a person, food, or craft was a "culture" would have only served to decontextualize and encourage single-dimension portrayals of that culture by denying the possibility of those broader webs of interaction. I was concerned about the possibility that the children, many trained by television to receive information in 10-minute segments, would watch rather than interact with the guests from diverse cultures and communities. I asked the designated teachers to spend the first day helping the children trace their roots, through their names and by interviewing a member of their family. I felt that through this process of self-exploration they could develop a series of questions that would give them the opportunity to interact with the guests.

Another concern of mine was that each morning of the week had been devoted to "cultural lessons" that took place inside a building within classroomlike rooms. The children had also been divided into three groups by age and kept separate for most of the mornings. The solution I reached was to devote two mornings during the week to in-class time for the instructors, who had requested time for formal instruction, and two mornings for field trips. During the field trips we went as a group into a variety of communities and met people from a variety of cultures in the contexts of their choice. Our field trips included visits with the rabbi at the local temple, with the director of the office for Chicano issues, with a traditional Celtic harp player, and with members of the Klamath-Paiute, Eskimo, and Karuk Nations and an afternoon canoeing and a day on one of the old growth forest/park areas that are easily accessible from Springfield. Visiting guests included Maria Sol (who did not make crepe-paper flowers but took this opportunity to share her life story) as well as other members of the Latino/Hispanic/Mexican American, Native American Indian, Indonesian, Micronesian, Asian-Pacific, Scandinavian, Serbian, Japanese American, and African American communities.

My motivation for facilitating these experiences was to expand recognition of culture from the standard "multicultural four"—African American; Native American Indian; Latino, Hispanic, Mexican American; and Asian-Pacific American—to representation more reflective of the diversity within each of these broad labels. I also hoped to introduce the children to international perceptions of cultural diversity, which are often based on distinctly different ethnic, linguistic, spiritual, and religious traditions. Participating in the camp were individuals whose ancestry was Swedish, African, Japanese, Korean, English, Manx, Dutch, German, Irish, Native American Indian, Hispanic, Mexican, Welsh, Italian, and Jewish as well as individuals whose primary cultural identity was Hawaiian, Trukese, Jewish, Mexican, Chicano, Hispanic, Klamath-Paiute, and Eskimo. I felt that Multicultural Kids Camp should be a celebration of each of these cultural voices.

I formally took the role of teacher twice during the camp. The first time was early on the first morning. All the participants sat in a circle and we discussed the power and fragility within a circle. We passed, hand to hand, with great tenderness, a fresh egg and talked about the care and respect the humans within a circle must have for one another. We talked about language and how "history" is "her-story" as well as "our stories" and "their stories." We looked at the differences between the Mercator and the Peter's world map projections, and we speculated on whose stories or perceptions of the world are usually portrayed in children's books. In order to support the idea of a common thread by which we could create a work symbolic of our rich cultural diversity, we talked about making the camp banner.

The banner consisted of the black silhouette of a large treelike shape sewn onto an electric blue background. I told them that I had chosen this as the background for our work because a tree is a central metaphor in many cultures and so could represent all of us. Nordic mythology incorporates the metaphor of the World Tree in its historical traditions. The Welsh worshipped seven trees, each with its own power (*The Mabinogi*, trans. 1987). The Chinese revere the mulberry, and the fig is considered a symbol of fertility in many cultures whose origins spring from the Middle East. The Hebrew calendar includes a day, Tu b'Sheevat, devoted to planting trees in honor of a special living person or as a memorial. Christians place the "tree of the knowledge of good and evil" at the center of their belief system. The mythology/history of the Six Nations speaks of the Great Elm; the Great Tree at the center of Sky-World; and the symbol of the Iroquois Confederacy, the Great Tree of Peace, whose white roots embrace the earth (Hertzberg, 1966).

Available throughout the week were pieces of felt and boxes of odds and ends. During the week, the children cut the pieces of felt into the shapes of leaves and used these as the foundation for creating visual representations of their cultural backgrounds. These "leaves" were glued onto the branches of the tree. The banner was completed by Friday morning and served as a powerful visual image of our multiple cultural voices. During our last morning meeting we shared our impressions of the week and asked the children what they had learned. Although some of them still insisted that they had come from West Covina, California, or Florence, Oregon, which in the immediate sense was usually true, most were able to grasp the concept that this camp represented a constellation of diverse cultures from throughout the world.

I reflected on the imposition of my ideals relative to the format of the camp, the formation of groups, the definitions of what was multicultural, and the teaching strategies. The children seemed comfortable; the reactions of the staff, however, were a bit more cautious.

## THE VOICES OF THE ADULTS: CELEBRATION OF DIVERSITY OR IMPOSITION?

As stated before, this project involved the integration of many strong voices. I would like to invite you, the reader, to listen to the individuals within the general clamor. Each of these people is represented by his or her own words. It is my belief that the true orchestration for creating a song that will transform our society lies in the recognition that we each have unique voices.

### Clergy and Laity Concerned

Throughout the 3 years preceding this experience, all three representatives from CALC, Carolyn, Maria, and Gloria, had expressed a need to change the manner of their involvement with Multicultural Kids Camp. Gloria felt that she had learned what she needed to know as a fundraiser for a nonprofit organization and that it was time to move on. She applied for, and received, a prestigious grant for a doctoral program in women's studies. Both Maria and Carolyn had also pulled back from their initial involvement. Both stated their reasons for this withdrawal as based in concerns about its format for the last 3 years.

As the sole Latino on the steering committee for Clergy and Laity Concerned, Maria was often asked to be the expert representing all Latino, Hispanic, and Chicano people—a position she found restrictive and unrealistic. As she said, "If I have to make one more paper flower . . . " She stated that the camp needed to change; "it has still been showing cultural stuff like foods and crafts." Maria felt that multicultural education "takes a lot of relationship building," and she wanted to do "a 4-year kind of plan where the ¹ week of Multicultural Kids Camp would be focused on one community." She really wanted kids to understand what the Latino community looked like right in Lane County.

Carolyn's concerns reflected the need she saw for social transformation through proactive involvement:

The curriculum of the camp is . . . just too busy. . . . Maybe that has gotten in the way of the patient development of deeper understanding. . . . Real multicultural education isn't just about dance, food, handicrafts; it's about understanding different ways of looking at the world, and I'm not sure that we've conveyed that as much as we would have liked to the kids.

These three women differed in their values and assumptions regarding Multicultural Kids Camp, and this produced the possibility for imposition.

### Willamalane Parks and Recreation Agency

The concerns of members of the Willamalane Parks and Recreation Agency were superficially related to the explicit Multicultural Kids Camp curriculum. They indicated that they felt the segmentation of culture into different experiences, what I described as the "Sesame Street" style, was appropriate. The needs of the Springfield people were met by this particular format; as Kate stated, "It is a camp experience."

### The Teachers

Paulette Ansari, George Ann Baker, Rich Glauber, Liliana Allende, and Nancy Bray expressed positive feelings about the actual teaching week and saw positive effects on themselves, the children, and the community. Paulette felt that Multicultural Kids Camp and the activities she chose to do with her own children provided references for future experiences. In talking about the seeming uninterest of her then 10-year-old son during a talk about Dr. Martin Luther King, and relating it to why she continued to teach and codirect Multicultural Kids Camp, she stated:

> I want to provide things that may not seem much to them now, but that they can look back on as meaning something to them. . . . I needed to be an adult, to have a history, before I could look back and really understand things that happened to me as a kid. . . . People would mistreat me because I am black and males will run right over you unless you're, well, they call it aggressive, but I call it assertive.

As one of four African Americans employed in what she called "nonjanitorial positions" in the large Springfield school district, she stated that "it's real important to make the multicultural statement in Springfield. They have more and more minorities . . . and the racism in Springfield is more pronounced and stronger in areas than it is in Eugene." Unfortunately, because Springfield school district does not allow employees who live outside the district boundaries to sit on their district policy committees and Paulette lives in the neighboring town of Eugene, she is unable to sit on the affirmative action board. Therefore, her voice is heard only through her work as a librarian at one of the middle schools, as a storyteller, and as a teacher in Multicultural Kids Camp. She felt that the racism she experienced extended to socioeconomic prejudice that caused problems for anyone from the relatively middle-class community of Eugene who worked in the predominantly working-class town of Springfield. As she described it, "They'll say, you live in Eugene like, hey, you live on the other side of the tracks or something. I mean seriously . . . and this is, like I said, with two Caucasians, so you can imagine how it is with me."

Nancy, a veteran Springfield teacher and also a resident of Eugene, was able to offer an idea of the long-term perspective:

> We are contributing toward small steps to a change. I'm seeing some changes at my old school, over the last 3 years. They now have bulletin boards out about appreciating cultural diversity, they are having a multicultural fair, and I'm not even there organizing, they're doing it, and a lot of those kids have come to the camp.

However, she also expressed concern with the Clergy and Laity Concerned/Willamalane Parks and Recreation affiliation: "What I would really like to see is a Multicultural Kids Camp in Springfield, but not necessarily with Willamalane."

George Ann didn't wish to have her views recorded. She did say that she enjoyed the experience and would be back to work with the camp the following summer. Rich and Liliana enjoyed being teachers as a "summer experience" and have taken the multicultural process into their other work. Rich now volunteers at one of the temples, teaching a children's group, and works with the local public schools as an "artist in residence," and Liliana is a teacher in a Spanish-English bilingual program for preschool children. They both found the intensity of the Multicultural Kids Camp process "exhausting, rewarding (not financially), well worth it," but after that summer, they "prefer to be involved in other projects."

### The Extended Community

This work was not isolated to the involvement of the specific people mentioned above. Within the communities of Eugene and Springfield are many groups dedicated to the struggle for human rights and the preservation of the environment. Unfortunately, many of these equally strong voices found the proactive agenda of the sponsoring agency inappropriate and impositional. An example of this perception was provided by a local businessmen's fraternity, which wished to donate money to the camp, but not to support the sponsoring agency. They wrote:

> We are not interested in giving money to Clergy and Laity Concerned; they are too controversial [on] things like Central America. . . . But from what we've heard you've got a really good program for kids . . . and we'd like to consider your program.

## REFLECTIONS ON THE PROCESS: MULTIPLE ISSUES, MULTIPLE PERSPECTIVES

Proactive involvement is part of what makes Clergy and Laity Concerned a dynamic and vital organization. However, the missionary-like zeal with which they approached racial awareness and proactive change was overwhelming for the other people involved in the camp process. During the formation of the Multicultural Kids Camp curriculum, Maria, Carolyn, and Gloria requested that the participating adults reflect on their values and assumptions before working with the children. The reaction of the Willamalane Parks and Recreation staff to this request was not enthusiastic. Antoinette and Kate felt that the morning workshop on values clarification, led by Carolyn and Maria in the weeks before the camp, shouldn't be necessary. As they stated:

It caused some of the people in the camp not to want to associate with each other. It carried over to our staff interactions throughout the summer. The experience brought up a lot of things that they carried in baggage. It makes people think. Maybe it's a little more in depth than we need to go, but it's hard to tell, you know, how far to go.

As far as Maria and Carolyn were concerned, it hardly went far enough: "With Willamalane Parks and Recreation there isn't that shared reality, so there are just a set of assumptions that are not appropriate to make" (Carolyn). Maria suggested:

Not everyone is together at Willamalane. I feel that if they're going to participate in that kind of a camp, then people need to be at least somewhat understanding of the value and commitment and the reason we're even doing it. I have gone to each camp and shared and that to me feels like it's always the same. I'm concerned about where those adults that are working with the kids are at and I did see some problems. Maybe they don't need to be there, or maybe they do need to be there, but I don't like to have people learn at the expense of someone else, especially with kids.

Carolyn was fully aware that "a lot of what CALC works on seems grim to people." However, she felt that it was vital for people to confront their personal prejudices and biases. She saw many positive aspects in the relationship with Willamalane Parks and Recreation, for example, the ability "to offer the kids a full-day experience" and meeting a need in the Springfield community for multicultural education. She also saw limitations in that affiliation:

It put some real constraints on us, though, in terms of the kinds of things we're able to talk about with the kids. . . . [In the past] we were able to talk about militarism, the causes of war, and peace making . . . to have the kids write letters to their senators about military spending versus social needs and we were able to do that without anyone getting upset about it. . . . I have some concerns about where some of their [Willamalane's] staff are coming from in terms of their sensitivity to some of these issues.

I also had to come to terms with my own attitudes and values toward this issue of imposition in multicultural education. As I stated in one conversation with Carolyn:

It's very challenging. . . . There's a reality represented in Springfield that seems to constitute a large part of the "American mind-set," and it's a constant reminder for me . . . that one has to move gently in making these changes, but not back away because there are children who can go any distance with you, and the boundaries of the adults are not necessarily the limitations of the children.

At that point, Carolyn stated, "You put the kids in a difficult position when you get them out of sync with their own families." I immediately responded in a manner that reflected my commitment to social change: "Yes, you have to be very careful about how it's done . . . but you can't always continue to teach the children of the people who already share your values."

As I said this I thought of one of my former sixth-grade students, "Ernesto," a bright, fearlessly articulate Chicano. During the year we were in the same classroom, he wrote a beautiful statement against racism that was eventually published in one of the state's larger newspapers and quoted in the House by our congressional representative. The summer after that school year I called his home to see if he wanted to earn some money and have the experience of being a camp counselor for a week. His mother, a warm woman whom I knew well, having taught one of her children every year, said, "Ms. Jones, you were good for my Ernesto, but his father wants him to be a man. He's going to go out for football this summer." Ernesto's father is probably much more attuned to the survival needs of his son in that predominantly light-skinned, working-class, fundamentalist logging community. I wonder how Ernesto is feeling and how he will cope. I share Susan's concern that I was too far removed from the real lives of these young people and their families. I worry about the values that I imposed on him through language, literacy, and cross-cultural experiences that may have taken him away from the worlds of his family and community. I also hope that his life will provide him with the opportunity for these values to resurface.

These reflections are reminders of the underlying question addressed in this chapter and of the motivating concerns for my involvement with Multicultural Kids Camp: How can we collaboratively develop and implement curriculum that is inclusive of all traditions, that is a celebration of multiple voices, and that recognizes the vital connections between human beings and our environment? This question is at the crux of all my work and that of my colleagues. Susan, Petra, Jan, Gretchen, and I are proactively involved in the support and recognition of our diverse communities, and each of us is exploring the issue of imposition. The only answer I have found is to allow people to speak for themselves. In that process of discovery I have also raised more questions surrounding my right to impose the power of thoughtful dialogue on children whose parents may not want to hear those voices and on a society that is based in part on the denial of diverse voices. The following passage was written during the camp experience, while we were picnicking among the old growth. It reflects the reasons for my continued involvement in curriculum development and with Multicultural Kids Camp.

## THE CHILDREN'S VOICES (AN IMPRESSION)

They are clustered around a rock intently searching for gold, or are scattered on the grassy slope, licking fingers sticky with the alluring (seductive) glue of melted marshmallow, chocolate, and graham cracker crumbs. They play alone and in pairs, their movement a dance that is distracting and compelling. Their high-pitched calls are muffled by the chatter of the icy McKenzie and absorbed by the deep-rooted pillars of the cathedral old growth. They are shimmering, glowing, flashing colors that cause the air to tremble and the earth to quiver with intensity—violent tremors of color capable of scorching heat and searing light. They are the rhythm and pattern of change, the heart and hope of the future.

## REFLECTIONS ON MY ROLE AS CAMP FACILITATOR/ CODIRECTOR AND ON THE PROCESS: FACILITATION OR IMPOSITION?

During the development and implementation of curriculum for Multicultural Kids Camp, my manner of emphasizing holistic and ecologically sensitive curriculum was felt to be impositional, not reflective of the ideals within multicultural education. The participating adults later shared with me that they "were wondering about the canoeing," as Antoinette inquired of me during one of our postcamp discussions. "Was that culturally related, and the hike at the old growth trail/park—I mean it was nice to go there, but would it have been more advantageous to go to some place where they would have a little more exposure to another culture?" I forget my exact response to Antoinette, but these were two events that I felt were appropriate to the curriculum.

There are many cultures whose realities are intimately intertwined with their environment. Cecil King (1989), in a presentation for the American Anthropological Association, described the Odawa (Ojibwe) language as one in which "the concept of animateness is limitless." The concept of separating human from everything else in order to obtain objective and verifiable truths is a Euro-American, Cartesian perspective. The continual process of separation has resulted in attitudes toward the environment based on ideals of immediacy and consumerism. Michael Apple (1990) states that our schools reflect mainstream cultural values: they have "always been caught up in the history of class, race, gender, religious relations . . . and the consistent pressure to make the needs of business and industry the primary concern of the education systems" (p. 526). As Tracy Faulconer (1992) notes in *Situating Trends in Environmental Education within the Ecological Debate*: "The language we use to frame environmental issues and our ideas about them will determine whether or not they [the children] perceive the ecological crisis to be a simple problem of supply and demand—producer and consumer—or as the complex socio-cultural, economic, scientific and religious dilemma that it is" (p. 201). Fortunately, George Ann, an enrolled member of the Confederated Tribes of Warm Springs, was willing to support me on the idea that canoeing is a cultural experience. The hike in the Cascade range, along an old growth trail, reinforced the tree metaphor. It offered another contextual learning experience to the children and incorporated my belief that there may be very little time left for human beings on this planet. Through this experiential process, I had hoped to teach the idea that we live in a complex, interdependent web of relationships that needs to be recognized, because I believe that we are currently risking the loss of major strands of what was once an ecologically balanced planet. One cannot describe old growth; it has to be experienced. I wanted these children to feel something that may soon no longer be available to human beings on this planet.

What I had trouble with was the expressed need of everyone else involved with the camp to categorically relegate multicultural curriculum to recognition of four specific "target" groups: African Americans; Native American Indians; Asian-Pacific Americans; and Latino, Hispanic, and Mexican Americans. Since there were a number of children registered as "interracial," or "biracial" as well as children and teachers from diverse Euro-American cultures, specific Asian-Pacific cultures, and Native American Indian Nations, I was concerned that categorical designation of culture for some participants might imply lack of culture for other participants. I was also concerned that replicating those broad, hyphenated labels would reinforce assumptions of dependent connections to mainstream American culture and undermine the strength of diversity within each of those multicultural labels. As stated by Ellen Carol Dubois and Vicki Ruiz (1990) in *Unequal Sisters: A Multicultural Reader in U.S. Women's History*: "We choose the term 'multicultural' . . . because we seek to focus on the interplay of many races and cultures . . . because we seek to assume that the term 'race' needs to be theorized rather than assumed" (pp. xi–xii). As suggested earlier, I feel that multicultural education should be "multi," an opportunity for the integration of many diverse cultures, traditions, and perspectives into curriculum.

## CONCLUSION

Multicultural education began as a powerful force, perilous to the dominant paradigm. However, in the last 10 years of teaching and learning, I have watched multicultural education become an umbrella term for an enormous variety of strategies, methodologies, and theoretical frames. In the process of acquiring legitimation there has been a loss of spontaneity, inspiration, and recognition of cultural diversity to the structure and demands of the uniform curriculum units which have been imposed. Compounding the imposition of categorization of culture is the tendency to rely on multicultural education packages. These curriculum packages are often used like instant cake recipes, pulled out when an administrator feels pressure to do something "affirmative" or a teacher runs short of Friday afternoon art projects. This "tag-on" approach reinforces decontextualized and categorical teaching-learning processes and assumes that culture and tradition are externals to be acquired rather than internal realities deserving recognition and respect.

I find any learning in categorical form to be restrictive because it reflects the compartmentalization of most curricula in the public schools. I am not alone in this concern. Curriculum theorists and practitioners alike (Apple, 1990; Catalano, 1992; Fry, 1992; Giroux, Penna, & Pinar, 1981; Jipson & Proudfoot, 1990; Kozol, 1991; Sleeter & Grant, 1987; Villanueva, 1992) have raised objections to the standard public school curriculum. Their voices reinforce what is suggested throughout this work. That suggestion is that schools can no longer be allowed to exist in isolation from community context and that curriculum should be transformed in order to acknowledge the interactive relationships of language, race, class, gender, culture, religion, and community.

As Nel Noddings (1990) states, understanding that "curriculum and community shape each other" allows us to "ask more intelligent questions about the nature and limits of each set of influences" (p. x). Robin Heslip (1991), in *As the Curriculum Turns: Reconstructing for Relational Education through Reflection and Resistance*, suggests that "curriculum represents a way of life that requires continual analysis and reconstruction by teachers, students, administrators and community members" (p. v). Ursi Reynolds (1991), in *Teachers' Perceptions of Kids and the Systems: Inclusion, Cultures and Curriculum*, notes that "it is essential for everybody's ideas and influence to count when it comes to the organization, actions, and dynamic of systems of schooling within which relations and learning are transacted" (p. 8). It is essential that the multiple voices of culture and community be heard and that education reflect these inter- and intra-personal interactions. As James Beane (1990) writes, without the inclusion of these multiple voices, curricular reforms are "doomed to failure" (p. 52).

I am concerned that curricula with the transformational power of multicultural education have fallen prey to the public school system. I feel that there is something very wrong with a school system that encourages categorization—the hierarchical language of a paradigm that results in decontextualization, disempowerment, and miscommunication—the concepts multicultural education attempts to transform.

I worry that multiculturalism may soon become a politically correct rhetorical term that will serve to support the dominant paradigm and reinforce the processes of assimilation and acculturation embedded within the standard public school curriculum—another example of what Octavio Paz (1985) refers to as the cult of progress. As Paz writes, "To strengthen the status quo is to strengthen a system that grows and spreads at the expense of the people who feed it [until] at last the philosophy of progress shows its true face: a featureless blank" (1985: 224–225). It is my contention that without the inclusion of the multiple voices of students, teachers, and communities, the traditional public school curriculum will remain a featureless blank—a tool for the perpetuation of a belief system that disregards context and relationship.

These statements remind us of the concerns addressed in this chapter: As parents, educators, and members of diverse communities, how can we develop curriculum that is inclusive of all cultural traditions, that is a celebration of multiple cultural voices? How do we respond to a need for cross-cultural communication and for education that is multicultural without replicating the traditional public school curriculum and imposing the limits of our own experiences and needs on the process?

The problem of imposition emerged at Multicultural Kids Camp on multiple levels: in staff direction of the children through planned experiences; through staff interaction with each other as we planned and implemented the program; and as we realized the implications of the standard concept of multicultural curriculum. The work with Multicultural Kids Camp provided a collective opportunity for people with various viewpoints to try to work together. No one was, or is, completely satisfied. We were too political for some people, not culturally responsive enough for others, and I feel that we have not even begun to tap the needed transformation toward a more holistic approach that will recognize the broad ecological web of voices that must be heard, if our planet is to retain the rich wisdom and diversity necessary for our survival.

## EPILOGUE

In January 1992, I received a call from Paulette Ansari. She was concerned that no one had come forward to coordinate Multicultural Kids Camp for the following summer, and she asked me if I wanted to be involved. My answer was a definitive yes. I felt that this was a powerful opportunity to reconnect with some of the individuals and communities that inspire my community and academic work.

There had been some significant changes made in the 3 years since the documentation for this chapter. The camp was no longer held in affiliation with Willamalane and no longer took place in Springfield. The focus of the camp was now global cultural diversity and peace education, and it was assumed that 3 of the 5 days would be spent out in the diverse communities in Eugene. The curriculum development and implementation processes were collaborative. Paulette Ansari, George Ann Baker, and Rich Glauber had been joined by Searsy Green ("an African American woman, a teacher, and the mother of three bright boys"), and Edward Wade (the racial justice coordinator for Clergy and Laity Concerned, an African American man, and a senior at the local university who described himself as "still surviving"). Once more, the frustrations were based in what was described as "this tip-of-the-iceberg approach"—a perceived lack of commitment—and a perceived need for the year-round building and maintaining of relationships with these children, their families, and their communities. Multicultural Kids Camp once more provided us with an opportunity to work collectively in order to build those connections, to create a space in which the children could establish relationships and nurture their growing awareness of self, of community, and of diversity. It also provided opportunities for discussion. We each wonder if current budget cuts (and our accompanying job fears) will allow us the freedom to continue with this work, and we worry about the degree to which the growing separatist movements in the Northwest portend regional/national xenophobia and eventual global genocide—*and* we plan how to continue with this work.


POSTEPILOGUE

It is August 9, 1994. I call Clergy and Laity Concerned and request information regarding Multicultural Kids Camp—I am now stepparenting and I would like our 7- and 10-year-old children to participate. I am told by a staff member: "We are now working more with adolescents, so attempting to do just a summer program for younger kids seemed inconsistent with our policies. We don't really want to work with the kids throughout the year; however, the different communities of color are planning on doing children camps." I ask if my stepchildren, Irish-Welsh and Norwegian, would be included in these camps and I am told that "well, sure, but none of them have really gotten started yet. Maybe next summer." I next call Willamalane to see if they are offering a program that emphasizes education that is multicultural. I am fortunate enough to reach Antoinette Hayward. She expresses her regret that the collaboration between Clergy and Laity Concerned and Willamalane only lasted a few years. As she says, "The training we received from CALC was great, but we have a really transient staff and there was little carryover to the next year. We needed the expertise; I'm not sure that CALC understood that." In the meantime, Proposition 9, the anti-almost-everybody initiative, although outlawed at the state level, has been passing in many of Oregon's small communities. Even as I continue to work for change by tutoring with the Indian Education Program, writing curriculum with nongovernmental organizations (NGOs) and grants for other projects, and "professing" in teacher education programs, I seriously consider becoming involved in one of the many private alternative schools springing up in this area and/or joining with other disheartened parents and home-schooling our soon-to-arrive youngest child.

## REFERENCES

Ansari, B. (1992). The racism free zone project. *Clergy and Laity Concerned, 16*(3), 31.

Apple, M. (1990, March). Is there a curriculum voice to reclaim? *Phi Delta Kappan, 71*(7), 526–530.

Beane, J. A. (1990). *A middle school curriculum: From rhetoric to reality.* Macon, GA: Panaprint.

Catalano, A. (1992). *Reflective, collegial professional development in pre-service teacher education: A relational perspective.* Unpublished doctoral dissertation, University of Oregon, Eugene.

Connelly, F. M., & Clandinin, D. J. (1988). *Teachers as curriculum planners: Narratives of experience.* New York: Teachers College Press.

Cornbleth, C. (1990). *Curriculum in context.* New York: Falmer Press.

De Brunhoff, J. (1933). *Babar.* New York: Random House.

DuBois, E., & Ruiz, V. (Eds.). (1990). *Unequal sisters: A multicultural reader in U.S. women's history.* London: Routledge.

Faulconer, T. (1992). *Situating trends in environmental education within the ecological debate.* Unpublished doctoral dissertation, University of Oregon, Eugene.

Fry, K. (1992). *Collaborating on the planning, implementation and evaluation of a multicultural curriculum.* Unpublished doctoral dissertation, University of Oregon, Eugene.

Giroux, H. A., Penna, A. N., & Pinar, W. F. (Eds.). (1981). *Curriculum and instruction: Alternatives in education.* Berkeley, CA: McCutchan.

Hertzberg, H. (1966). *The great tree and the longhouse: The culture of the Iroquois.* New York: Macmillan.

Heslip, R. (1991). *As the curriculum turns: Reconstructing for relational education through reflection and resistance.* Unpublished doctoral dissertation, University of Oregon, Eugene.

Jipson, J. A., & Proudfoot, R. C. (1990, March). *The challenge and promise of educational reform.* Paper presented at Northwest Holmes Group, Seattle, WA.

Juster, N. (1972). *The phantom tollbooth.* New York: Random House.

King, C. (1989, November). *Here come the anthros.* Paper presented at the annual meeting of the American Anthropological Association, Washington, DC.

Kozol, J. (1991). *Savage inequalities: Children in America's schools.* New York: Crown.

*Mabinogi, The.* (1987). (P. K. Ford, Trans. and Ed.). Berkeley: University of California Press.

Miller, J. (1990). Teachers as curriculum creators. In J. T. Sears & J. D. Marshall (Eds.), *Teaching and thinking about curriculum: Critical inquiries* (pp. 85–96). New York: Teachers College Press.

Noddings, N. (1990). Foreword. In J. T. Sears & J. D. Marshall (Eds.), *Teaching and thinking about curriculum: Critical inquiries* (pp. ix–xi). New York: Teachers College Press.

Orwell, G. (1949). *1984*. New York: Harcourt Brace.

Paz, O. (1985). *The labyrinth of solitude and other writings* (L. Kemp, Y. Milos, & R. Belash, Trans.). New York: Grove Weidenfield.

Proudfoot, R. (1990). *Even the birds don't sound the same here: The Laotian refugees' search for heart in American culture.* New York: Peter Lang.

Reynolds, U. (1991). *Teachers' perceptions of kids and the systems: Inclusion, cultures and curriculum.* Unpublished doctoral dissertation, University of Oregon, Eugene.

Schmuck, R. A., & Runkel, P. C. (1985). *The handbook of organizational development in schools.* Palo Alto, CA: Mayfield.

Sleeter, C. E., & Grant, C. A. (1987). An analysis of multicultural education in the United States. *Harvard Educational Review, 57*(4), 421–444.

Tolkien, J. R. (1966). *The lord of the rings.* Boston: Houghton Mifflin.

Turner, F. (1986). *Beyond geography: The western spirit against the wilderness.* New Brunswick, NJ: Rutgers University Press.

Villanueva, A. (1992). *Case studies of Chicano educators who have successfully transisted the public school system and who have not lost their primary cultural identity.* Unpublished doctoral dissertation, University of Oregon, Eugene.

# CHAPTER 4

# Here I Go Again:
# Supervision, Defining a Cultural Role

*Gretchen Freed-Rowland*

As an educator for over 20 years, I have come to seriously question the imposition of underlying assumptions and expectations of the Euro-anthrocentric culture and the role of education within it. Unfortunately, not all of us recognize the cultural as well as the gender embeddedness of language or the necessity of looking at the "discontinuities" (Foucault, 1980) of our past so that we can reclaim questions and voices. Without our histories, cultures, and languages we cannot really understand what questions should be asked, who is allowed to ask them, and who is allowed to answer them.

The storytelling context in which I grew up allowed for all the levels of potential meaning in those stories to evolve and emerge. As I needed them, another of their meanings would come clear. I can now see how much they have shaped my life and values. I can see how learning is an ongoing process dependent on context. How can you really understand what I mean? How can I represent my view with just the decontextualized "bare bones," the facts, the points you want me to get to? Besides, who am I to deny you the pleasure of a story which has those other layers of inference and possibility? Who am I to deny or make invisible the diversity, all the different ways by which different people come to know what they know?

I have a story to tell. I am an (Anishinabe) Ojibwa-(Hatcanjgara) Winnebago woman. U.S. history and cultural maps renamed us Chippewa but we know ourselves as Anishinabe or Ojibwa, except when we deal with the Bureau of Indian Affairs (BIA); then we have to be Chippewa again. I am a "half-breed," half red and half white, according to my birth certificate. I am also an "urban Indian," because there are only two categories, reservation or urban, neither of which describes much of anything, even on federal statistical charts for which such categories have been developed. The term "urban Indian" tends to assume that language and tribal rituals and ceremonies have been displaced. It assumes that urban Indians cannot also be traditionals. I have lost much in two generations, and the rules keep changing as to who the federal government will recognize as an "Indian." I do have my tribal enrollment number, which is recognized by my grandfather's tribe. The federal government quantifies me as one-quarter Winnebago blood, and without that I would no longer be an Indian legally.

There are many of us for whom traditional American educational rhetoric and assumptions do not validate our cultural experience and values. Consequently, we do not exist in other people's eyes as we believe we are. This creates a dissonance in the classroom that neither the child nor the teacher has been taught to identify and understand (Cazden, John, & Hymes, 1972; Philips, 1979/1983; Spindler, 1982). This has a ripple effect within the school, between administration, faculty, parents, and community (Wolcott, 1967/1984). For example, the relationship between the American people and Native American Indians has always been one of conflict. The never changing, romanticized historical images of Plains Indians as "savages" on horseback or of Longfellow's Hiawatha in the dark, mysterious forest haunt us; as do the images of Indians as mystical shamans, keepers of our ancient wisdom, or as dirty, drunk, fat, dark-skinned people hanging around the forts or, today, hanging around the bars in towns. These are some of the prevalent stereotypes of Native American Indians which our children still must face, even in their schoolbooks. Such stereotypes deny us our voices; we don't "sound" or "look" like we are supposed to sound and look. Where are the "real" stories about "real" Indians? Why are not the "real" Indians' voices heard in schoolbooks and in the media? Why are such "racist" stereotypes still imposed on us?

As part of a teaching team, for a class in multicultural education at the University of Oregon, I continually experienced the shock that I have again become invisible. It is particularly painful in small groups, where, in talk about American Indians, we are always "they" and "them." I'm not only invisible but dead, lost in Western lore. Even when we are discussing current issues for Indian peoples and children, members of the group, unconsciously, lump all Indian cultures together in the past tense and always use the pronoun "they."

Ken Kesey in *And One Flew over the Cuckoo's Nest* (1973) did a masterful job of capturing this notion of how it feels to be invalidated, to become invisible, in the scene where the so-called deaf and dumb Celilo Indian tells about when he was 8 years old and the government agents went out to Celilo Falls (now flooded) and discounted his presence even though they were talking to him and around him about things personal to him. He decided then he was invisible in the white man's world. Many of us can identify occasions where our use of language and our ideas have been treated as irrelevant or inappropriate. Our voices are not heard. If it happens too many times, in too many contexts, we truly become invisible. For some of us, not only are we invisible because we are Indians, but also because we are women (Munro, 1990). The "other things" that happened in the classroom and on the playground were and always are more about that "other, hidden curriculum" for us than about what teachers thought they were and are teaching.

As an Indian woman caught between two cultures, and for whom history of this "place" (Berry, 1977/1986) goes back thousands of years, I keep asking myself, Have I been trapped into being an instrument of cultural genocide for my own people and my own beliefs? I am trying to be a bridge, a healer, yet here I am "playing" the educated Indian woman "talking" in the privileged written text, because in this culture that is what I am supposed to do. My people turn their backs on me when I act like this with them; yet my grandparents, my mother, and her sisters taught all 19 of us children that "we can't just stand by and watch things happen." As members of an Indian family out in the white man's world, we have an obligation to at least be heard.

I was born on a reservation, but I was already privileged by my grandfather's position as superintendent for all Northwest Indian tribes and by the level of education and experiences of my extended family. I knew explicitly, by the age of 7, the politics of being an Indian. I hadn't yet learned about being a "half-breed." I knew about broken treaty rights and that we had to stick together and speak up "outside the family." We were allowed to be with the grownups only if we were quiet and listened. As the oldest of 19 grandchildren, during my first 8 years, I stayed with my grandparents on the reservation a great deal of the time. I learned many things by being quiet, listening and watching. I remember there were so many stories and always lots of humor and jokes, some of them about white people.

We were also a Christianized family, and our parents were well educated, as were our grandparents, in the Euro-American tradition. They believed education would save our people. We were also well schooled in the proverbs of the Bible and Walt Disney. I thought Jesus Christ was a white man with long reddish blonde hair in a long white gown who really understood Indian peoples' ways—how one has to live in and for the family, for the (Indian) community, and for all the others less fortunate than us.

Before the age of 5, with tremendous curiosity and no fear, I would go far and wide away from camp or home on foot or horseback. I don't remember being told but I remember stories from which I learned to withdraw quietly from an animal's presence or be still. I knew if I got lost on horseback that "Snippy" would take me home. I knew that "Crazy Nellie" wasn't to be feared the way the other "res" (reservation) adult Indians said she should be. My "sense" was validated by my grandmother. She allowed me to go to Nellie's house and begin another piece of my education.

I learned as a child from Nellie and others not to be fearful and to recognize there is more than one way of knowing and doing—of being in the world. I also learned as a child that life is about getting hurt, that we would be called names, hit, and denied entrance to places, but that what mattered was "standing up and being counted." Perhaps for these same reasons, I have since learned that I am uncomfortable with simplifying my thoughts so as to be able to "talk" in a straightforward way. How we use language reflects our understanding of reality, our comfort zones. Language speaks us as we speak it (Whorf, 1964). I have a hard time not putting "my two cents' worth" into the discussion.

This, then, is the context I feel I must provide to frame how the issue of impositionality became not singular but multilayered for me, as it impacted my experience as a supervisor of teachers. It also impacted their experience of me as their supervisor and of themselves as teachers and as students.

In order to talk about the issue of imposition in my experience as a supervisor of teachers in a master's degree teacher program, I need to create a context for why I struggled so with what I saw to be conflicting views as to what school, teaching, and learning "ought" to be about and what my role "ought" to be as supervisor in a relational model (Proudfoot, personal communications, 1988–1991) of teacher education. In the relational model of education the core beliefs and theoretical framing are that we are all cultural beings; that we must acknowledge and respect diversity; that we are all teacher-learners, even the children; that learning is about learning; that it is an ongoing process, not a product; and that curriculum is emergent. Therefore, the relational model respects collegiality, difference, and the sharing of perspectives, rather than a hierarchy of expertise and judgment. Philosophically, because of their participation in this particular master's program, the three women in this study had to endorse, at least to some degree, the relational model of education as collegial-human relational-integrative-multicultural-cross-cultural-Eurocentric-gender-sensitive (Proudfoot, 1986; personal communication, 1988). The program is process- not product-oriented. It is inductive—the content is the emergent curriculum—a fusion of the relevant research literature with what the student teachers bring to their seminar from their personal and teaching experience. The program offers a cadre of professors, on-site supervisors, curriculum specialists representing different cultural perspectives, and peer teachers to support the teacher's growth in the public school setting. Part of my responsibility was to be a classroom supervisor for 4 hours once a week for 9 months. So there I was, in a new place, part of a multicultural team in a nationally acclaimed graduate teacher master's degree program at a major university. At the same time, I recognize that I'm back in that old place . . . struggling with the realization that once again, my cultural reality, my own voice, is not one easily shared in the academic arena, much less out in the public schools.

As a supervisor, not only was I to observe, take data, ask what the teacher would like me to focus upon, and to debrief, but also to help the teacher draw on theoretical and other seminar content as a means for deconstructing curriculum materials and curriculum requirements. I also participated with the teacher's students, team taught, modeled teaching strategies, had the teacher critique me, and brainstormed ideas having to do with particular student, parent, or administrator's needs and with curriculum and lesson planning. Ideally, we built a team and went through a process in which a model was created which, upon reflection, can be drawn upon, refined, and utilized to understand what teaching and learning "ought" to be about.

The 2 years of supervision discussed in this study were in three fairly traditional classrooms. The teachers with whom I worked are Anne, Fran, and Lyla, and the principals are Norm and Ms. Brown. The data upon which this study was based were derived from my supervision records for 1988–89 and 1989–90. The analysis of my records from a personal cultural perspective highlighted what was problematic and what was appropriate in a collegial-relational model of supervision. This chapter reflects my struggle with traditional teacher education assumptions about teacher intervention and the imposition of my "cultural baggage" and intentions. What I brought to these teachers was 20-plus years of teacher lore and current research literature that supported my understanding of teaching and learning. This study also deals with what the teachers and their principals thought a supervisor as expert "ought" to provide.

The relational model, in suggesting what education "ought" to be about, is not what these teachers had experienced, for the most part, as undergraduates in education or in their teaching experience. Nor had it been encountered, to any degree, in their later educational experience other than in this particular program.

The first problem arose when the three women students I was supervising were critical of the main tool for informal record keeping and retrospective evaluation —a journal. Anne and Fran were so adamant that the journal was a waste of already precious time that they refused to do it even though it was a program requirement. This was allowed on an individual basis as a way to be sensitive to individual needs and to negotiate an alternative within the framework of the model.

The relational model is an affirmation of who I am and what I have learned as an Ojibwa-Winnebago woman and as a public school teacher for 15 years. The teachers and principals in this study had these comments about the model:

- "confusing"
- "not clear"
- "threatening"
- "fuzzy"
- "Tell me"

- "What is it you want me to do?"

- "I need a lesson plan"

My role, as I understood it from the relational model, was not to direct or even give advice directly unless sought out by the teachers. I was to be the facilitator and supporter of the teachers' development with sensitivity to their own style, experience, and maturity in a particular school-district-community setting. I wanted these teachers to feel comfortable and trusting enough to allow their strengths, weakness, fears, and triumphs to emerge so that we could talk about them in a reflective way. I wanted them to realize that all that we say, do, and believe is a subjective and culturally learned understanding of the world and that their understanding may differ from that of some of the students they taught. I wanted them to realize I didn't have "right" answers for them. I wanted to help them articulate their needs and their sense of what they did well within a context of what they believed. Ideally, I wanted to help them recognize and be comfortable with this as part of a lifelong learning process in which they would grow and in turn model the process. In that way they could begin to help their students break through the implicit cultural message that teaching is about being an expert, knowing the right answers (which are often disguised, as in the teacher's manual), and thus having the power, instead of being about asking wonderful questions and sharing a diversity of ideas and possibilities.

This was not an easy task for me. I was caught between not wanting to be directly impositional and therefore trying to find indirect ways of fostering dialogue and asking questions, and recognizing that any framing that I did was impositional. I struggled with my need to contextualize, their impatience, sometimes, with me, and their need for both approval and immediate concrete "stuff. " My own teacher training years ago and the years of education I have experienced in my life also intruded on the process. I wanted to help but I felt it was also important to remember how long it had taken me to undo at least some of the expectations I had learned to respond to so well and to finally feel confident and comfortable in my own style.

For although I was brought up as part of an extended Native American family, I was also schooled during the '50s in rural and city cultures in Oregon. I remember being 7 years old and told why we had to do our best in school and always tell the truth. I remember the feeling of always being tense and ready as I left the house and went outside to be with "white" people. It was similar to the feeling I would later experience getting up on the starting block in high school swim meets. I was about 8 or 9 when I first stayed out of school to go with my mother and grandmother to protest another government action against treaty rights and promises of our "Great White Father in the East."

For me this all translated into "You have to be better than white kids; you can't fool around and be caught in any kind of situation that could be misconstrued. You have to finish college no matter what; and you must help those who haven't had your privileges—those less fortunate than you, particularly Indian peoples." Consequently, my teaching style was framed by my own cultural experiences and interpretation at a very early age and emerged through my concern for each whole child/person in the community of my classroom.

I became aware of how problematic my "oughts" for the classroom initially were and of their roots in my Euro-American teacher training. I was a product of a time and place when it was still acceptable to put a hand on kids and joke with them, but also to expect conformity to certain explicit rules of behavior. I was fortunate to work in one school long enough to have the support of the counselor, administration, students, and community for "my way" of teaching and evaluating.

As an instructor and supervisor and as a graduate teaching fellow in two departments for 5½ years, I believed I had experience and a perspective which I had a responsibility to share. At the same time, being sensitive to the different ways in which people effectively negotiate learning and doing and to their priorities, I also have difficulty in being more direct or in intervening in the work of others. To me, Lyla, Anne, and Fran were teachers, not student teachers. They had already been screened by a committee for this particular master's program, and on that basis for the most part, were hired by experienced principals looking for a teacher who would fit the needs of a particular school, community, and group of students. It was my responsibility, then, to get a feel for how best to facilitate both the fit and the teacher's strengths and emerging style.

For example, Anne's students already had a reputation of being a difficult group to handle and one with lower than average skill levels. Anne gave them more freedom than I would have regarding how they sat and moved around the classroom. They were very noisy and interactive when making transitions from one lesson or group to another or moving from one part of the room to the other. Based on my "expert" "clinical supervisor" experience (Acheson & Gall, 1980/1986), university program checklists, the literature on effective schooling and behavior modification, and my early classroom teacher experience, I could have initiated some brainstorming around how to tighten up her classroom management and accountability skills. Instead, I continued to observe, collect data, and journalize about my conflicting thoughts regarding responsibility and teaching styles. I repeatedly asked myself questions about the relationships among the kids, the classroom, and the learning dynamic. Could Anne accept my frame of reference? (It has been my experience that direct intervention tends not to work, at least not in the long run.) I later discovered, in spite of their noise and interactive style, the students consistently got to where they were going in record time. I timed them. By not intervening right away, I learned some powerful lessons about what was good teaching for Anne in a collegial-relational model. Those lessons affirmed my beliefs about my job as a supervisor.

The language of the clinical supervision model and of literature on effective teaching implies that the teacher is an objective, neutral transmitter of disembodied skills and knowledge, who should acquire strategies that could be immediately utilized. Unfortunately, it is this same literature, language, and experience that framed the three teachers' and the principals' expectations. In this case, the teachers wanted concrete practical formulas and remedies, something that at the end of the year felt like it was a reusable package.

Norm, one of the principals for whom I have a great deal of respect, was critical of the "professional" support the teachers and supervisors received from the university. It was his sense that it is precisely in the first years of teaching that teachers should be given a great deal of instruction and feedback around the models, theories, and strategies they learned about as undergraduates. I agreed, but I believed we disagreed on the process and product. His sense was that Anne, in comparing notes with another earlier teacher in the program, felt she wasn't getting enough concrete information, programs, and techniques that she could use in the classroom. However, he was not as uncomfortable as Ms. Brown about not having "paper" support for what went on in the classroom— those pieces of paper containing checklists and recognizable educational jargon that can be put into their files. Teachers and principals seem to want packages of the newest trends that the teacher can try out under the university expert's supervision, yet still within an identifiable and familiar structure.

Things the teachers said they would have liked more of were lists of resources, handouts and photocopies, units, lesson plans, recipes for teaching curriculum (not kids) and classroom management, and maybe a handbook or how-to guide for being an integrating-relational-collegial-teacher-learner:

- "I would like to have to be able to lay out what my supervisor gave me."
- "It didn't feel like I had passed the test."
- "I didn't know what to expect, so I'm not sure I got what I was supposed to."
- "To have learned things that I couldn't have learned on my own."
- "It's too fuzzy to have the pre- and post-observations and final evaluation conference be an oral discussion with just rough notes based on a journal and self-analysis in relationship to what did the kids learn versus what did I teach and what rules did I remember to follow."

Questions kept surfacing: What did I bring to this year of teaching a specific group of children in a particular setting possessing its own constraints? What did I learn teaching is really about? What do I know now that I didn't know at the beginning of the year, or at winter break, or at the end of the year? What do I feel good or confident about now? How do I feel I have changed? What do I know about my style versus other styles, including that of my supervisor? What do I need to work on? What are my weaknesses? In relationship to what? What are my plans for next year and how can I simplify my role and enhance those of my students—looking at the prescribed curriculum and how it went; looking at my attempts at variations? To better meet individual students' needs, what would I want to do differently? How could I accomplish that without a big expenditure of time, money, and resources?

Yet, as with students, the last thing the teachers and I really wanted was to be told what to do, nor did we have time to follow through on some of the ideas we really liked. They had enough to do in just figuring out what was expected by the principal and how to juggle the pieces the day was cut up into so that the minutes for each subject would add up and they would be ready when the children from the other classes trooped in for spelling or reading. Anne, in particular, had an enormous task deciding how to teach to an impossible range of math skills and do the district "individualized" math packages within the time frame given. The teachers were overwhelmed with the enormity of what they didn't know. They knew that no amount of preparation made them ready for what actually ended up happening. No preservice classes really had taught them about what the kids brought with them to the classroom and what happened when all of "it" got stirred together: the teacher, the time schedules, the other teachers, the chaos in the halls, the bathrooms, the lunchroom, and also what the teacher thought he or she was supposed to be doing. From fall through winter, in particular, we would hear in the seminars, not just from my teachers, but from all of them: "Everything is out of control!" "I can't do it all." "How is anybody supposed to do all of this." "I have no time to do anything extra." "I never see my family or my friends." "I must be missing something." "Help me!" "This wasn't what it was like in student teaching." Can they be blamed for feeling the supervisor ought to be able to "do" something? Weren't those their expectations of what teaching would be about—being able to do something and being able to make a difference?

What good is a supervisor who comes in and instead wants to brainstorm around the teacher's problems and his or her own efforts to solve them and encourages his or her ideas for the next time? Teaching lessons scattered throughout the year and giving rough, informal notes were not tangible enough. Having someone there to observe, participate, and give feedback as an ongoing process didn't seem structured or professional enough to the teachers or to the principals. Yet my experience with the brainstorming sessions, rehashing problematic attempts, and with the journal or some sort of personal record-keeping process has been that they work and are much richer and less limiting as evaluating tools. They allow for ongoing interactive (both oral and written) review and reflection in a way that the standard "efficient" models for evaluation, the checklists, do not. (Keeping the dreaded journal, for those who did, made a considerable difference in these areas of greatest concern, as a means of reflecting on what they had learned, how they had grown, and what they each could have used more of.)

How could I help them understand the importance of looking beyond the district or school requirements when they were not sure of what those really were? How could I convey that some of the very important content of successful teaching is still left to an implicit immersion process and that over time they would learn what they needed to know? Preservice coursework and student-teaching experience had not prepared them for effectively dealing with parents, substitutes, the clerical and bookkeeping expectations, and the different personalities that make up the political-social culture of the school. How could I enhance their confidence that they should, and could in time, tailor their curriculum to the needs and interests of their students; that it was possible to use different approaches and materials, while still staying within the required guidelines; and that curriculum was not a thing but an ongoing process?

In the end, somehow, my trying to facilitate the teachers in working through issues and in doing the work themselves felt to them like they had missed something. I had not done my job. Their sense of what an "expert" ought to do translated into a feeling that I should have imposed my expertise and my style, and not have brainstormed with them, answering questions with questions. My experience framed what I saw and heard and therefore the questions I asked and the stories I told. But their experience and expectations framed what they heard me say as well. Since we did not document our verbal interaction over my notes and observations, they didn't have access to their own responses to those sessions if they didn't keep a journal. My role was to support them in what they chose to do and not to do, and to help them be aware that they were making choices. Their style of teaching was evolving. Yet I realized that by the questions I asked, I was framing the focus of what we talked about. So I tried to get them to ask for what they wanted or to frame the discussion. It was not easy to get them to do so.

Upon reflection, perhaps, I realize that the principals may be right about what "real" teaching "ought" to be about. What is the point of all the theory, microlessons, models of teaching, peer coaching, scope, sequence, closure, and individualizing lesson plans for mainstreaming, and so on, if there is no follow-through, if there is no place and time to really use it, and if there is no acceptance of the perspective that strategies may fail a few times before we can decide whether or not they will ever work or if they are appropriate. Research indicates that new teachers fall back on how they were taught or, in other words, what was modeled for them (P. Munro, personal communication, fall 1989).

The system does not acknowledge what we do well and what is working. It teaches us to focus on what is not working and what we do poorly. It is counterproductive because it teaches us to devalue ourselves when we don't fit at the top of the competitive numerical scale or have the "right" answers. The focus is narrow and harsh. It is not about ideas and how we got them; it is about having the correct end result, the product. It is about getting to the next level, not the thinking and doing process of how to get there.

The problem is clear. How can teachers value a supervisor who refuses to tell them what to do to improve and who insists on getting a feel for their style, their students, and their classroom before saying much of anything? In other words, as the supervisor, I, too, am held accountable for a product at the end of the day.

Schooling, especially at the academy, gets knowledge mixed up with the information dispensed. Teaching becomes the providing of information to students either by the teacher lecturing or asking limited questions or by the student reading and answering questions thought of by someone else. These methods, like tests and measurements, are also class- and culture-bound. Learning is assumed as a result of this interaction. This model of teaching is the standard one with which we are all very familiar and from which we have, in fact, learned. But can we truly call this discourse, let alone dialogue?

Given the ever persistent factory or banking model of education and the politicization of such papers as *A Nation Prepared* (Carnegie Forum, 1986), *Meeting the Challenge of a Nation at Risk* (National Commission of Excellence in Education, 1984), and others; given that many of us see the number of students for whom "back to basics" makes no sense at all; given the changing demographics of the United States and the world; and given the impinging global economic and ecological crisis, I have asked myself: What should I have done differently? What should I have said to the teachers with whom I worked, and for whom, in the end, the system holds me accountable? Should I have played the expert, as was their expectation, instead of imposing my own cultural perspective on them by refusing to be the expert? Should I have softened the model with which they had no previous experience and for which they were not prepared? As supervisor-teacher-learner-colleague-elder peer-storyteller-listener, I should be a catalyst for reciprocating dialogue—for a discourse in which we can construct, console, brainstorm with, remind, review, and support each other. In reality, I cannot be a dispenser of information—only a sharer of my lore, a teller of stories. From my cultural perspective, it is inappropriate to speak for anyone else, to be an expert, yet that is what the academy, and society at large, expect of us. We each become the experts of something very small.

## REFERENCES

Acheson, K., and Gall, M. (1986). *Techniques in the clinical supervision of teachers: Preservice and inservices applications.* New York: Longman. (Original work published 1980)

Berry, W. (1986). *The unsettling of America: Culture and agriculture.* San Francisco: Sierra Club Books. (Original work published 1977)

Carnegie Forum on Education and Economy. (1986). *A nation prepared: Teachers for the 21st century.* New York: Author.

Cazden, C., John, V., & Hymes, D. (Eds.). (1972). *Functions of language in the classroom.* Prospect Heights, IL: Waveland Press.

Foucault, M. (1980). *The history of sexuality: Vol. 1. An introduction* (R. Hurley, Trans.). New York: Vintage/Random House.

Kesey, K. (1973). *And one flew over the cuckoo's nest.* New York: Viking Press.

Munro, P. (1990, April). *Common differences: Curriculum decision making and feminist pedagogy.* Paper presented at the American Educational Research Association, Boston, MA.

National Commission of Excellence in Education. (1984). *Meeting the challenge of a nation at risk.* Cambridge, MA: U.S.A. Research.

Philips, S. (1983). *The invisible cultures: Communication in classroom and community on the Warm Springs Indian reservation.* New York: Longman. (Original work published 1979)

Proudfoot, R. (1986). *Model for the synergy of relational education: The dynamics of cultural interaction and connection.* Unpublished manuscript, University of Oregon, Eugene.

Spindler, G. (Ed.). (1982). *Doing the ethnography of schooling: Educational anthropology in action.* Prospect Heights, IL: Waveland Press.

Whorf, B. (1964). A linguistic consideration of thinking in primitive communities. In J. Carroll (Ed.), *Language, thought, and reality: Selected writings of Benjamin Lee Whorf* (pp. 65–86). Cambridge, MA: MIT Press.

Wolcott, H. (1984). *A Kwakiutl village and school.* Prospect Heights, IL: Waveland Press. (Original work published 1967)

# CHAPTER 5

## Speculations:
## Negotiating a Feminist Supervision Identity

*Petra Munro*

### GOING TO THE BEACH

To speculate. The double-edged meaning of this word—to meditate and reflect as well as to spy, watch, or observe—captures the tensions and contradictions I experience in my role as supervisor of preservice teachers. Like others (Bowers & Flinders, 1990; Britzman, 1991; Gorman & Haggerson, 1993), I am engaged in reconceptualizing supervision as a process of mutual, interactive dialogue for the purposes of learning more about the context and complexity of the teaching act. Yet like Gretchen, I struggle with the imposition of dominant cultural meanings and expectations of "super" "vision" that situate me in that unfamiliar terrain of expert, voyeur, gatekeeper, and guard. To be the object of knowledge, the object of the gaze, and the object of surveillance—that is what I know. As it is with Susan, the taking up of an identity in which I am to function as an "agent of social control" is positioning myself in the role of the oppressor. Thus, to take up an identity as a supervisor is to be positioned within externally persuasive discourses (Bakhtin, 1981) which reify the very relations of power which I as a feminist seek to disrupt. Thus, the goal of this chapter is not to posit a "feminist supervisor identity" but to speculate on how being positioned as a supervisor is a continual negotiation of power relations and relations of gender.

My own grappling with the inherent contradictions of supervision actually began while I was a high school social studies teacher. It was 1984, my first year of teaching. I was looking for a master's thesis topic related to my interest in bringing about transformative curricular change. The director of instruction at the suburban Chicago high school where I was teaching was anxious to try out a new form of supervision called "peer coaching" (Munro & Elliot, 1987). We teamed up and I began to do "teacher-research" before I had ever heard of the term. Peer coaching held out the promise of collegial, collaborative supervision in which teachers could continually engage in the study of their craft. Ironically, peer coaching emerged in our district simultaneously with "outcomes-based education." Hargreaves and Dawe (1990) point out the peculiar paradox of teachers being encouraged to collaborate at precisely the moment when there is less to collaborate about. Accountability, outcomes-based education, and "back to the basics" prescribe what to teach and how to teach and leave little room for reflection, innovation, and imaginative collaboration. Do terms like peer coaching, peer supervision, mentoring, tutoring, and collegial assistance, which are currently a high-priority objective in American schools (Anderson, 1993), merely resituate observation and regulation so that teachers in effect become "agents charged with policing one another's oppression" (Smyth, 1991: 95)? According to Smyth (1991), power, although dispersed, still functions as a form of control reminiscent of the system of "indirect rule," which gives the appearance of decentralization but in effect does little to challenge dominant relations of power. It was with a desire to understand what I experienced as these contradictions that I returned to graduate school.

It was in the spring, in Jan's course on women and children in the workplace, that I first began to understand the complex and contradictory ways in which relations of power function and how power relations are always gendered. Our discussions throughout the semester led me to Gerda Lerner's *Creation of Patriarchy* (1986) and Madeline Grumet's *Bitter Milk* (1988). Simultaneously, I was taking Harry Wolcott's course on teacher culture and pursuing my interest in gender issues from an anthropological perspective. Henrietta Moore's *Feminism and Anthropology* (1988) was particularly pivotal in refocusing my analysis from looking at how gender is experienced through culture to asking how culture is experienced and structured through gender. Rosaldo and Lamphere (1974) articulated the culture/nature, male/female, public/private dichotomy which functions as the basic ideological grounding for the subordination of women to men. My struggles to understand the power dynamics of supervision took on a new dimension. As the summer began, I looked forward to the feminist theory seminar as a site for grappling with the implications of feminism for supervision. Little did I realize that what would become home for me and a site of resistance (hooks, 1990) would serve to displace others. But the summer began and off to the beach we went.

It was on the Oregon coast, at the beach house that Jan had rented for a week in August, that the summer seminar (Karen, Gretchen, and myself) met to grapple with the ongoing issues of imposition. The sound of the waves, Eric's (Jan's son) demands that we swing with him or build sand castles, and the tempting treats we had all brought prompted the right distance from "home" to share our experiences of the past year. Gretchen and I sat at the picnic table outside what Jan called her "beach shack." Because it was August, we were thinking about our fall graduate assistantships as supervisors of student teachers. The uneasy feelings crept over us. I reflected back on my past year of supervising secondary student teachers and the continual tensions I had felt in wanting to empower students to confront issues of racism, sexism, and classism in the social studies curriculum while also trying to implement my feminist pedagogical beliefs in which students are constructors of their own knowledge. Like Susan and Karen, I struggled with how to work for social change while not committing the sin of imposition through imposing my political ideologies or cultural biases.

For Gretchen, imposition was not the issue. To be directive or to intervene in the work of student teachers would be to delegitimate their experience. I probed, "What if a student were blatantly racist in class? You wouldn't do anything?" Gretchen's response was that she saw her role as trying to understand the meanings that students give to their actions. "Wasn't not addressing racist comments tantamount to perpetuating racism?" I retorted. Didn't being a feminist working for change mean we had to identify, locate, and resist modes of oppression? These three steps which provided me with a clear-cut method for battling injustice were from Gretchen's point of view a decontextualized recipe which stripped oppression from its location in language, historicity, and culture. That discourse functions in complex and contradictory ways was not quite clear to me just yet (I was still in my stage of resisting Foucault. Why, I wondered, were all these feminists still having to legitimate their work through using male theorists?). Gretchen and I went back and forth. I tried to find some exception to her adamant response that no, under no circumstances would she be directive. Like the waves in the background, we kept going round and round, not getting anywhere (though of course I still thought we would get somewhere). Our locations seemed irreconcilable.

Our discussion at the beach prompted us to write an AERA proposal on imposition. I welcomed the opportunity to "reflect" on my experiences as a supervisor from my newfound insights as a feminist. What did feminist theory have to do with supervision? Why was I still uneasy with supervision despite terms like "reflective practice" (Schon, 1983) and "peer coaching" which were directed at reshaping supervision models to reflect a more collaborative, egalitarian vision? In what ways did gender shape understandings of power and authority that are embedded in supervisory concepts like observation, conferencing, feedback, and evaluation? How did "super" "vision" impose itself on me and locate me in an identity which left me speculating as to whether it was possible to be a feminist and a supervisor? Thus, I locate my story in my experiences as a supervisor of secondary social studies student teachers in the 1988–89 year.

## THE CONFLICT: A LONG WAY FROM THE BEACH

After a brief preconference in the teachers' lounge, Jeff and I headed toward his classroom. Considering that it was my first observation of his teaching, Jeff seemed very calm. I chatted idly as we walked to his classroom. My nervous banter was probably more to calm myself than to make Jeff feel at ease. This was my first term supervising student teachers, a job I took very seriously. As we neared the classroom, I asked Jeff what he would like me to focus my observation on. "I'm afraid not everyone is getting involved," he replied. "Could you keep track of who is and who isn't participating?" "Sure," I said as we rounded the corner into the classroom, where the students were seated and appeared ready to go.

"Today's lesson will cover the reasons we got involved in a war with England for our independence." Jeff leaned against the table at the front of the room as he began his chronological account of the events leading up to the American Revolution: the French and Indian War, the Stamp Act, the Boston Tea Party, the Boston Massacre, and finally Lexington and Concord. Students sat politely, some taking notes, others with their eyes fixed in the distance. "When war broke out in 1776, we were the underdog, a team without a defense and no quarterback, but we had spirit, a spirit which united us in the quest for justice, liberty, and the pursuit of happiness." Jeff continued, "War is very similar to a football game: there are two teams, and each has its strengths and weaknesses and its strategies. Let's compare the two teams in the Revolutionary War."

During the debriefing in our postconference, Jeff concluded that the lesson had gone well because he was able to make it relate to students' lives by using the football metaphor. I agreed that making learning relevant to students' lives is very important, and continued, "Do you think it was relevant to all the students in the class?" Jeff looked puzzled, and I probed further by suggesting that perhaps not everyone understood football. "Oh," he replied. "I never thought about that." "If a student doesn't understand football [I included myself as an example], how likely is it that they will be able to participate in the lesson?" I asked. "Yeah, I see your point," Jeff replied.

This scenario was not uncommon among the student teachers whom I supervised. Although well-intentioned, the student teachers often taught lessons from a masculinist, Eurocentric perspective and perpetuated discrimination unknowingly through what I considered class, gender, and racial stereotypes. Just as disturbing as the more blatant forms of discrimination were the subtle ways in which teachers reinforced dominant patriarchal world views by subscribing to a pedagogy which structured knowledge as absolute and discrete, privileged the rational over the intuitive and the abstract over the experiential, and gave credence to a linear, dualistic historical view of the world. In the above case, the use of the football metaphor reduced the complexity of human events and interactions by allowing the teacher to present the war as "two teams," thus perpetuating an epistemological view of the world which is dichotomous and simplistic. In working with preservice teachers (both male and female) who teach history primarily from a Euro-American, male, militaristic perspective, I felt compelled to "raise the consciousness" of my students. Initially, my readings in production theory and the "new sociology," articulated in the practical subdiscourse of "liberatory pedagogy" (Apple, 1979; Comstock, 1982; Freire, 1973; Giroux, 1986; McClaren, 1989), guided my work with preservice teachers. Positioning myself as a social change agent, I was able to rationalize my imposition. And, although I felt uncomfortable being directive regarding the student teachers' curriculum and pedagogy, I wondered if not imposing was even more impositional on those whose voices were marginalized and excluded from the curriculum.

In working to "raise the consciousness" of preservice teachers to the implicit cultural assumptions and androcentric bias inherent in their teaching, I faced the contradiction of advocating a feminist perspective which honors students' experiences as a way of validating students as creators of their own knowledge while, at the same time, wanting to impose my "oughts" (or absolutes) in the name of bringing about transformative social change for a more equitable society. I found myself caught in a continual and never ending spiral of postmodern thought as I tried to avoid the binary of the relativism versus essentialism trap. Influenced by other feminists, I saw my work with student teachers as a site from which I could reconceptualize the research and teaching process in such a way that acknowledged "difference" and "positionality" without capitulating to political imposition or relativistic indifference (Ellsworth, 1989; Flax, 1990; Lather, 1989; Miller, 1987).

My experiences working with preservice teachers were woven within this continual dilemma of how to raise issues central to my beliefs about "good" teaching—that learning is a collaborative endeavor developed in a relational, experiential context that allows multiple and diverse voices to be heard yet avoids an absolutist viewpoint which risks re-creating the oppressive nature of essentialism. This chapter discusses my struggle in negotiating the contradictions inherent in maintaining a feminist perspective with the goal of social change while at the same time respecting the rights of others to construct their own knowledge. Does the collaborative or reciprocal approach advocated by many feminists address the inherent hierarchical nature of the traditional teacher–student relationship? Can the issue of imposition be resolved or are student–teacher relationships impositional by nature? How do I deal with a situation where a student's construction/interpretation of experience is different from my own and in direct conflict with my goals as a feminist? This chapter examines each of these questions within the context of my experience as a supervisor and teacher of secondary education student teachers.

## IN THE NAME OF FEMINIST PEDAGOGY

Most feminists assume the oppression of women and have as one of their major goals the correction of both the invisibility and distortion of female experience in ways relevant to ending women's unequal social position (Lather, 1986; Rosaldo & Lamphere, 1974; Weiler, 1988). In striving for equality, many feminists have rejected the "add-women-and-stir" approach, which assumes an acceptance of patriarchal standards and a conformity to their expectations and requirements (Gross, 1986; Harding, 1987). Acknowledgment and validation of women's experiences have necessitated a basic restructuring of theoretical and analytical approaches which reflects a world view in which knowledge evolves in relations, knowledge is socially constructed, multiple ways of knowing are acknowledged, and the personal and subjective are validated (Belenky,Clinchy, Goldberger, & Tarule, 1986; Gilligan, 1982).

What does this world view imply as feminists bridge the gap between educational theory and classroom practice? Like Jan, I was drawn to Carol Shrewsbury's (1987) concept of feminist pedagogy which envisions "a classroom characterized as persons connected in a net of relationships with people who care about each other's learning as well as their own which is very different from a classroom that is seen as comprised of teacher and students" (p. 8). Curriculum which reflects the relational dimensions of the classroom as opposed to a hierarchical, abstract, and objective perspective is based on an understanding of the interactive, dialectical process of teaching which is placed in the daily lives of teachers and students. The curriculum in the feminist classroom is grounded primarily in the belief that curriculum emerges in the interactions between student and teacher. In the words of Madeline Grumet (1988: 172):

> Curriculum is a moving form. That is why we have trouble capturing it, fixing it into language, lodging it into our matrix. Whether we talk about it as history, as syllabi, as classroom discourse, as intended learning outcomes, or as experience, we are trying to grasp a moving form, to catch it at the moment that it slides from being the figure, the object and goal of action and collapses into the ground for action. . . . Curriculum, considered apart from its appropriation and transformation by students, curriculum defined as design, a structure of knowledge, an intended learning outcome, or a learning environment, is merely a static form.

This does not imply that the curriculum is relative or without direction, for implicit in a feminist viewpoint is the goal of bringing about social change. Thus, for many feminists the goal of curriculum is to raise the critical consciousness of students for the purposes of bringing about social change for a more just society (Lather, 1988; Weiler, 1988). This critical consciousness is based not on abstract or theoretical notions of democracy and change. Students' personal lives are not shed like coats and left in the cloak room as students enter the classroom. The personal experiences and feelings of students are central to understanding forms of oppression and bringing about social change.

Thus, a feminist pedagogy encourages a curriculum which incorporates multiple voices and diverse points of view. Curriculum is not designed to provide the "truth," the answers, or the absolute knowledge. In the words of Maxine Greene (1975: 183):

> I am suggesting that the ordering of material that is curriculum be presented as a series of potential perspectives on the world as lived by our students. I am suggesting that the students, in dialogue with their teachers, be enabled to understand the ways in which the disciplines make available principles, protocols, schemata by means of which they, as persons present themselves, can interpret the multiple realities of their lives.

This perception of curriculum nurtures the relational dimension of the classroom and avoids the dualistic thinking dominant in patriarchy, which separates the personal from the public, experience from knowledge, and emotion from thought.

As I began my supervision of student teachers, I felt committed to promoting the incorporation of a feminist viewpoint as one means of trying to bring about a more just society. As I conducted my supervision with student teachers, I was interested not only in the equal participation of boys and girls or the equal treatment of both genders in textbooks, but in the incorporation and acknowledgment of alternative world views, including those which feminists have highlighted as being central to women. In the daily classroom practices of student teachers, this meant I was encouraging history to be taught from multiple perspectives, with awareness of diversity, and, consequently, with use of a variety of teaching styles which validate students' knowledge and personal experiences.

## THE SCENE

As a supervisor of secondary education social studies teachers, I observed student teachers in the field, conducted a required weekly seminar, and read students' journals. The seminar had no set curriculum although I was given the impression it was to be a place for student teachers to debrief about their anxieties, problems, and successes as they made the transition from the university environment to the "real" world of teaching. The seminar met weekly for 2 hours and generally followed a small-group discussion format.

The first group of student teachers, six in all, helped me ease into my supervisory role by ignoring my discomfort at being in the position of "expert."

For Gretchen, being the "expert" was culturally inappropriate. I struggled with the contradiction of being a woman (one who lacks power) and being positioned as a supervisor (one who has power). Terms like power and authority are located in and dependent on gendered understandings in which male behavior is constituted in opposition to female behavior (Butler, 1990). To be female is not to have authority. Thus, to be a woman in a position of authority is necessarily a contradiction in terms (Bloom & Munro, 1995). Negotiating these conflicting subjectivities became the site from which I bumped up against taken-for-granted notions of power and authority. Despite my reconceptualization of supervision from a technocratic to a collaborative endeavor, my emerging poststructural understandings reminded me that all relations are embedded in power dynamics.

## IMPOSITION: LET ME COUNT THE WAYS

### Speculation 1: The Irony of the "Reflective" Supervisor

As the student teachers arrived at our first seminar, I was sure some of them were misplaced. Four of the six student teachers were clearly older than I. As we confirmed that we were all in the right place, introductions revealed that these "older" students had worked successfully in other professions, several had families and teenage children, and all were articulate about the reasons they wanted to go into teaching. My stereotype of the young college student who enters teaching to have summers off or pursue coaching or because he or she "loves" kids quickly faded as I realized the firm dedication of these students. I thought to myself, what do I have to offer? In assuming that my role would be to "empower" beginning teachers, I was aware of having committed my first sin of imposition.

My opening words at the first seminar still echo in my mind: "I can't teach you to be a good teacher; my role is to help you become the teacher you chose to become." In advocating a self-directed, reflective approach to learning how to teach, I hoped not only to allow students to become constructors of their own knowledge, but also to establish an approach to teaching which would promote the pursuit of good teaching as a lifelong endeavor. Rather than teaching them "skills" or "prescriptive recipes," my goal was to develop students' ability to be critical and to contemplate what implications their teaching had on students and on issues of race, class, and gender.

I faced an immediate conflict: What right did I have to impose my political values on the student teachers? How could these student teachers be free to construct their own knowledge when I was molding and directing them to attain a certain "consciousness"? My initial resolution to this dilemma was to adopt the model of the reflective practitioner (Schon, 1983). Schon's notion of "reflection in action" is a process whereby teachers engage in continual inquiry about their actions and tacit knowledge and what this means for their practice. Drawing on Dewey's understanding of the dialectic between experience and theory, Schon's model initially presented a model of supervision which acknowledged the social construction of knowledge. I hoped that the student teachers would reflect on their practice through journal writing, self-evaluation, and learning to ask certain questions of themselves. In assuming they would reflect and recognize sexist, racist, or other oppressive acts, I was able to cleanse myself of the guilt of imposition, for in theory wasn't I just teaching them to reflect?

In practice, the notion of the reflective practitioner soon became problematic. What happened—with Jeff, for example—when reflection did not lead students to recognize the embedded sexist, racist, or otherwise oppressive implications of their teaching? Implicit in the metaphor of reflection is the concept of the mirror image. Luce Irigaray (1974/1985) suggests that the danger of the mirror, "in whose sight everything outside remains forever a condition making possible the image and the reproduction of the self" (p. 328), is that reflection is done in isolation and yields only one image, that of the subject. This "reflexive rationality" suggests that learning is self-directed and is the product of rational, autonomous thought conducted in isolation, independently of others. As Toril Moi (1985: 132) says, the mirror image "hints at a basic assumption underlying all Western philosophical discourse: the necessity of postulating a subject that is capable of reflecting its own being." Although allowing me to escape the discomfort of imposing my values, the notions embedded in the reflective practitioner model were in direct contradiction to my beliefs that knowledge evolves in the interaction of relationships and is arrived at through an intersubjective process.

In hindsight, I recognize that advocating a reflective approach to supervision relieved my uneasiness with imposing my own values of teaching on the student teachers with whom I was working. I neglected to consider, however, that the mirror "empty of altering reflections . . . is in the service of the same subject to whom it would present its surfaces, candid in their self-ignorance" (Irigaray, 1974/1985). Students reflecting on their teaching saw only a partial picture, which not only excluded multiple images of the classroom, but also reproduced deeply embedded cultural assumptions regarding notions of an autonomous, rational self capable of self-reflection.

As their supervisor, I also believed I could help the student teachers develop their reflective skills by acting as a mirror for them. Ironically, this position as reflector of knowledge repositioned my relation to knowledge within traditional gender norms in which women are assumed to be facilitators of knowledge but incapable of becoming knowers themselves (Martusewicz, 1992). Like Gretchen, I hoped to be nondirective by merely collecting data as to what was happening in the classroom and presenting the events to the students just as they occurred. Yet, as with traditional supervision models (Acheson & Gall, 1987), there is still the assumption that the supervisor reflects back what has happened in the classroom, "holding it up" so that the student teacher can see his or her image and analyze it. Gretchen's continual remarks about the culturally embedded nature of language reminded me of the fallacy of the mirror metaphor. The mirror image maintains a correspondence theory to reality. Paul Ricoeur (1974) reminds us that experience can never be captured since it is continuously being mediated through language. Unfortunately, the mirror metaphor reinforces the notion of the "objective" bystander who can present a detached and neutral account of the events of the classroom. In effect, the supervisor still assumes the role of "expert," with its implicit power base, instead of placing the learning experience in a reciprocal, mutually interactive framework. By excluding myself, my viewpoint, my reflections, from these student teachers' learning process, I limited their reflections to one viewpoint, their own. By minimizing my own subjectivity I directed the focus of the analysis solely toward the "subject," the student teacher. In effect, despite the "empowering" intent of "reflective practice," the student teacher remains the object of scrutiny of the spectator or supervisor.

I do not want to dismiss the process of reflection, but if it focuses only on the subject, then we maintain the myth of the individual capable of reflecting autonomously and in isolation. To make explicit the cultural assumptions which perpetuate a patriarchal world view, the mirror must function to reflect a diversity of images. Now I acknowledge that whether I try to be an "objective" outsider or include my own voice in the dialogue, both approaches are impositional to some degree. As spectator, however, I objectify the students and impose distance, neutrality, and a false sense of "expert." By placing myself within the relationship, not only do I reduce the subject/object dichotomy, but the reflections become many, allowing students to see multiple reflections rather than remain captives of their own image.

### Speculation 2: Interpreting the "Other"

As mentioned earlier, the students I worked with possessed clear and strong ideas about teaching and reasons for entering the profession. They were by no means "empty vessels" waiting for me to fill them with knowledge. Bonnie, a 22-year-old white, middle-class, Christian student, stated that her goal in teaching social studies was

> to help students recognize that all people are equal. We need to get rid of the ethnocentrism. I want my students to realize that being white and male isn't superior. It's important to teach things critically and from many points of view. Once that's been done, students can make up their own minds.

Karl, at age 36, has chosen teaching as his second career. For Karl the challenge in teaching high school students is to show students how social studies can be a vehicle for making sense of and putting together events that affect them. Through studying history, students can gain a better understanding of themselves and the world around them.

Karl emphasized making history relevant to students so that they could make connections between the past and the present.

In many respects, the student teachers were philosophically aligned with my own perspectives about teaching. They would not have called themselves "feminists," but in principle we agreed about the importance of making learning relevant (i.e., considering the whole child); being sensitive to issues of gender, race, and class; including all students by using a variety of teaching and learning styles; and validating students as creators of their own knowledge.

Conflict arose as I observed dissonance between student teachers' teaching behaviors in the classroom and the values they supposedly advocated. One recurrent example was that student teachers tended to follow the history textbook although they admitted that this chronological approach was not very stimulating for students. Was I watching "deskilling" (Apple, 1978) in action? Or perhaps the cooperating teacher was exerting pressure on the student teacher to teach "by the book." My agenda for debriefing sessions focused on trying to ascertain the roots of this perceived discrepancy. Through the use of probing questions—How did you feel about the lesson? Did you accomplish your goals? What would you have done the same or differently?—I could often gain insight into what I perceived as the apparent contradiction between teaching style and philosophy.

With Karl, however, this was not the case. In one U.S. history lesson, he stood glued to the podium for the entire class session while lecturing on the early causes of westward expansion. In the debriefing, it was obvious that Karl was pleased with the lesson; he believed he had cited many interesting "facts" and related persons of the past to current figures known to most students. Of course, my interpretation of the events differed. From my perspective, Karl had lectured the students and by neglecting to involve them, had made it difficult for them to find the lecture relevant. (In fact, their body language told me that they perceived it as far from interesting.) Yet at the same time, I believed I had to accept his interpretation of the situation.

This situation presented me with an obvious dilemma. I felt Karl's interpretation of the classroom situation was inaccurate and distorted the reality of what was actually happening. Yet on the other hand, I did not want to deny or diffuse Karl's claims by suggesting that his construction of his experiences was not valid and by favoring *my* interpretation of the events. However, I wanted Karl to agree with me and in the postconference was unwilling to capitulate until we had both agreed he had not presented the lesson in a manner relevant to students. Although I recognized the inherent relation of domination by imposing my "construction" on Karl, I believed my duty was to help him recognize his teaching strategies and change them toward a more student-centered approach. And, as a friend, I felt it was my obligation to point out the contradiction between his beliefs and his actions. Unlike Gretchen or Susan, who sought to understand the other's point of view, I insisted from my position as social change agent that I knew what he needed to do.

If my ultimate goal was to bring about change, then I felt it was my duty to raise his "consciousness" about what was really happening in the classroom and encourage change. The assumption I made was that Karl was not "conscious" and that I, as the supervisor working for social change, had the inside track on "helping" him. Feminists like Angela McRobbie (1982) and Elizabeth Ellsworth (1989) have pointed out the inherent contradiction in a feminist viewpoint which strives for reciprocity but maintains that we have the "inside track" on empowering others. McRobbie (1982: 52) asks: "How can we assume that they need anything done for them in the first place? Or conversely that we have anything real to offer them?" The very agency of individuals to come to a critical consciousness of their own (Gramsci, 1971) seemed undermined by talk of the need to "empower" and "emancipate" (Ellsworth, 1989; Gore, 1993; McRobbie, 1982). My patronizing stance directly conflicted with the egalitarian, reciprocal, nonhierarchical position I advocated as a feminist who was attempting to validate students as knowers.

How did I resolve the issue? On reflection, I recognized that I was trapped in the notion that Karl and I could rationally discuss the situation and come to a common, shared interpretation. Elizabeth Ellsworth (1989: 306) suggests that although "dialogue" gives the illusion of equality, in fact it leaves intact the authoritarian nature of the teacher–student relationship. Biddy Martin and Chandra Moharity (1986: 208) warn feminists that we should be engaged in "creating new forms of collective struggle that do not depend upon the repression and violence needed by dialogue based on and enforcing a harmony of interests." Like other feminists, my goal is to acknowledge and encourage a diversity of voices and multiple interpretations of reality. Therefore, the purpose of dialogue becomes not consensus, but acknowledgment of difference as a way to explore what Sandra Harding (1992) calls "situated knowledges"—in other words, the willingness to reason from the other's point of view (Benhabib, 1992; Freed-Rowland, 1990; Jones, 1990). Feminists concerned with avoiding relativism and political inaction have suggested that this focus on difference is problematic due to its potential relativism (Alcoff, 1989). In encouraging students I work with to listen to their own voices and trust in their subjectivity, I do not intend to promote relativistic indifference. Nor do I agree with many postmodernists who suggest that because our subjectivity is constructed by social discourses beyond our control, we have no intentionality whatsoever (Alcoff, 1989). As Mascia-Lees, Sharpe, and Cohen (1989) suggest, although feminist theory shares similar concerns with postmodern ideas, feminist theory differs from postmodernism in that it acknowledges its grounding in politics. Thus, a relativity leading to political irresponsibility or nihilism is inherently contradictory to a feminist perspective which has as its primary goal bringing about change for a more equitable society.

As I continued my work with Karl, I tried to voice my interpretations without expecting Karl to necessarily agree with them. We discussed that it was OK not to interpret events in the same way. To avoid being indifferent or "objective," I acknowledged my interpretations of classroom situations, but when I acknowledged that Karl's interpretation was just as valid as mine, it no longer was an issue of imposition, except perhaps a case of mutual imposition. In recognizing that each of us has only "partial knowledge," we had to work together in a reciprocal way so that we could construct the pieces into a whole—not an absolute or complete whole, but a fluid, ever changing construct of reality. Rather than seek "unitary wholeness or dialectical resolution," Patti Lather (1989) sees the necessity to "intervene in ongoing movements, to keep things in process, to disrupt, to keep the system in play, to set up procedures to continuously demystify the realities we create, to fight the tendency for our categories to congeal" (p. 2). Curricular acts take on new meaning in this context in which fluidity and movement replace transmission and reproduction.

By acknowledging that realities are multisubjective and incongruent, I struggled to let go of my need for the "right" and "absolute" answer or solution and to be honest with students, not misleading them into thinking that there was one interpretation of events. This included learning that disagreeing with someone does not necessarily mean one is competitive or adversarial. My work toward a better understanding of how to achieve this sense of difference without opposition continues.

### Speculation 3: Imposing Friendship

The problem of imposition was clearly highlighted by my discomfort with being in a position of authority and power. Generally, the concept of power is conceived to be that of "power over," rather than "power with" or empowerment. My perceived power as supervisor is grounded not only in the authority invested in my role as a result of the hierarchical position, but also in the view that knowledge is a commodity that the supervisor has and the student teacher does not. My fear of imposing my interpretations on Karl was, partly, rooted in the acceptance of dominant notions of power. My original coping strategy to decrease this discomfort was to rationalize my role as teacher-supervisor as facilitator of knowledge, not as an "expert." Like Jan, who adopted the teacher as midwife metaphor to ease the tensions of being positioned as expert, I adopted the term "facilitator" and thus reenvisioned my relationship with students as egalitarian and collaborative; consequently, I thought, imposition would no longer be a problem.

I quickly realized, however, that the tensions I felt as "authority" figure continued in my capacity as friend and facilitator. I now battled the dilemma of defining my responsibilities as friend or facilitator. Did establishing a reciprocal and collaborative relationship mean that power was equally distributed and so resolve my problem of having power over? Or, as John Smyth (1991) suggests, is the shift to more collegial forms of supervision through collaboration merely a way to mask continued managerial ends of supervision which are in fact seeking to harness teachers more effectively to the work of economic reconstruction? Does changing the definition of "who" does supervision really change relations of power?

As I worked to resolve this dilemma, it became apparent that I was confusing the notion of authority with authoritarianism. If authority is viewed not as rooted in the individual, as Hannah Arendt (1968) suggests, but as part of a collectively shared memory, then the "power" of those in authority can be viewed not as power over but as power with. Power emerges in the shared experiences which enhance the understanding of the authority of our traditions and experiences. Of course, we don't all share the same traditions, nor do we all equally share the same notions of authority. But by placing authority in collective memories, we encourage an intersubjective view of the world grounded in the realities of people's lives, not located in abstract notions of justice. Power is not a single possession, nor is it located in a unitary, static sense; rather, it is continually negotiated and positioned in the apparatuses of regulation themselves (Walkerdine, 1990). Thus the discourses of reflective practitioner and of teacher as facilitator or midwife necessarily function in complex and contradictory ways. Yet because power is decentered and plural, so, in turn, are forms of political struggle. This understanding of power is attractive because, as Nancy Fraser (1989) suggests, it widens the arena within which people confront and seek to change their lives.

Therefore, power is something feminists don't necessarily have to be against. Toril Moi (1985: 148) maintains that "feminism is not simply about rejecting power, but transforming the existing power structures—and in the process, transforming the very concept of power itself." Along these same lines, Carolyn Shrewsbury (1987: 8) suggests that feminists are questioning the traditional notion of power by reconceptualizing a concept of power that does not embody relations of domination. If women, as Gilligan (1982) and others have pointed out, view the world through connectedness rather than hierarchy, then the meaning of power takes on a different construct. As Shrewsbury (1987: 8) suggests, "feminist pedagogy embodies a concept of power as energy, capacity, and potential rather than as domination. . . . Under conceptions of power as capability the goal is to increase the power of all actors, not to limit the power of some."

What does this reconceptualization of power, as a shared construction of reality which enhances the authority of all, mean in my work as supervisor? If we conceive of the relationship as a mutual exchange of constructed meanings intended not to highlight opposition, but to seek an intersubjective understanding which enhances notions of shared experience, then authority becomes grounded not in the individual, but in the constant negotiation taking place within a relationship. We cannot and do not want to avoid imposing our values, lest we risk reconstructing the objectifying relations characterized by patriarchy by hiding behind the mask of objectivity. Therefore, my power is based not on imposing my viewpoint, but in the authority of my experiences and my recognition of the common understandings we strive for in our daily interactions.

### Speculation 4: The Fallacy of Empowerment

Perhaps my greatest dilemma in trying to avoid being impositional was the affirmation I received from several student teachers for being impositional. At the end of his student teaching, Jeff reflected:

> You took the extra time and effort to push me into trying new approaches and methods in teaching and continually challenged me to attempt to go beyond my current conceptions of what teaching was and accepted nothing but my best effort.

Although this type of feedback eased my guilt about imposing, it did not resolve the problem. I was still "stuck" with trying to justify what right I had to impose my perceptions of teaching on others. Despite my understanding of myself as a facilitator or collaborator, I had naively assumed that students would accept my perspective as the "truth" without questioning it. Fortunately, this was not the case.

In working with the students, I soon realized that although they listened politely and intently to my feedback and suggestions, they made choices as to what they would reject and what they would integrate into their repertoire of teaching "skills." The students' assertion of their own interpretation of events and rejection of my definition of events highlighted my presumed hegemony. Like others (Waite, 1993; Zeichner & Tabachnick, 1985), I am closer to understanding that my preoccupation with imposing obscured the agency of student teachers to construct their own meanings. My fear of imposition was based in part on the assumption that students were empty vessels and that my predetermined answers and solutions would become theirs. I feared, as does Patti Lather (1988), that "reproducing the conceptual map of the teacher in the mind of the student disempowers through reification and recipe approaches to knowledge" (p. 569). What this viewpoint neglects, however, is the resistance of many students to accept carte blanche the viewpoints of the teacher—that is, what David Flinders (in press) calls the "slippage" between imposition and agency.

The old questions—How do I impose? Is it right to impose?—changed. Now I ask, Could I impose even if I wanted to? The inherent authority in my position as supervisor had led me to believe that I could impose. Yet my experience watching student teachers pick and choose from my suggestions and viewpoints made it clear that they were not lumps of clay which I could form.

## CONCLUSION: SHATTERING THE SPECULUM

In the following semesters, I approached my role as supervisor with considerably less inclination to "save the world" by producing good teachers. Instead, I engaged in a mutual exploration of the multidimensional, problematic task of teaching. I shared my experience, not "expertise." My purpose in sharing was not guided by the hope that these new teachers would emulate me. Instead, I hoped they would consider my experiences as yet another interpretation of how one makes meaning of the complex task of teaching.

My struggle between avoiding imposition and capitulating to being the "neutral" observer continues. I recognize the futility of positing these as distinct dichotomous extremes when reality presents a continuous muddy field. I hope that by sharing our struggles regarding issues of imposition, instead of seeking analytic distance, we will enhance our understanding of the complexity of human relationships from which we emerge and are attempting to make meaning.

Have I become less forthright in presenting my position on what constitutes "good teaching"? No, I have not. Removing myself, my biases, and my standpoint from the supervision process would eliminate the possibility of being involved in the interactive relationship which is the basis for generating new understandings and knowledge. Without a position, a standpoint, speculations, there would also be no discourse.

## REFERENCES

Acheson, K. A., & Gall, M. D. (1987). *Techniques in the clinical supervision of teachers* (2nd ed.). New York: Longman.

Alcoff, L. (1989). Cultural feminism versus poststructuralism: The identity crisis in feminist theory. In M. R. Malson, J. F. O'Barr, S. Westphal-Wihl, & M. Wyer (Eds.), *Feminist theory in practice and process* (pp. 295–327). Chicago: University of Chicago Press.

Anderson, R. (1993). Clinical supervision: Its history and current context. In R. Anderson & K. Snyder (Eds.), *Clinical supervision: Coaching for higher performance* (pp. 5–19). Lancaster, PA: Technomic Publishing.

Apple, M. (1978). The new sociology of education: Analyzing cultural and economic reproduction. *Harvard Educational Review, 48*(1), 495–503.

Apple, M. (1979). *Ideology and curriculum.* London: Routledge and Kegan Paul.

Arendt, H. (1968). *Between past and future: Eight exercises in political thought.* New York: Viking Press.

Bakhtin, M. (1981). *The dialogic imagination* (C. Emerson & M. Holquist, Trans.). Austin: University of Texas Press.

Belenky, M. F., Clinchy, B. M., Goldberger, N. R., & Tarule, J. M. (1986). *Women's ways of knowing: The development of self, voice and mind.* New York: Basic Books.

Benhabib, S. (1992). *Situating the self.* New York: Routledge.

Bloom, L., & Munro, P. (1995). Conflicts of selves: Non-unitary subjectivity in women administrators' life history narratives. In A. Hatch & R. Wisniewski (Eds.), *Life history and narrative.* (pp. 99–112) London: Falmer Press.

Bowers, C., & Flinders, D. (1990). *Responsive teaching.* New York: Teachers College Press.

Britzman, D. (1991). *Practice makes practice.* Albany: State University of New York Press.

Butler, J. (1990). *Gender trouble: Feminism and the subversion of identity.* London: Routledge.

Comstock, D. (1982). A method for critical research. In E. Bredo & W. Feinberg (Eds.), *Knowledge and values in social and education research* (pp. 370–390). Philadelphia: Temple University Press.

Ellsworth, E. (1989). Why doesn't this feel empowering?: Working through the repressive myths of critical pedagogy. *Harvard Educational Review, 59*(3), 297–324.

Flax, J. (1990). *Thinking fragments: Psychoanalysis, feminism and postmodernism in the contemporary west.* Berkeley: University of California Press.

Flinders, D. (in press). Industrial dimensions of supervision. In G. Firth & E. Pajak (Eds.), *Handbook of research on school supervision.* New York: Scholastic.

Fraser, N. (1989). *Unruly practices: Power, discourse and gender in contemporary social theory.* Minneapolis: University of Minnesota Press.

Freed-Rowland, G. (1990, April). *Here I go again: Supervision, defining a cultural role.* Paper presented at the American Educational Research Association, Boston, MA.

Freire, P. (1973). *Pedagogy of the oppressed.* New York: Seabury Press.

Gilligan, C. (1982). *In a different voice: Psychological theory and women's development.* Cambridge, MA: Harvard University Press.

Giroux, H. (1986). Curriculum, teaching and the resisting intellectual. *Curriculum and teaching, 1*(1 & 2), 33–42.

Gore, J. (1993). *The struggle for pedagogies.* New York: Routledge.

Gorman, N., & Haggerson, H. (1993). Philosophic consideration in the practice of clinical supervision. In R. Anderson & K. Snyder (Eds.), *Clinical supervision: Coaching for higher performance* (pp. 37–50). Lancaster, PA: Technomic Publishing.

Gramsci, A. (1971). *Selections from the prison notebooks.* New York: International.

Greene, M. (1975). Curriculum and cultural transformation: A humanistic view. *Cross Currents, 25*(2), 175–186.

Gross, E. (1986). What is feminist theory? In C. Pateman & E. Gross (Eds.), *Feminist challenges* (pp. 190–204). Boston: Northeastern University Press.

Grumet, M. (1988). *Bitter milk: Women and teaching.* Amherst: University of Massachusetts Press.

Harding, S. (1987). *Feminism and methodology.* Bloomington: Indiana University Press.

Harding, S. (1992). *Whose science/whose knowledge?* New York: Cornell University Press.

Hargreaves, A., & Dawe, R. (1990). Paths of professional development: Contrived collegiality, collaboration, culture and the case of peer coaching. *Teaching and Teacher Education, 6*(3), 227–241.

hooks, b. (1990). *Yearning: Race, gender and cultural politics.* Boston: South End Press.

Irigaray, L. (1985). *Speculum of the other woman* (G. Gill, Trans.). Paris: Editions de Minuit. (Original work published 1974)

Jones, K. (1990, April). *Curriculum development in a cross cultural context.* Paper presented at the American Educational Research Association, Boston, MA.

Lather, P. (1986). Research as praxis. *Harvard Educational Review, 56*(3), 257–277.

Lather, P. (1988). Feminist perspectives on empowering research methodologies. *Women's Studies International Forum, 11*(6), 569–581.

Lather, P. (1989, March). *Deconstructing/deconstructive inquiry: The politics of knowing and being known.* Paper presented at the American Educational Research Association, San Francisco, CA.

Lerner, G. (1986). *Creation of patriarchy.* New York: Oxford University Press.

Martin, B., & Moharity, C. J. (1986). Feminist politics: What's home got to do with it? In T. G. Lauretis (Ed.), *Feminist study/critical studies* (pp. 191–212). Bloomington: Indiana University Press.

Martusewicz, R. (1992). Mapping the post-modern subject: Post-structuralism and the educated woman. In W. Pinar & W. Reynolds (Eds.), *Understanding curriculum as phenomenological and deconstructed text* (pp. 131–158). New York: Teachers College Press.

Mascia-Lees, F. E., Sharpe, P., & Cohen, C. (1989). The postmodernist turn in anthropology: Cautions from a feminist perspective. *Signs, 15*(1), 7–34.

McClaren, P. (1989). *Life in schools.* New York: Longman.

McRobbie, A. (1982). The politics of feminist research: Between text, talk and action. *Feminist Review, 12,* 46–57.

Miller, J. (1987). Women as teachers/researchers: Gaining a sense of ourselves. *Teacher Education Quarterly, 14,* 52–58.

Moi, T. (1985). *Sexual/textual politics: Feminist literary theory.* New York: Methuen.

Moore, H. L. (1988). *Feminism and anthropology.* Minneapolis: University of Minnesota Press.

Munro, P., and Elliot, J. (1987). Instructional growth through peer coaching. *Journal of Staff Development, 8*(1), 25–28.

Ricoeur, P. (1974). *The conflict of interpretations.* Evanston, IL: Northwestern University Press.

Rosaldo, M., & Lamphere, L. (1974). *Women, culture and society.* Stanford, CA: Stanford University Press.

Schon, D. (1983). *The reflective practitioner: How professionals think in action.* New York: Basic Books.

Shrewsbury, C. (1987). What is feminist pedagogy? *Women's Studies Quarterly, 15*(3 & 4), 6–14.

Smyth, J. (1991). Instructional supervision and the redefinition of who does it in schools. *Journal of Curriculum and Supervision, 7*(1), 90–99.

Waite, D. (1993). Teachers in conference: A qualitative study of teacher-supervisor face-to-face interactions. *American Educational Research Journal, 30*(4), 675–702.

Walkerdine, V. (1990). *Schoolgirl fictions.* London: Verso.

Weiler, K. (1988). *Women teaching for change: Gender, class and power.* South Hadley, MA: Bergin & Garvey.

Zeichner, K. M., & Tabachnick, B. R. (1985). The development of teacher perspectives: Social strategies and institutional control in the socialization of beginning teachers. *Journal of Education for Teaching, 11*(1), 1–25.

# PART II

## APPRECIATING DISSONANCE: MULTIPLE PERSPECTIVES ON COLLABORATION

Women today read and write biographies to gain perspective on their lives. Each reading provokes a dialogue of comparison and recognition, a process of memory and articulation that makes one's own experience available as a lens of empathy. We gain even more from comparing notes and trying to understand the choices of friends. When one has matured surrounded by implicit disparagement, the undiscovered self is an unexpected resource.

—Bateson, 1990: 5

We continued: "This symposium presents five life histories. Our choice of personal narratives is an expression of our commitment to validating women's voices. As Bateson (1990) suggests, it is the marginalization of women's voices which continues to position us for oppression. Our presentation is an attempt to model a truly collaborative, self-reflexive, intersubjective process. Thus, we offer our stories and our personal interpretations of their significance to us and to the teaching/learning process."

And so we began our presentation in Milwaukee at the annual conference of Research on Women and Education in November 1990. A year had passed since we had first begun to work together. We had survived AERA and we struggled to make sense of our hopes for collaboration and the realities of group tensions and dynamics. Although we shared a commitment to social change, the process of working together was not unproblematic, and it raised important questions regarding what it means to translate concepts like "collaboration," "connectedness," and "community" into everyday practice. Drawn to the hope of redefining traditional patriarchal power dimensions so as not to be characterized by hierarchy and competition, we were confounded by the emergent dynamics which threatened our work together. Collaboration, our alternative to imposition, our lived praxis, now imposed on us by forcing us to look not only at the theory of imposition but also at the presence of it in our relationships and in the realities of working together.

This chapter presents our dialogue with each other, delivered in Milwaukee as we reflected on our work together. Invigorated by the presence of supportive women, hopeful that we could heal old wounds, we examined the emergence of our identity as a work-group and our continuing struggle to validate and support each other. Our collaboration had raised three central questions. We respond to them here through our individual, sometimes contradictory, descriptions of our work together.

1. How is the process of collaboration achieved and maintained by a diverse group of women representing different ideological perspectives and cultural realities?

2. How can individual identity and difference be acknowledged and validated while we maintain commitment to shared purposes?

3. How can we continue to support and empower each other while confronting external obstacles to our project?

Rather than generate prescriptions for feminist group-practice, we hoped to reveal the complexities of the collaborative process. Our hope was that if we could understand the process, perhaps we could maintain the threads of our group despite the unraveling that was already occurring. As educators concerned with bringing about transformative social action, we faced the question of how to work together without violating each other's rights to construct her own meanings and live within her own reality.

Preparing for the Milwaukee symposium gave us the opportunity to pause in our work to discuss the positions we had assumed relative to each other and to our ideas and ideologies. We acknowledged the commonalities that brought us to this project but also the diversity and tensions between us that provided us with the chance to grow but, in the end, brought us to crisis. In presenting our collective project and our ongoing reflections on our experiences with each other as teacher-learners, we hoped to portray those very differences and the shared commitment between us that honored them.

Our narratives presented the stories of our experiences of those years of working together. In their contradictions and affirmations, we believe they blended together as a response to the questions we posed. However, they are also incomplete, and the story has not ended. We continue to work together to complete this book, still seeking to understand ourselves as we reflect on how we teach and learn together.

Imagine that you are in Eugene, Oregon, having tea at the Napoli Cafe. At the next table are a group of five women, obviously old friends reunited after a long separation. You cannot help but listen in on pieces of their conversation, intruding on your conversation almost like a dramatic soliloquy.

◕◡

JAN: *I remember how we got acquainted. It was the dean's "beer and brat" party in 1988. I always liked the idea of his having beer and brats; in those days it reminded me of Wisconsin, which I was still missing. Gretchen dragged several of you over so you could ask me about my language development course. Later, I realized that what you were interested in was not necessarily early childhood education but the opportunity to share some of your own stories and ideas about teaching. I was pleased and excited when some of you seemed to also have an interest in doing research from a feminist perspective. I guess you each reminded me, in some way, of myself as a graduate student—tentative, exhilarated by all of the new ideas, concerned with being "smart" enough to make it. I remembered the vow several of my women colleagues back in Madison had made as we finished our doctoral programs: to actively support women students as they learned the necessary academic rituals. We were all so angry with the usual privileging of male students, the way they were mentored, taken to conferences, taught how to write journal articles. We wanted to have the same support—it had taken us so long to figure it out, after we finished our degrees.*

*I also remember that first day at the coast, when we met at the beach shack to begin the process of socializing you into "good academics." We discovered our shared interest in questions about whether we were imposing too much on our students in our work as teachers.*

*Gretchen was so indignant that we had suggested she should "tell" her student teachers how to improve their teaching. It took the rest of us a longer time to figure out that that was imposition, too. I wish Susan had been there. It is hard to believe that we weren't all part of the group from the very beginning.*

*My best memory was of that second trip to the coast when you all gave me the shawl. You don't know how important that was to me—realizing you all appreciated the work we were doing. It wasn't just another "please the teacher" trip. In those days I was sure I was there to give continual support, but I never really expected anything in return. It was during that trip that I realized how powerful our group had become.*

*And remember the day we presented at the Center for Women in Society— Gretchen, you were so dramatic in your traditional beaded jewelry, arms waving to emphasize your points. And Petra, you really kept us going with your sense of direction and ideas. And at Bergamo—I felt so guilty about not taking you all along—sort of like when you buy one of your kids a birthday present and don't get something for the others. It was then I really began to struggle with your separate realities and various needs. It made me acknowledge the different types of relation-*

ships I had with each of you and also my need to respond in my own way to the differences between you. I realized that you were no longer, in my mind, this amorphous group of students whom I was mentoring through graduate school but that you each brought something special and unique to our interactions.

What did I learn from our project? I learned about myself—I found I was amazed that our process of collaboration worked at all with such a diverse group of women, that we were sometimes, even often, able to set aside the competition and jealousy that has often plagued similar relationships between women. Or am I overromanticizing again? I also found it to be the hardest part of my work. What was most difficult for me was letting go of control. As the oldest in my family and the one who always had to get home, start dinner, be responsible for my sisters and brother, I have struggled, it seems forever, with my need to be in charge so that unnamed disasters won't occur. I can remember being upset when you did not meet my expectations of the "good graduate student," couldn't get to our meetings, or seemed to dismiss my preoccupation with getting "the work" done.

Also, I recall sensing, that as major professor, I should chide you to get your dissertations done, yet I did not want to be too active in assuming that role, which seemed so unpleasant and impositional. I reminded myself it was OK to let you have some space to create your own time line as long as you knew I was there to help when you needed it. Our research project was good therapy for my obsessiveness—often you all were the ones that were on task, and I was the one behind, overwhelmed with the complexities of my daily life and getting my own work done. I often found myself feeling I was disappointing you every time I couldn't meet our self-imposed schedules.

I did not expect to have such intense emotional reactions to our group. My experience as a graduate student had been so uninvolved. I was angry when I gave up my son's school open house for the group meeting, and some of you decided to go to a dance performance and didn't tell the rest of us until later. I remember saying to Petra that I wouldn't have done that—I would have honored my responsibilities. It's that old imposition of my values and style on the rest of you again, I guess— thinking it was all about getting papers written rather than working out our relationships and, thus, our ideas with each other.

Our interactions were good much of the time, however. I think we learned early on that we needed to have time together to be focused, and that we owed each other attention and respect. I sometimes wondered, in the beginning, about whether we all shared a similar commitment to the project; it seemed that it was always Gretchen, Petra, and I that were on task, critiquing one another's writing so vigorously—except I wasn't putting mine out for critique—or maybe it was that I wasn't finding time to produce anything. In a sense, I projected what Karen and Susan might have felt, a need to perform, an absolute insistence on cooperation, a pressure to let go of my self-protective individuality. And then when Gretchen started to pull back from us, I understood why, but at first I was hurt by the choice she felt she had to make to support her cultural community. I remember those early *questions and the dilemmas that arose for me as I tried to figure out who I was in that crazy university world and those mornings at the Napoli, trying to sort out how to talk about how I took our work seriously and expected as much from you, too, and asking myself, would you resent my interfering in your work? And yet I believed that you demonstrated your regard for someone else by being straight with them.*

*I remember reflecting on my rather informal advising style: Should I be so friendly and direct with my students? Could I get away with it or would my colleagues think I was too "unprofessional" or "undignified"? I remember the difficulty I was having with what Lee Ann Bell (1989) calls the "impostor syndrome," my belief that I didn't really have anything important to offer unless I pretended I was the great scholar, and I couldn't do that. I didn't feel like a wonderful authority on anything, although I believed I could always get people to think for themselves because of the many questions I asked. You all helped me discover what my real job was—sharing my experience with you all and perhaps helping you in the process—being a companion on your struggle through the academic rituals that seemed to surround us all the time.*

*I realize now how much of my identity was tied up in perceptions of need: what I "needed" to do; being needed myself; and meeting others' needs. I also remember being angry—about how much time it took, about how I was always the one who was "on"—and fearing I was creating a dependency that would be, in the end, destructive. Working with the group made me confront some very core issues. What does it mean to be a mentor-mother, a companion? How much of myself can I afford to give to my students? It was often hard to deal with this project straight on. It reminds me sometimes of how I feel about my maternal role with my own children. The "motherly satisfaction" I've experienced in seeing them (my daughters and my women students) succeed has seemed at times suffocating, and their needs for reassurance and support, at times when I really wanted to let go and be taken care of myself, were sometimes terrifying.*

*I can remember being very tired and often wanting to "settle down into my real job,"—you know, lock myself in my office and churn out journal articles or something. Sometimes I thought that was what was meant by living a "normal life"—that is, one that did not include a hundred other people. But I also remember feeling such warmth and comfort from you all—like at that last meeting at Gretchen's. The goats nuzzling us as we ate our potluck dinner by the campfire. Gretchen's caring and trust in us as she shared her new friends and the stone figures she had chosen for us, reminding us that even though she is not always with us, we are always part of her, of each other's lives. The worrying and fussing and the complaining we do about each other—signs to me that the mentor role no longer fits me, if it ever did. We have learned to care about each other even as we admit to differences that, at times, sadden us and, at other times, enrage us.*

*What I remember best of all was the absolute joy of being a part of the group—all the energy and love as we affirmed each other's work; as we shared our values and* beliefs in our work as women teachers, in our respect for difference, in our interest in narrative and exploring our personal experiences, in our commitment to making schools a better place for kids; and as we acknowledged our interdependence and our need for each other's inspiration and support.

As I look back at our work together, I am once again aware of how we've renegotiated and remapped our work, our goals, and even our expectations around time and personal space. I am empowered by how we have been able to make our own experiences central to our understanding of our roles as teachers. I am gratified by our growing appreciation for each other's uniqueness. And yet, it has been for me primarily a journey toward self-awareness, a way of knowing myself through my experiences with others.

༂

PETRA: *The sun was shining brightly through the sliding glass door. It was going to be a lovely afternoon for a tea party. I had carefully chosen my most delicate lacy tablecloth to go with my grandmother's antique china. The flowers in the center of the table brought out the deep purple and rust shades in the china, creating a perfect setting for high tea. After checking the table one last time, I continued to chop chocolate into small bits for the orange chocolate muffins. I was anxious for the smell of baking muffins to fill the house and complete the perfect ambiance for our tea. I envisioned the five of us sipping our tea, sampling the delicious finger sandwiches Susan would bring, and drinking sherry as the afternoon sun set.*

*At ten minutes to three the phone rings; it is Gretchen—she isn't feeling well and will not be able to make it. I am disappointed but reassure her that "I understand that she needs time alone" and to "let me know if there is anything I can do." I reluctantly remove one place setting. The table looks awkward, incomplete. Will our group now feel incomplete? Is it still "the group" if it is only the four of us?*

*What do I feel? I have a mental conversation reassuring myself that I really do understand why Gretchen can't make it, yet I acknowledge that there is some anger: "Don't we have a commitment to the group? Shouldn't our commitment to the group come before our individual needs? Why do I feel that my sense of responsibility is greater or different than that of others in the group?" The timer of the oven drones in the background. After checking the muffins I continue my mental conversation: "What's my anger **really** about?" Perhaps it is just my disappointment or hurt because I have put so much effort into **my** tea party. I wanted to create the perfect afternoon and now it is no longer so. I realize that my creation is not really my own.*

*As I reflect on that particular afternoon, I recognize that it represents a microcosm of the ongoing work of our group—replete with its high expectations, disappointments, and critical questions about the collaborative process. As I look back on the tea party I wonder how we were able to maintain a group identity in spite of our differing needs, other obligations, and the external forces which impacted us. What was and is necessary for a group to be collaborative? Do we need a common goal? Does it require that we all contribute equally? Must we have a similar understanding of terms like commitment? Dialogue? Responsibility? What role did dissonance, rather than consensus, play in maintaining the fiber of our group?*

*The tea party serves as an apt metaphor for our work together. It captures the romantic visions I had of working together with a group of women: visions of stormy intellectual dialogue, a safe space in which to challenge our ideas and nurture our thoughts, a space in which we could discuss "possibilities" of social change without being labeled "unrealistic." I hoped the group would allow me to gain confidence in my intellectual abilities, to trust in my own capabilities without needing the constant reassurance of a male figure. I wanted to develop the strength of self-validation, a necessary skill if I was to survive the dark corridors of the "white ivory tower."*

*We began our study and support group as a result of what I thought was our common interest in feminist theory. I remember vividly our late-afternoon sessions in the beer gardens of Eugene trying to make sense of Lather, Alcoff, Flax. I avoided words like hegemony and hermeneutics, not sure how to pronounce them, let alone what they meant. I was sure I was a slow learner and was tiring everyone with my constant questions for clarification and my need to put all the theories in a chart so I could get a linear overview. Yet I was excited by what I was reading. Jan, Gretchen, and I often raced and clamored over each other as ideas and connections went rushing through our minds, our thoughts faster than our words could express. Karen looked distant, shocked. I sensed her suspicion of feminism. I had begun to find my voice, my validation. Was she losing hers in the process? How much was my voice becoming an imposition?*

*If our interest in feminism had initially brought us together, our varied reactions threatened to pull us apart. As Susan joined us after the summer, our group had a new focus, putting together a paper for AERA. The question arose: Do we all have to be feminists? My initial reaction was, how can we not be? Each of us had experienced discrimination. We were all trying to survive in an environment which still honored male ways of thinking and being, in which male voices were heard more than female, in which our ideas were more often cutoff, interrupted, or ignored, yet sometimes stolen.*

*As our fall sessions continued I was confused as to why Karen and Susan weren't active participants in our marathon work sessions discussing readings and critiquing papers. I pondered as to the reasons they "rejected" feminism. I was resentful that they did not share their thoughts and feelings. Wasn't this a group; wasn't part of our responsibility as members of the group to contribute? Our differing views of feminism seemed to put a slight edge on our meetings. Wasn't the reason we were together to discuss feminist theory? If we didn't share an interest in feminism, what was our purpose?*

*In hindsight it seems so obvious to me that there would be differences in our motivations for participating in the group and that it was natural that we didn't share the same views on feminism. I guess as I read hooks, Trinh Minh-ha, and Spivak the true meaning of the words "difference" and "multiple realities" didn't quite translate to my own little world. The theory had a life of its own separate from the interactions in our group.*

*Yet in spite of our differences we survived. We have not all become feminists, but in fact our understandings of ourselves, our varied positions, our perspectives, have coalesced. I now understand that Susan considers herself to come from an "object relations psychoanalytic perspective," that Gretchen considers herself first an Ojibwa-Winnebago woman and then a feminist postmodernist, that Karen still feels uncomfortable with any label. My understandings of these varied perspectives have enriched my understandings of the multiple ways in which we experience the world. Although Susan and I share a similar experience as a result of our German upbringing, I cannot share her Jewish experience, but I now appreciate that for her, her oppression as a Jew is more salient than her oppression as a woman.*

*Our group did not reach these understandings at our cozy tea parties. I believe these evolved at our late-night meetings in which we were constantly trying to make sense of our silences, angers, and absences. It was difficult to discuss our differences for fear of inflicting hurt, pain, and misunderstandings. My understandings at least have come through the experiencing of these women, and knowing them long enough to understand the context in which their lives evolve. Our entangled evenings were balanced by our lovely tea parties. Our collaboration was reminiscent of a teeter-totter, always seeking to resolve the tension between our similarities and our differences, yet somehow sensing that a perfect balance would stop the motion, bring us to a standstill. Dissonance, rather than consensus, emerged as being essential to the collaborative process.*

*Collaboration was not always cozy tea parties. In fact, as part of this group process I have come to recognize that my needs and my expectations for being nurtured are the antithesis of our tea parties. Although superficially the tea parties provided a warm, cozy atmosphere, they were constructed, artificial, my creation, my need to create an illusion. The nurturing I needed came as a result of the intense dialogue and feedback I received during our evening sessions throughout the fall and winter of 1989–90 as we wrote rough drafts of our AERA papers and critiqued them. The first time my paper was critiqued I remember the disappointment at receiving rough drafts of my paper which had few or almost no comments. For me this was a sign either that people had not taken the time to read my paper carefully or that my thoughts were not worthy enough of comment. I left that meeting confused as to why people had joined a study group if they really didn't want to take an active part in the process. It was not until we critiqued other papers that I realized that my assumptions about the lack of feedback on my paper were misguided. As I gave Susan her rough draft with comments and marks covering the page, proud that I had done a thorough job and really taken the time to engage myself in her work, she looked devastated. For her all my markings were not a sign of caring, but a brutal critique. It became clear why my paper had so few marks. Our differences again became apparent.*

*How did we work through these differences? As a collaborative group, I believed, we had the goal of sharing equal responsibility. Although Jan had provided the impetus for our group by offering a course in feminist theory, our continued work together was conceived as a collaborative effort in which we were all colleagues working together and sharing equally the responsibilities. However, another source of tension was the differing amounts of responsibilities each of us took. In the end, it always seemed as if Jan was ultimately responsible. My need to be organized, to not wait until the last minute, to have everything under control, often put me in the position of taking responsibility for being "tasky," setting deadlines, and having work done on time. The more resentful I became of this role, the less committed I felt to the group. For me, taking responsibility is a sign of commitment. Letting one or two people take the responsibility represents a lack of sensitivity. But again, somehow we managed to stay together. That fall and winter we committed to developing another AERA presentation and I wondered how that process would unfold.*

*Despite the difficulties and discomforts we shared, I find it difficult to think of dissolving our group. I can't imagine what the past years might have been like without the support of this group. Would I have had the confidence to submit several articles for publication without their feedback that "yes, my papers were academic enough and did say something of value"? Would the writing I do now reflect my voice, my experiences, if not for the validation of my experiences in this group? I look at my current teaching; I feel it is more collaborative, more sensitive to different voices. Would I have risked having 10 male students do art projects in a secondary social studies methods class? Our group process is mysterious to me, subtle, in a way that is at times almost discomforting to me. Perhaps it is like magic, illusive to the human eye but something felt deeply in the heart. Like so many of our experiences as teachers, students, and researchers, it can't be explained, just known.*

༄

**KAREN:** *We met early during the fall of 1990 to decide how to represent the ongoing collaborative processes we were experiencing. In a crowded coffeehouse, over calendars whose daily boxes are filled with obligations and responsibilities, whose pages are covered with layers of post-its with additional must-do lists, we worked to find a convenient meeting time. We decided on a Wednesday evening, a meal composed of our favorite foods—black beans, rice, tortillas, crab salad, Dos Equis, wine, fruit, and ice cream—and to gather at Susan's. We were to meet between 6:30 and 7:00, in order to allow Susan time to return from her work with the teenage moms. It was a lovely gathering, all 40 minutes of it that I experienced between the time I arrived and dashed off for a previously scheduled obligation. Gretchen also left early.*

*Three days later, in my university mailbox, I discovered a summary of the ideas that Jan, Petra, and Susan had shared that night. Think about two scenarios, they suggested, one that reflects the positive, and one the negative aspects of working with the group. All right, I thought, this time I won't let them down, I'll work with contrasts, I won't lay my "relational" infinite-possibilities more-comfortable-with-chaos-than-truths trip on them. Despite my profound disbelief in dialectics, in "truths" discovered through a progression of opposites, and my reluctance to deal in proverbial black-and-white relationships and dichotomous realities, I thought, for them, I'll do it, I'll decontextualize! I took a deep breath and in the quiet eddy surrounding the computer, amid the turbulence of the elementary education office, within the 2 hours I had before our next meeting, I tried to represent my feelings about the group. These are the two experiences that came to me.*

*The first: a nurturing, homey time. I was comforted by the background murmurs of Susan and Jan, seated on a log up near the cliff. Soothed by the familiar rhythm of the ocean and embraced by the salty mist carried toward the bay on the crests of the incoming waves, I wondered, but didn't worry, about not hearing or seeing Petra. I couldn't imagine that our supremely competent, organized, and linear representation of German American efficiency (humor and dedication) was lost, and once more I was sorry that Gretchen had been unable to join us. I let myself drift into that lull between sunset and dark, between sight and touch. The rocks were still warm from the rare, windless day. I carefully stood on the darkest, knowing from years of long, languid beach days that they would be radiating with the glow of that day. Their warmth provided a sense of solidarity and familiarity. Petra appeared. I felt home, with friends, colleagues I trusted and respected.*

*We climbed the path up the cliff, relying more on instinct than sight. It was a reminder of how limited we allow our senses of the world to be when we assume that paths will be paved, segmented into even steps, and brightly lit by technology. We opened a bottle of wine (actually two, one red and one white), toasted each other, felt Gretchen there with us, and on two benches, lit only by a flickering candle and the faint luminescence of the North Star, gave Jan our gift.*

*In contrast: an exhausting, confusing, and frustrating experience. The community meeting ran late. I should have anticipated that, but I hadn't. It was 9:45 p.m., cold, wet, and gloomy, and home was a 30-minute hydroplane up I-5. I had promised to be meeting with the group—to be there at 8:00 at the latest. I hit warp speed, caught the green lights, slid through yellows, spun down the back roads, racing into Susan's, to a wall of resentment and misunderstandings that magnified my own frustration with the horrible situation I felt I was in. I was ignored, once more marginalized and silenced. I sat next to Gretchen, knowing that she would buffer for me, protect me from their hostility, and later provide a reality check. I wanted to trust these people. They seemed like good women. Yet their university ties and personal connections were with the very people who had spent the last 3 years using my work, my time, my energy and passion, as though I existed solely to fuel them. The meeting earlier was a grim reminder of the last difficult years trying to integrate community work in multicultural education with the doctoral program. At that earlier meeting, I had felt trapped, knowing that I had to be there because of my long-term involvement with the sponsoring community agency; knowing that I ought to support the speaker, a mentor during my graduate program; knowing that by not joining the group, I was letting down people who seemed to genuinely care; knowing that I had been fooled before. Feeling exhausted by the stress, the tugs, and the internal dissonance, I withdrew.*

*Do these two scenarios represent my involvement with the group? In a way. If one expects brief glimpses to be moments of truth, paragraphs to represent tangled, muddled, poignant, and joyful life experiences—then they offer a glimmer of the magical place Petra referred to, a place we created for sharing tears, laughter, growth, and inspiration. But they fail to represent the power that each of our personalities and diverse perspectives brings to each encounter—the words can't capture the tensions, the dissonance, the diversity, and ultimately the strength I feel we experience in the collaborative process.*

*How did it begin? For me it was an opportunity to spend time with some people I love and some I wanted to get to know better. The institutional excuse was a course on feminism, taught by Jan and hidden under the title of "Research in Early Childhood Education." It was summer 1989; Petra, Gretchen, Jan, and I met over beer and chips on the deck of one of the local pubs. I sat there, engulfed in their voices, watching their thought processes, their eyes gleaming with the validation of their personal experiences, concerns, and dreams as expressed by feminist authors. Though personally not hearing myself in those readings, I enjoyed their pleasure and occasionally, so that Petra and Jan would know that I was paying attention, offered thoughts such as "This time, let's try diagramming those feminist theories in a circle rather than a grid pattern" or "I wonder how that woman would choose to represent herself in terms of colors and sounds—or how would you or I attempt to do that." Mentally I created three- and four-dimensional representations of what I thought they were saying to each other, what I thought each one was hearing— often wondering where gaps, gulfs, and misunderstandings come from; where they go; and how dialogue seems to create a circle for them to become common threads, bridges, and intuitive leaps—connections.*

*I sat there, feeling engulfed by their passion, knowing from years of juggling multiple realities, that the readings, the intellectual parenthesis, offered me a unique opportunity to hear their hearts in an environment that felt safe for each of us. Knowing also that when I had enough of this parade of theorists, I would create a polite excuse to leave and that Gretchen would make a joke that would help take any hurt out of my leaving before "the time was up." Feeling also that Petra and Jan were women I wanted as friends and feeling very unsure about how to make friends—wondering if the institution, our common ground, allowed the tears and the sharing and the years it takes me to develop a feeling of friendship.*

*We decided to work on an AERA presentation for Boston in 1990, and Susan joined the group. Thank heavens, I thought, a strong, competent, caring, and compassionate woman who does not define herself as a feminist. She felt like a sister. I was so glad that she was working with us. The presentation, yes, that was important, a vital part of doctoral socialization, a necessary item for my resume, my pedigree of intellectual competence—but I had already been to an AERA conference, and was a bit disenchanted. All that validation through theory, so much rhetoric about transforming education and so little modeling, men and women in ties, intently staring at each others' right breasts. It took most of the first morning to realize that people were here to "network," see and be seen, and were primarily interested in noting name tags. Jan assured me that we would not do a podium presentation, that change can come from inside the structure, and we all agreed that modeling a dialogue format was a good beginning.*

*We spent months critiquing each other's work, trying to shed our academic survival baggage and write from the heart—writing from places I'd never shared with anyone outside of my community. For me, it was a painful process. I had always divorced myself from my academic work, read the teachers, not bothered reading the texts, gone for the A, the smile of approval, the nod, the perks, the institutional recognition, the short-term benefits that have nothing to do with the rest of my life. Jan, Gretchen, Petra, and Susan demanded integration, they couldn't be fooled, there was no A to shoot for, the silver ring was myself, and I couldn't walk away from them because they were equally involved in the process.*

*Jan created institutionally acceptable spaces for us—I worked under reading and conference labels designed to fit into my doctoral program, and learned more from this process than I had during the previous 3 years of standard coursework. We began to know each other, to read discomforts, and to know when and how to support each other. We started to share our lives, slowly building a new place, a space that blended the academic and personal. We started to rely on each other and we also started to draw strength from our membership with the group and use our voices with assurance and conviction. As a result, we were perceived as becoming too powerful, too close, too strong, too capable, too competent, too female, too exclusive—there were resentments, jealousies, and misunderstandings from friends, faculty, lovers, and colleagues. We held together, gathering strength and validation, support and clarification, from each other. In the month's time bracketing AERA, we all completed and passed our comprehensive exams, determined our dissertation topics, and assertively redefined relationships with partners, colleagues, and lovers. By May 1990 we were exhausted—this summer pulled us in different directions.*

*And here we are. I've learned that these women don't really expect me to decontextualize, to assume the institutional mask, in order to be a part of the group. I suspect that if I were to play the "active listening" game, utilize the acceptable mainstream cues—leaning forward, paraphrasing, clarifying, nodding at appropriate intervals, and maintaining continuous eye contact—the contrast with my normal behavior would be so startling that they'd become genuinely, and justifiably, worried about my level of commitment as well as my mental, emotional, and spiritual stability. I've learned that what these women expect and deserve is what they give, sincere and honest dialogue—and that the struggle is just as painful a process for each of them. Most of all, I'm grateful that we've created a safe space in which to reflect, to share our concerns, to speculate, to inspire, and to grow together.*

*Have we achieved ultimate collaboration? No, I feel that we've just experienced glimpses of what we're capable of becoming, individually and as a group. Our work together has provided windows for understanding ourselves; the collaborative process has provided a frame for heartfelt human interaction. I couldn't have survived without these women. Their passion, their pain, and our process have become part of who I am. I carry them with me in my work. I am a stronger woman for their friendships, and a gentler power due to their presence in my life. The differences, the dissonance, and the diversity have created a tension that is empowering, that strengthens all our voices. We're more than the sum of parts; we're alive with multiple possibilities, rich with multiple voices. To harm one is to damage the others—to bring joy to one is to inspire the rest. To walk away, to withdraw now, is comparable to strangling in isolation—inconceivable in a group process where each thread has become an integral part of the whole.*

∾

SUSAN: *This is my fourth attempt to write this, and even as I write, each word is heavy with doubt and anxiety. What makes this reflection of our collaborative process so difficult? I **never** rewrite papers; in fact, much to Petra's chagrin, I rarely edit them.*

*It's Tuesday evening and I feel sad; the Oregon rain falling with slow persistence, as it does, mirrors the tears collected on my chest. Today, I met with my clients, my subjects, my students, the 15 adolescent mothers for the last time. The image of Rachel's glisteny, big-eyed stare as I say my final "words of wisdom"—"when that stuff from your past catches up with you, you have to dig around in it and talk about it, and I know you'll come out stronger and healthier"—remains in my head and heart.*

*These young mothers have been at the core of my personal and professional world for 19 months; as I take distance from them in order to write my dissertation, the questions which plague me daily in my confusing existence as practitioner-researcher resurface. In which world am I more at home? Among direct-service providers (counselors, social workers, teachers), I treasure our shared visibly present purpose—in this case, supporting the development of adolescent mothers—but long for dialogue in which we examine critically our roles and services, critique the notion of parent education, admit that classism contaminates the agency, or address unhealthy messages we inadvertently communicate to our clients. In this, my "university" group, I felt exhilarated by our discussions of imposition, often affirmed as a writer, and consistently strengthened simply by the idea of women working together. Yet I feel different again.*

*I withdraw psychologically as words which lack meaning for me and labels which do not adequately reflect my experience dart back and forth. How personal are the voices here? If we do not hear each other's voice clearly, are our voices being heard? Is this collaboration about change? If so, is the change on a conscious level only? Can we fairly describe our process with terms like commitment, collaboration, and appreciation of difference if we, too, do not look at the less than conscious processes in our interactions with each other, dig around in them, and, ultimately, truly know each other?*

*It's two weeks before the Women Educators conference in Milwaukee in November 1990, as I walk into Gretchen's living room. The psychological confusion has become increasingly more intense with each meeting; am I joining four women with whom I have collaborated for 13 months or am I joining my family at dinner? Am I the good daughter again, being neither seen nor heard but tolerating the blessing and burden of knowing and holding what each is feeling? In any group, it seems, I feel burdened by the feelings of others; in the language of object relations theory, I hold unconsciously the feelings—resentment, anxiety, fear of abandonment—which others find intolerable or unacceptable in themselves. Collaboration, thus, is only possible when I can confront others about their emotional experience and, hence, unburden myself. That is at tremendous psychological risk for me, and it surfaces the questions of safety and trust with which each of us struggles in some way.*

*I reflect on my history with this group, joining the process in the fall, unfamiliar with and, like Karen, suspicious of the feminist theories leading to the imposition project. I began my involvement with that same question, asking of Jan, why me? What does my work have to do with this? The task was exciting. seeing the different meanings imposition had for each of us in our roles as teachers, supervisors, counselors. Yet I wanted a tea party, too, an herbal tea party; "sisters" sitting around on soft pillows, Rudy, my cat, roaming from one to the other, the Indigo Girls on the stereo, sipping tea out of mugs and dipping blue corn chips into tofu pâté, being real, confronting each other, helping each other grow like it's the '70s in Marin again, where I grew up—the way I always wanted it to be then, too.*

*What it really looked like, for better or worse, was something different. I take care of Jan because she is anxious and overworked, like me. I had to be there for her, work harder, talk about psychology, make cracks about men who are "fixated at formal operations," worry about everyone and each other, want her approval, treasure the honesty, the directness, the unwritten promise to be straight with each other, except the dynamics with Petra are confusing.*

*The three of us together and psychological survival take precedence over collaboration, as I try to balance the present with unconscious trips down memory lane with my mother and grandmother. I'm not as smart; I'm too soft, too affective, much too affective. I withdraw because I cannot tolerate the competition. Competition? Competition has no place among women collaborating for social change! Petra and I compete covertly, expressing feelings of inadequacy in different ways, hanging in there, crying, withdrawing, feeling alternately angry and guilty. Will this relationship work? Will it ever be easy? We keep bumping up against each other's identity, the German-Jewish disconnection, an area that remains untouched.*

*At times, it has felt easier with Karen because I often sensed something "Jewish" about her. I felt drawn to her, perhaps due to the shared family craziness, growing up, not as blondes, under the California sunshine. But it gets confusing, evasive, foggy, and I am not sure how close we are. I loved the playfulness, how we at times colluded with each other covertly to distract the collaborative process, to resist the feminist labels, to be the bad, irresponsible "adolescents."*

*Yet we ultimately come through. Karen, especially, is such a gifted writer, and a nurturer, especially when it came to Gretchen, whom I really don't know. We've never talked, so have we really collaborated? I love who I think she is, and I realized at some point that I do understand her when she talks or when she writes. It/she validates who I am, that it's okay that I wave my arms around when I talk and start saying something without knowing where I'm going until I get there. It's my language, my culture. When Gretchen compliments or supports me, it resonates with truth and wisdom. I would like to know her more.*

*This collaboration process is about relationships. The products—the papers, the book, the conference presentations—are less significant than the group processes, the interactions. This group has different meanings and serves different purposes for each one of us, yet I would assert that some of the meanings and purposes are not consciously available. What ultimately remains with me is the mirror, the reflections of who I am, my needs, my resistance (psychological, not political), my fear (as well as my inadequacies and my gifts). The issues I hear loudly here are not expressed in words such as inclusion, safety, and commitment. They are communicated in projections, repression of feelings, nonverbal gestures. I cannot safely collaborate as long as you all do not know my experience of this group, and I know yours only partially.*

*What has been the richer? I have gained much on conscious and unconscious levels in the last 13 months. As probably is the case with many of us, I have always had more difficulties in my relationships with women; I feel so easily burdened, resentful, insecure, overwhelmed. During the time we have worked together, I have seen increasingly clearer why I have come together with these four women, what I am meant to resolve. For me, collaboration is an ongoing process of psychological as well as intellectual growth, but not without bumps and regressions. The "herbal tea party" is never proper or mellow. It is messy underneath. I pull back, withdraw when it feels overwhelming and I feel insecure. Or I pull attention from everyone, relying on my humor, as I always did in my family, in the classroom, in my group, at staff meetings. I want to feel nurtured, to receive papers with no corrections on them, to hear people telling me I'm wonderful over and over again, so I still won't believe it.*

*I would not have accomplished what I have without this group. There is courage in numbers, in these numbers especially. External obstacles and neurotic impulses are balanced with encouragement and understanding. Jan has tears in her eyes as I share something one of the moms said in group; Petra takes time to go "power shopping" with me; Karen refers to my cat as one of her favorite broad-chested males; Gretchen gives me permission to tell stories, to leave out periods, and talk in Jewish commas—series of things without a breath in between—and yet, not to be afraid of doing the parentheses thing. They all listened to my doubts (my personal obstacles with this process) and, at a time when I desperately needed it, kept me company.*

*Perhaps I have underestimated how much this process has given me, on a conscious level; yet I do believe we have taken turns leaving, needing, imposing. When I separate my reactions from the task at hand, it's not so bad, and I can finally see what's in it for me, what's for me. My questions persist, however; is it only acceptable to have voice if the words are pleasingly distant, allowing women to avoid what, from my perspective, makes collaboration difficult, sometimes painful? Can we talk about women collaborating if we cannot communicate in the immediate and be clear, clean, and honest in our interactions? For Rachel and the other young women/mothers in my group, and, I maintain, for us as well, collaborating first with the internal self is the beginning of the path toward true personal and social change.*

∽

GRETCHEN: *How did we ever come together in the first place? As it happens, it was for different reasons, different agendas. I was interested in feminist pedagogy and theory because I felt I needed to know about it to be a competent female Native American professor. I knew from what I had already been exposed to that the academic feminists were breaking open the Cartesian paradigm in ways that the civil rights movement could not. I also learned skills in our group that I had never been able to try before. I learned about writing, discussing, presenting. I learned them, in part, because I was getting a more honest response to what I do, even within the give and take of our different moods and levels of tolerance. It was through our work together—reflecting, discussing, writing—that I realized what I had become from my early Native American values, beliefs, perceptions, and constructions of meaning. Stories, indirect teaching, emergent curriculum, and my sense of autonomy come from being part of a community. My purpose, therefore, is to support that community. I lose my sense of identity when I rebel against that responsibility and try to be too much of an individual.*

*What were my expectations? What were my conflicts—areas of holding back, distrust? Of what? There is this feeling in the pit of my stomach. Yet I had no distrust of any of the women. In fact, I was impressed with the integrity of their work, their beliefs, and their lived lives. I was also impressed with their writing ability and mortified by how differently I had to begin, what my understanding of the task was, and of my contributions. I was never disappointed in what they did or did not do.*

*Yet there were submerged issues and anxiety with silences. But I struggled with how to interpret them and the resulting discomfort instead of asking what the silences mean. I had questions about the definition of what is real or fiction, of how we interpret commitment and its expression, of bursts of feelings over issues that are not shared by the others, of feelings silenced because each of us in our turn felt we didn't dare express the depth of our feelings about certain issues. My fear was of not being good enough, of being too different, of alienating what was becoming such a powerful support and influence in my life and in my writing. What were the interpretations of all of this from each of us within the context of our "forming" group? What of the needs of each of us to have a turn, to be a focus? What of the tension around the differing abilities and our understanding of what it means to be academically focused and organized? What of our assumptions around taking each other's time for our other ongoing work? What of the difficulty in dealing with conflict, discomfort, hurt? How to approach it? Hurting others. Hurting ourselves. Do we even know when we are hurting ourselves? At what point does it matter? The perspectives, cultural and otherwise, on individuality, community (my own, the women's), on the perceived academic/work requirements and the family-animal-community demands and responsibilities and choices, too—how do we balance these? Our group process was the unacknowledged source of unexamined learning and assumptions, of expectations about our performance and allegiance, of connections between the fragmented segments of our lives that often do not touch.*

*My life's experience has been one of being in several realities and of struggling for some kind of balance. The postmodern questioning and thinking frame is one that I have been struggling with all of my life. The questions for me have been multilayered, but centered on my being caught between Native American and Northern European–American mainstream cultures. I struggle with what I believe are my moral, political, and sacred responsibilities to community. These are, from my cultural perspective, what I have to address in order to meet my responsibilities to myself.*

*I learned from these four women, through our work together, that we all share fears about our own worth and adequacy in our writing, about how we will measure up to the abilities and expectations of others. I became aware of our individual concerns about our differing definitions and interpretations of individual and community, of rights and obligations, of responsibilities and commitments, and of dialogue and silences. We struggled to understand how they manifested themselves and matched our expectations, and we struggled with how we withdrew from conflict and how we came back together. How was it, with our differences of styles and rules for discussion and being heard, that we stayed together and created such wonderful stuff? How did we come to understand each other's support and not only trust but look forward to each other's critiques? For me, one of the reasons it worked was because we had weekly deadlines that had to be met. Fortunately, the lack of elaboration of the work to be done in between didn't get judged. Instead what we brought was treated as our best effort, given the circumstances.*

*Our sharing and critiquing illuminated and shaped our next drafts. Contrary to assumptions about "too much collaboration," we brought to the critiquing process an appreciation of our differences, and it gave us new perspectives, methods, language, and clarity with which to think and talk about. We each came away from long-into-the-night sessions exhausted but heady with exhilaration for each other's seemingly giant steps between drafts. We came away filled with our own ideas and desire to write more. Through this ongoing process, we developed the sense of finding* our own voices. What I brought to each session was very raw. Was it fear, organizational skills, priorities, resistance? I lacked experience and asked, What would it take to get the job done? What are the time needs for me? I still do not know. The group critiqued in such a way that they allowed me to work through with them my ideas, my interpretations of what I was doing. I found I could literally see and hear from them how I might structure my contribution.

It was all right to accept help from each other and it was OK to refuse, too. It was wonderful when my explanations made sense to them. We discussed our ways of being and doing and our reasons for withdrawing from issues, why we were sometimes unable to remain with the group. I was able to continue because for the first time in my life I had a support group of women whose minds I admired and trusted, who could, in the end, accept our different styles and stick up for themselves when they needed to talk yet not be competitive in the sense of being the most right.

Sometimes, however, I felt like an outsider. At those times, I withdrew. One of the issues was over the ownership of ideas and culture, the label of "expert." I am uncomfortable publicly admitting to a need for ownership that excludes. Yet I recognize the political necessity of the issues that surround these questions. I am aware of how I am different with different groups, Indians and whites, men and women.

I had never worked with a group of women scholars before or even studied with others to any extent. I had always trusted my own ability to cram ideas for an exam and had never had the time to do drafts to share with anyone. I didn't know how to do that. It seemed such a huge responsibility . . . I always resisted. I questioned the source of my resistance. Could this reflect what was modeled in my family and in my mother—this distrust of any woman outside our Native American community and family? Had I learned that we weren't really free to choose to whom we could go for support? Was it my ambivalence and confusion around what it was to be a good/nice Indian woman? What is a friend? A relative? What is a colleague? How did friendships emerge out of these processes? What were our responsibilities to each other besides getting our writing done?

Each woman in our group is committed to the integrity of her beliefs, her education, and her life's experience. Our work together has strengthened that in each of us, I believe. I also believe that to be one of the central threads of our bonding, with each other. With our similar enough work ethics, our values, and our commitment we have created heated, exciting brainstorming sessions that leave us exhausted, dazed, angry, hurt, and eager to come back to work with each other because of the vitality and integrity of our discussions.

But I still have questions. How were we alike? What did each of us find in the others that made it possible to be there week after week in the midst of preparing for term papers, comprehensive examinations, thesis proposals, topsy-turvy feelings, and personal lives (barely)? How did we work out such an intense small-group process in such chaos? What helped us to survive those moments? How was this a model for what we should do as mentors, as teachers?

## REFERENCES

Bateson, M. C. (1990). *Composing a life*. New York: Atlantic Monthly Press.
Bell, L. A. (1989). *The gifted woman as imposter*. Unpublished manuscript.

# PART III

## GETTING LOST

To keep from getting lost in the usual ways one must follow a route of estrangement from dominant codes of meaning and look again at the microhistory of cultural production and the critical histories of reception.

—Gilmore, 1994: 6

In fact, the "other" can get lost in research whose stated purpose is exploration on its own terms. This is because, by the very act of engaging in critical, emancipatory, empowering research, researchers take a particular ethical stance toward their informants, defining them as disempowered or oppressed, regardless of how the informants define themselves.

—LeCompte, 1993: 13

❧

The recognition of truths as partial, contested, intersubjective, and illusive has raised challenging methodological questions for researchers engaged in interpretive inquiry. Postmodern and feminist thinking increasingly makes the interpretive task tricky as old theories and master narratives have been displaced. The current crisis of representation has necessitated that we estrange ourselves from taken-for-granted assumptions regarding subjectivity, ethics, and textual production. Recognizing that as researchers we are engaged in inscribing culture, and never merely describing it, we have continually struggled with issues of power, authority, and knowledge. To "get lost" is to continually interrogate and distance ourselves from the positions we take up as researchers as a means of locating sites of power and privilege.

This section of the book includes five chapters reflecting on issues of imposition and positioning which emerged from a variety of emancipatory research projects in which we were engaged. They reflect a point of departure—

a departure from our collaborative work toward an application of our emerging individual understandings of imposition in our individual research agendas. Yet despite our separate interests and our various theoretical perspectives, we shared a common concern for seeking alternatives to the traditional, hierarchical research relationships that have been characterized as potentially exploitative and as a reification of patriarchal power relations.

As researchers, we confronted three basic issues regarding the impositional nature of traditional research paradigms. First, the very process of research raises the basic questions of why and for whom we do research. Can any research process equitably serve the interest of all those involved? Second, inherent in the process of research is defining one's theory of knowledge. What counts as valid and useful knowledge? How is that knowledge acquired, verified, and textually represented? If we believe that knowledge is socially constructed, how do we represent and acknowledge the multiple viewpoints that emerge in the research process? Finally, what is the nature of the relationship between the researcher and the researched? Does the reciprocal or collaborative approach to the research relationship advocated by feminists and critical ethnographers address the issues of imposition inherent in the traditional research relationship, or are research relationships impositional by nature?

These chapters discuss the dilemmas we faced as we tried to balance our roles as researchers and our concerns with social transformation with our understanding of the importance of acknowledging the social construction of meaning. The inherent conflict in being committed to liberatory, critical research while not imposing on others raised serious ethical issues for us as we searched for egalitarian and nonexploitative research methodologies. In grappling with these issues each of us sought alternative research methodologies in participatory, collaborative life-history, and autobiographical research. Yet what initially appeared to us as acceptable alternatives became challenging sites for illuminating new questions and issues.

Grounded in our experiences as researchers, the chapters in Part III explore the contradictions, struggles, and negotiations inherent in trying to conduct research which reflects our beliefs as women and researchers. Petra Munro discusses the dilemmas which arose in her attempts to conduct life histories with retired women teachers. Karen Froude Jones reflects on her attempts to establish collaborative research relationships with the participants in her life-history project of first-generation elementary school teachers. Susan Victor looks back on her participatory research project with teenage mothers and wonders whose interests really were served. Janice Jipson explores processes of positioning and imposition in autobiographical research. Gretchen Freed-Rowland addresses issues of truth and representation. In each of these chapters we describe our ongoing struggles to demystify the research process by including our subjective, emergent voices.

## REFERENCES

Gilmore, L. (1994). *Autobiographics: A feminist theory of women's self-representation.* Ithaca, NY: Cornell University Press.

LeCompte, M. (1993). A framework for hearing silence: What does telling stories mean when we are supposed to be doing science? In D. McLaughlin & W. G. Tierney (Eds.), *Naming silenced lives* (pp. 9–28). New York: Routledge.

# CHAPTER 6

# Multiple "I's":
## Dilemmas of Life-History Research

*Petra Munro*

As I read the letter confirming my participation in a paper presentation of the Qualitative Special Interest Group at the 1991 American Educational Research Association, I was somewhat surprised at the title of the session, "Validity in Qualitative Research." "Validity," I thought. "Me, talk about validity. They must have gotten me confused with someone else." I went back to my original proposal; I hadn't mentioned the word validity. Validity was not a word in my vocabulary, or in my methodological framework. Three years of working as a graduate student with Harry Wolcott, coupled with my own immersion in feminist literature, had led me to agree that "to ask about validity in qualitative research was to ask the wrong question" (Wolcott, 1990: 135).

Validity, as an epistemological concept, assumes an absolute, fixed truth which can be measured, validated, and verified (Grumet, 1990; Wolcott,1990). Feminists, among others, have sought to disrupt the safest ideas about truth and to force them to stand up to examination against other facts, standards, experiences, and perspectives (Lather, 1993; Personal Narratives Group, 1989; Smith, 1993).[1] The recognition of truths as partial, contested, intersubjective, and illusive has raised challenging methodological questions (Anderson, Armitage, Jack, & Wittner, 1990). If truth no longer exists, do concepts like validity vanish from the ethnographic landscape, thrust into the endless abyss of relativity? In this era of blurred genres, what then become the criteria for judging the "truthfulness" or validity of research?[2]

As I began my recent field work—collecting the life histories of women teachers—I found that the truth had little to do with getting the story right and everything to do with the relationships I was developing.[3] In this chapter, I suggest that validity has little to do with understanding "the" truth, whether partial or otherwise, but rather with understanding how the research process illuminates our "ways of knowing." My relationships in the field not only provide the primary source of data, but as G. E. Marcus (1982) suggests, in the process of self-reflection they become the epistemological base from which interpretations and claims originate. The "truthfulness" of my research became dependent on making explicit the relational dimensions of my fieldwork by revealing the intersubjective and political dynamics of the research relationship.

As I began this research, I was sensitive to the feminist goals of establishing collaborative and nonexploitative research relationships, placing myself re-flexively within the work to avoid objectification, and conducting research which would be transformative (Lather, 1986). Yet these goals were not unprob-lematic. Trying to establish collaborative research relationships presented me with ethical dilemmas for which I was unprepared. First, did my desire for collaboration mask the unequal power relations which assumed that I could impose a type of relationship on my participants that they were perhaps not willing to accept? Second, did my political standpoint and feminist categories threaten to subvert the meanings my participants gave to their lives and roles as women? Was I undermining my goal of trying to understand the meanings women give to their experiences by limiting the categories to my feminist perspectives? Lastly, in trying to represent the intersubjective process in the text by including multiple voices, was I reducing the stories of these women, focusing attention on my story rather than theirs? This chapter recounts my emerging struggles with these dilemmas. But first let me set the scene by describing the context in which this work took place.

## INVISIBLE MENDING: THE SEARCH FOR A METHOD

As a feminist, I was interested in seeking a method which would allow me to recover the marginalized voices of women teachers and the meanings they give to their experiences. Jane Marcus (1984) refers to this process of recovering women's voices as "invisible mending." My initial attraction to qualitative research methodologies had been their acknowledgment of multiple and partial truths, of the intersubjective nature of the construction of knowledge, and of the need for contextual and holistic descriptions. Yet my explicitly feminist viewpoint, with its focus on transformation, seemed at odds with ethnography's focus on description. As I sought a methodology which would allow for and value personal voice, be collaborative, and foster transformation, life history seemed to present the most viable alternative.

The current focus on acknowledging the subjective, multiple, and partial nature of human experience has resulted in a revival of life-history method-ology (Sparkes, 1994). What were previously considered criticisms of life history—its lack of representativeness and its subjective nature—are now viewed as its greatest strengths (Geiger, 1986; Plummer, 1983). Life history's primary goal is an account of one person's life in her or his own words elicited or prompted by another person (Langness & Frank, 1981; Plummer, 1983; Watson & Watson-Sparks, 1985). Life-history studies provide an opportunity to explore not only the effects of social structures on people but also the ways in which people themselves create culture (Mandelbaum, 1973; Sheridan & Salaff, 1984).

For feminists seeking to recover the lost voices of women who have been denied access to public space because of "patriarchal notions of women's inherent nature and consequent social role," life history has provided one alternative methodology (Smith, 1987: 7). In addition to being useful for studying persons whose history has been marginalized (McLaughlin & Tierney, 1993), life histories are particularly well suited to illustrating some aspects of culture not usually portrayed by other means, such as women's view of their culture (Langness & Frank, 1981). According to the Personal Narratives Group (1989), life histories are especially suitable for illuminating several aspects of gender relations including (1) the construction of the gendered self-identity (2) the relationship between the individual and society in the creation and perpetuation of gender norms, and (3) the dynamics of power relations between men and women. I hoped that life history's potential for illuminating the dynamic interaction between human agency and hegemonic forces would highlight the experiences of women teachers as they negotiated and resisted imposed meanings.

Life-history method can also provide a research methodology which addresses feminist concerns that research be situated contextually, challenge the norm of objectivity by acknowledging the intersubjective process of meaning-making, and be collaborative and reciprocal. Lastly, by providing opportunities which allow people to become "visible and to enhance reflexive consciousness" (Myerhoff, 1982: 101), the life-history process can address feminist concerns that research be empowering and transformative.

## ENTERING THE FIELD

The selection of the "life historians" working with me in this project was as much arbitrary and serendipitous at the time as it now seems logical.[4] For the sake of brevity, I shall focus on two of the four participants in the study.

In hindsight, it comes as no surprise that I first heard of Brenda while overlooking the Minnesota chain of lakes from several thousand feet in the air. On our first meeting, Brenda talked of viewing life as a landscape, viewing the world through a geographer's eyes, where use of time and space reveals much more than the spoken word. As I casually described my current interest and work to the mother of one of Brenda's students, my seat mate on a flight from Milwaukee to Portland, she insisted that I must speak with Brenda; she would be just the person I was looking for. How could she have known the connections that linked our lives? I wondered, Could I call a perfect stranger, someone I had never met, and ask her to tell me her life story? Why would someone confide in and trust a total stranger with her life story?

Clio, the second life historian with whom I am working, came to my attention by more conventional methods. A phone call to the local school district asking for the names of retired women social studies teachers resulted in her name. I was surprised at her immediate willingness to meet with me to learn about the project. Even more surprising was her willingness, after only one hour together, to sign the Protection of Human Subjects consent form, in which she agreed to do a minimum of five interviews, allow me to do supplementary interviews with family, friends, and colleagues, and share personal documents. What were her motivations? I wondered.

At our initial meeting I explained the nature of the project and my hope that we would work collaboratively together. By being honest about my expectations and eliciting theirs, I hoped the life historians would be full participants in the research process. In addition to stating my research aims, I explained that they would receive copies of all transcribed interviews and that the final narratives would be given to them for feedback.

Throughout the following months I met with Clio weekly for several hours in her home, interviewed several former colleagues, and participated in several of her social events. Because Brenda lived 120 miles away, I met with her every other week for 3 or 4 hours and visited her for extended periods in which I observed her in her school setting and interviewed her colleagues, administrators, and students. Both life historians were generous with personal documents, sharing pictures, favorite books, letters, and their own writings and publications.

Often it was they who took the initiative in directing the research process. Their initiative in suggesting and arranging supplementary interviews often made me wonder, though, just who was "in control" of the research relationship. Brenda arranged for me to interview her principal on my first visit to her school. Both the participants suggested names of others whom I should interview in order to gain a better picture of who they were. Despite my goal of collaboration, I thought to myself, Wasn't it me who really was supposed to be in control? I began to question not only how collaborative our relationship was but also my true intentions in pursuing collaboration. I began to reconsider the assumptions and nature of the collaborative relationship as I faced this first dilemma regarding the role of power in the collaborative process.

## IMPOSING COLLABORATION

Feminists have been particularly sensitive to seeking alternatives to the traditional, hierarchical research relationship, which they see as potentially exploitative and as a reification of patriarchal power relations (Christman, 1988; Lather, 1986; Stacey, 1988). Ethnographic research, due to its focus on understanding the insider's or emic meaning, has shifted the traditional focus of power from the researcher to the researched. Agar's (1980) notion of the informant as "one up" inverts the traditional hierarchy by creating the subject as expert; however, the dualism and dichotomy of the research relationship are still maintained. The alienation between the researcher and researched resulting from this subject/object polarity is what I sought to avoid (Gitlin, 1990).

Like others engaged in collaborative research, I was hoping to establish an egalitarian, reciprocal research relationship which acknowledged the mutual and two-way nature of the research relationship (Duelli Klein, 1983; Golde, 1970; Reinharz, 1979; Robertson, 1983). The informant is neither a passive, objectified function of data, nor the insider on which the researcher is dependent for insight. Both the researcher and researched are active participants in the research relationship, and knowledge is viewed as socially and intersubjectively constructed.

One way in which I hoped to acknowledge the collaborative nature of the research relationship was by having each of the life historians keep a personal journal of her reactions to our ongoing work together. In addition to engaging them in the research through reflective writing, I hoped the journals would provide me with an understanding of the intersubjective nature of the research process. Despite what I thought were my well-intentioned goals, both participants rejected this suggestion, saying I could ask them questions, but they did not wish to write independently.

My first attempt at establishing a collaborative relationship was thus flatly rejected. I sensed that my request was perceived as a demand which did not conform to my participants' conceptualization of the research process. My heightened sensitivity to avoiding an exploitative research relationship had not taken into account the fact that my participants had their own reasons and agendas for participating in the study. In essence, my assumption of the need for a collaborative relationship underscored my perception of them as disempowered, thereby disregarding their power to determine the nature of the relationship.

My focus on collaboration had not taken into account that the life historians would develop their own framing of our relationship. When I arrived at Clio's home for our first interview, she was in the process of preparing coffee and warming freshly baked bread. She commented, "I thought about using my good china, but then decided that this was work and settled on using the everyday dishes." Brenda, answering the phone during one of our interviews, replied that she was working and would have to get back to the caller later. For these women, we were not engaged in chatter between friends, but in serious work. These incidents highlighted for me the multiple meanings which the participants created for understanding their role in the research process. What I thought would be enjoyable talk they conceived of as work. I was now faced with understanding the implications of their positioning themselves in a working relationship. Did they see themselves as coworkers, as employees with me as the employer, or as colleagues? Perhaps more important, how did they define work? What did work mean to them? What was the importance of their categorizing our relationship as work? What implications did this have in reconceptualizing the roles and responsibilities of both the researcher and researched? These questions made clear the negotiated and constructed nature of the research relationship.

In establishing a collaborative relationship, I believed I would also share my story. I engaged in life-history research because of its reciprocal nature involving mutual storytelling (Connelly & Clandinin, 1990). Connelly and Clandinin (1990: 4) emphasize the importance of the mutual construction of the research relationship by warning the researcher to be "aware of constructing a relationship in which both voices are heard." In addition to the paradox of the researcher "constructing" a mutual relationship, collaboration becomes particularly problematic when a life historian is not interested in hearing the researcher's story. Often when I spoke to Brenda, telling her about myself, she seemed uninterested and looked confused as to why I should talk so much when I was there to hear her story. Was I imposing my story on her? Was it to be the case that I as researcher became objectified in my role as passive listener? In my attempts to construct a collaborative relationship, whose needs were really being served?

I struggled to define the nature of our relationship. My own understanding of collaboration implied that the nature of the relationship be that of friends. This conflicted with their perception of our relationship as work. The business-like nature of our relationships seemed at odds with my goal of collaboration. My evolving understanding of Brenda's and Clio's framing of our relationship as work led me to be cautious in being too friendly. If this was a truly collaborative relationship, I felt the need to recognize and respect their desire to maintain a working relationship.

I wondered whether my search for collaboration had turned into what Marilyn Strathern (1987) calls "a metaphor for an ideal ethical situation in which neither voice is submerged by the Other" (p. 290). Was collaboration a delusion in which I could mask my discomfort with the hierarchical nature of the research relationship by submerging our differences? Or was the ultimate goal of the research process merely a selfish one designed to gain understanding of myself by detour of the other? Strathern (1987) reminds us that feminists traditionally are suspicious of the ethnographer's desire for collaboration and fearful of being appropriated and spoken for. In my case, I was the feminist, and yet the fear that I would in some way misrepresent or take advantage of them seemed to persist.

My efforts to establish collaboration seemed in vain. Was it to be as McRobbie (1982) and Stacey (1988) have suggested, that no matter how hard we try to establish an egalitarian relationship, the research relationship is inherently unequal and potentially exploitative, that despite our attempts to establish friendships, the perceived status and power differential between the researcher and researched will always influence the research relationship? These questions became particularly problematic as I attempted to situate myself in the research and acknowledge the intersubjective nature of the research process.

## COLLABORATION: GETTING *TOO* CLOSE

Researchers engaged in ethnography or participant observation have long revealed the dualistic and contradictory nature of the researcher/researched relationship by discussing the emotional as well as intellectual complexities of working in the field (Bowen, 1964; Golde, 1970; Powdermaker, 1966; Shostak, 1981). Ethnographers engaged in close and long-term relationships with "informants" have stressed the delicate nature of the field relationship, which demands openness and trust even while it demands distance in order to retain analytic competency (Everhart, 1977). The researcher is warned not to become too close to the "subject" lest he or she lose the objectivity necessary for analysis.

Feminists engaged in ethnographic work have pointed out the exploitative and unrealistic nature of pretending to be the "objective" bystander (Abu-Lughod, 1990; Fine, 1994; Roman & Apple, 1990; Stacey, 1988). The rejection of a grand narrative, in light of the fact that realities are historically and culturally situated, has resulted in feminists pursuing subjectivity in order, as Abu-Lughod (1990) puts it, to "reclaim objectivity to mean precisely the situated view" (p. 15). In trying to be truly collaborative, I believed this meant not only acknowledging the subjective nature of the life historians' experiences but also revealing my own situated position.

There seemed to be a tension between the need to place myself in the research process and the potential of revealing too much, thus predisposing the participants to my analytic categories. Although I knew, in theory, that notions of objectivity were false, I was afraid of imposing my analytic perspective by getting *too* close. My goal was to understand how *they* perceived their lives as teachers. In some ways, revealing too much about myself seemed in conflict with my goal of using a life-history methodology which would allow the life historian to speak for herself. I faced the contradiction between wanting an open and honest relationship and wanting one that would allow me to maintain the distance I felt I needed.

The tension between wanting to be open and honest, yet not to predispose the life historians to my biases, was problematic even before I began the research process. I was cautioned that my strong feminist position might "blind" me, causing me to see only what I wanted to see. I often wondered if others conducting research were warned that they would focus too much on class if they were Marxists or too much on culture if they were ethnographers. Why was my predisposition any more dangerous? In contrast, I felt that by openly acknowledging my subjectivity, I would be able to tap the intersubjective process by "attuning [myself] to where self and subject are intertwined" (Peshkin, 1988: 20).

Women writing about other women (Bateson, 1989; Chevigny, 1984; Heilbrun, 1988) have described the process of understanding another woman's life as one of empathy and identification with, and ultimately separation from, their informants. I sensed that without the process of identification, difference could not be illuminated. The identification or connection, the subjective experience I sought, seemed central to understanding them and to writing their life stories. These connections were, however, in part dependent on my willingness to reveal my own story. Again, I wondered, how much should I share?

I struggled. During the first interview and explanation of the project, I was careful not to reveal too much. I was cautious not to identify myself as a feminist, for fear that this might raise red flags or signal what I hoped to hear. In the interviews I held back comments and my own experiences, and tried to maintain neutral facial expressions so as not to lead them on or dispose them in any significant way. I wanted the themes to emerge from their stories. What role, if any, did they see gender playing in their lives as teachers? What meanings did they give to their lives as teachers? Would these stories emerge naturally if I told them too much? Like Kathy Anderson (Anderson, Armitage, Jack, & Wittner, 1990), I questioned if it was truly the life historian's understanding of her experience that I was seeking, or if I was structuring the interview so that the subject told the story that conformed to my orientation. Throughout the interviews it was difficult to listen without trying to make sense of the women's stories and place them within my theoretical framework. I often worried that this tendency was interfering with my ability to listen carefully to what the life historians were actually saying.

This was complicated by the fact that after the first interviews I tentatively identified three major themes. In the interviews that followed I felt my questions were guided by my need to gain a clearer understanding of these themes rather than allowing the participants to talk in a more open-ended manner. At the start of our fourth interview Brenda mentioned that she wanted to talk about her travels, a significant part of her story, which she felt she hadn't discussed. I, on the other hand, was anxious to hear more about what she had called her "allies" and the role they played in her life as a female teacher. She deferred to my request, yet I wondered afterward how collaborative our interview had been.

In wanting to truly honor the voices of these women teachers, I faced another dilemma as I began supplementary interviews with former students, colleagues, and administrators. My original intention was to conduct these interviews in an effort to enhance the subjective and contextual picture of the women I worked with. The life historians freely recommended persons they believed would help me and would be open to being interviewed. As I started these supplementary interviews, I began to question my own motives. When I asked Brenda's principal to tell me the story of how Brenda became division chair, I actually wanted to hear the other side of the story in order to identify incongruencies which might help me see the role gender played in Brenda's school life. I was also curious how the principal's description of Brenda would differ from her own or mine, as I hoped to gain more insight into Brenda's own frame of reference.

These supplementary interviews were—and continue to be—very helpful in illuminating the subjective nature of our experiences, yet I wonder what role they have in a collaborative research relationship. I wonder if they undermine the purpose of feminist narrative inquiry, which seeks to validate women's voices and experiences as truth. Sheridan and Salaff (1984) maintain that "contradictory statements and actions are not necessarily false fronts that should be eliminated. On the contrary, sensitive recordings of inconsistencies in what people say or do may show how perceptions of objective reality actually reflect different levels of more complex realities" (p. 17). This notion of expanding subjectivity by increasing the reflexive process by holding "reality" up to multiple mirrors certainly provides the opportunity to reflect the infinite and complex understandings of reality (Ruby, 1982). However, I worry deeply about the potential loss of women's voices in this array of infinite possibilities. Does the pursuit of subjectivity lead us into the abyss of relativity? More important, can the collaboration of women and the findings of our research be acknowledged when all voices are equally valid?

Seeking subjectivity through collaboration continues to raise provoking questions. Although I have not found a resolution to my continuing efforts to make sense of the research relationship, I am more cautious about naming the process collaborative or even suggesting that the research process can ever truly be collaborative. I say this especially in light of the fact that the research relationship in the field is only one aspect of the collaborative process. Genuine reciprocity entails not only sensitivity to the research relationship but also an account of the research process and relationship in the final text. The problem of representation, of both the stories and the intersubjective process, presented me with my final dilemma.

## "WHERE'S MY LIFE IN ALL OF THIS?": COLLABORATION AND TEXT

In trying to achieve a collaborative research relationship, the process and product of the research cannot be separated. In trying to recover the collaborative aspects of research in the text, the analysis and write-up have often been the exclusive concern of the researcher. According to Judith Stacey (1988), "the lives, loves, and tragedies that field work informants share with a researcher are ultimately data, grist for the ethnographic mill, a mill that has a truly grinding power" (p. 23). Leslie Roman (1989) points out that the ethnographer is written into the text, but rarely appears as a social subject in relation to those that he or she researches. An accounting of the relationship, its dynamics, and its role in achieving understanding is traditionally left out due to its subjective nature. Feminists (Anderson, Armitage, Jack, & Wittner, 1990; Harding, 1989; Mies, 1983) have warned against the dangers of dematerializing research accounts by stripping them of the economic, cultural, and political conditions under which field work has been conducted.

In seeking to establish a collaborative text, I was concerned not only with placing myself in the text, but with questioning what role the life historians should play in the analysis and writing up of the text. As I have just suggested, it is in the final product, or text, that collaboration has proved the most difficult (Crapanzano, 1980; Langness & Frank, 1981; Visweswaran, 1988). In attempting to construct a truly feminist, collaborative text, I conceived of three essential elements: my own self-reflexive account of the story, the intersubjective creation of the story, and the actual stories of the life historians. How to present these in a manner which did justice to each, while not reducing to a secondary position the story of the participants themselves, presents a continuing dilemma. How do I balance the stories of the life historians, my reflexive account, and their recollections of the research process without relegating their stories to a lesser position?

Susan Geiger (1990) suggests that at one end of the spectrum of textual representation lies erasure of the participant through anonymous generalizations from her story that objectify her as just another "text." At the other end lies total identification or attempted merger in an attempt to erase not the person herself but the reality of differences. In order to avoid either of these extremes, I hoped to represent the voices of the life historians in the text by incorporating their feedback on the transcripts, to engage them in a discussion of the salient themes, and ultimately to have them comment on the final narrative and include their reactions to it in a written form.

At this point, the reaction of the life historians to my including them in the interpretative process has been their acknowledgment that it is a subjective process; therefore, their own interpretations are no more valid than mine. Brenda commented at our last session, after discussing what I felt were the emergent themes, that she saw parallels between the research process and the classroom. Just as she expected students to create their own meanings and take what they needed from the classroom experience, she trusted that I would do the same.

In being left alone to the task of constructing their life histories, I am acutely aware of not wanting to succumb to "vanity ethnography" (Van Maanen, 1988). I am also self-conscious about experimenting with the text in a way that might seem disrespectful or alienate the participants. I wonder, for example, how they would feel if I presented them with an integrated text that interwove the multiple voices throughout the text. Would they see this as diminishing their story? If I used innovative postmodern textual representations, such as cartoons, poems, or pictures, interspersed throughout the text as a means of representing the complexity of our stories, would they find this a fair representation of their lives? In choosing to represent these narratives in alternative forms, am I elevating my need to make a political and theoretical statement or am I trying to do justice to the stories of women teachers?

## NO CONCLUSION

The dilemmas discussed here present no easy resolutions, if, in fact, there are solutions at all. The questions of representation, self-reflexivity, and subjectivity in the collaborative process are ongoing questions. Will degree of reflexivity or subjectivity, or mode of representation, provide a "better" criterion for establishing "truth"? What about the goal of feminist research to be emancipatory or empowering? What criteria will be established to assess this? Again, I believe we are posing the wrong questions if we seek only to replace one form of measurement with another, for we are still trapped within an essentialist notion of truth.

My quest for understanding the collaborative process has not led me to new definitions or methods for establishing truth, be it partial, absolute, multiple, or situated. It has led me to a deeper understanding of ways of knowing and how these are deeply embedded in the relational acts of the research process. My understanding of the multiple ways we create, negotiate, and make sense of the power relations in our lives has been enlarged. I only hope that my feminist position continues to situate me in and alert me to these crucial issues. For it is only from this position that I can even attempt to achieve the collaboration which I seek.

## NOTES

1. The challenge to positivistic notions of an absolute and fixed truth have also been explored extensively within the field of anthropology. For further discussion of these issues see Geertz (1973); Marcus & Fischer (1986); and Clifford (1986).

2. Many reconceptualizations of validity in a postpositivistic context have been undertaken. Lather (1986), discussing the methodological implications of emancipatory research, has suggested a need for "catalytic" validity. Critical ethnographers, as reviewed by Anderson (1989), concerned with the empowerment of those researched have suggested the notion of "critical validity" to reveal the political nature of research and expose its nonneutrality. Lincoln and Guba (1985) have maintained that the degree to which research is "objectively subjective" provides the basis for validity. They have suggested that triangulation, reflexivity, and member checks could assess the validity of qualitative inquiry. Since time and space are limited in this presentation, it is not feasible to undertake a thorough review of this literature. My purpose in this chapter is not to offer new categories to test validity, but to suggest that the concept itself is not a useful one in research that seeks understanding and meaning.

3. This research is part of a larger study that I conducted for my dissertation (Munro, 1991). This research was funded in part by the Center for the Study of Women in Society at the University of Oregon. I would like to acknowledge David Flinders, Harry Wolcott, and the Women's Study and Research Group at the University of Oregon for their honest and insightful feedback, which was central to the development of this chapter.

4. The term "life historians" is suggested by Marjorie Mbilinyi (1989) as an alternative to the objectifying labels of "informant" and "subject."

## REFERENCES

Abu-Lughod, L. (1990). Can there be feminist ethnography? *Women and Performance: A Journal of Feminist Theory, 5*(1), 7–27.

Agar, M. (1980). *The professional stranger.* New York: Academic Press.

Anderson, G. (1989). Critical ethnography in education: Origins, current status and new directions. *Review of Educational Research, 59*(3), 249–270.

Anderson, K., Armitage, S., Jack, D., & Wittner, J. (1990). Beginning where we are: Feminist methodology in oral history. In J. Nielson (Ed.), *Feminist research methods* (pp. 94–112). Boulder, CO: Westview Press.

Bateson, M. C. (1989). *Composing a life.* New York: Atlantic Monthly Press.

Bowen, E. S. (1964). *Return to laughter.* New York: Doubleday.

Chevigny, B. (1984). Daughters writing: Toward a theory of women's biography. In C. Ascher, L. DeSalvo, & S. Ruddick (Eds.), *Between women* (pp. 357–381). Boston: Beacon Press.

Christman, J. (1988). Working the field as female friend. *Anthropology and Education Quarterly, 19*(2), 70–85.

Clifford, J. (1986). Introduction: Partial truths. In J. Clifford & G. Marcus (Eds.), *Writing cultures: The poetics and politics of ethnography* (pp. 1–26). Berkeley: University of California Press.

Connelly, F. M., & Clandinin, D. J. (1990). Stories of experience and narrative inquiry. *Educational Researcher, 19*(4), 2–14.

Crapanzano, V. (1980). *Tuhami: Portrait of a Moroccan.* Chicago: University of Chicago Press.

Duelli Klein, R. (1983). How to do what we want to do: Thoughts about feminist methodology. In G. Bowles & R. Duelli Klein (Eds.), *Theories of women's studies* (pp. 105–116). London: Routledge and Kegan Paul.

Everhart, R. (1977). Between stranger and friend: Some consequences of "long term" field work in schools. *American Educational Research Journal, 14,* 1–15.

Fine, M. (1994). Re-inventing the hyphen. In N. Denzin & I. Lincoln (Eds.), *Handbook of Qualitative Research.* New York: Sage.

Geertz, C. (1973). *The interpretation of cultures.* New York: Basic Books.

Geiger, S. (1986). Women's life histories: Methods and content. *Signs, 11*(2), 334–351.

Geiger, S. (1990). What's so feminist about women's oral history? *Journal of Women's History, 2*(1), 169–182.

Gitlin, A. D. (1990). Educative research, voice and school change. *Harvard Educational Review, 60*(4), 443–466.

Golde, P. (1970). *Women in the field: Anthropological experiences.* Chicago: Aldine.

Grumet, M. (1990). On daffodils that come before the swallow dares. In E. Eisner & A. Peshkin (Eds.), *Qualitative inquiry in education* (pp. 101–120). New York: Teachers College Press.

Harding, S. (1989). Is there a feminist method? In N. Tuana (Ed.), *Feminism and science* (pp. 17–32). Bloomington: Indiana University Press.

Heilbrun, C. G. (1988). *Writing a woman's life.* New York: Ballantine Books.

Langness, L. L., & Frank, G. (1981). *Lives: Anthropological approach to biography.* Novato, CA: Chandler and Sharp.

Lather, P. (1986). Research as praxis. *Harvard Educational Review, 56*(3), 257–277.

Lather, P. (1993). Fertile obsession: Validity after poststructuralism. *Sociological Quarterly, 34*(4), 673–693.

Lincoln, Y. S., & Guba, E. G. (1985). *Naturalistic inquiry.* Beverly Hills: Sage.

Mandelbaum, D. (1973). The study of life history: Gandhi. *Current Anthropology, 14*(3), 177–206.

Marcus, G. E. (1982). Rhetoric and the ethnographic genre in anthropological research. In J. Ruby (Ed.), *A crack in the mirror* (pp. 163–171). Philadelphia: University of Pennsylvania Press.

Marcus, G., & Fischer, M. M. J. (1986). *Anthropology as cultural critique.* Chicago: University of Chicago Press.

Marcus, J. (1984). Invisible mending. In C. Ascher, L. DeSalvo, & S. Ruddick (Eds.), *Between women* (pp. 381–397). Boston: Beacon Press.

Mbilinyi, M. (1989). "I'd Have Been a Man." In Personal Narratives Group (Eds.), *Interpreting Women's Lives* (pp. 204–207). Bloomington: Indiana University Press.

McLaughlin, D., & Tierney, W. (1993). *Naming silenced lives: Personal narratives and processes of educational change.* New York: Routledge.

McRobbie, A. (1982). The politics of feminist research: Between text, talk and action. *Feminist Review, 12,* 46–57.

Mies, M. (1983). Towards a methodology for feminist research. In G. Bowles & R. Duelli Klein (Eds.), *Theories of women studies* (pp. 117–125). London: Routledge and Kegan Paul.

Munro, P. (1991). *A life of work: Stories women teachers tell.* Unpublished doctoral dissertation, University of Oregon, Eugene.

Myerhoff, B. (1982). Life history among the elderly. In J. Ruby (Ed.), *A crack in the mirror* (pp. 99–117). Philadelphia: University of Pennsylvania Press.

Personal Narratives Group. (1989). *Interpreting women's lives: Feminist theory and personal narratives.* Bloomington: Indiana University Press.

Peshkin, A. (1988). In search of subjectivity—one's own. *Educational Researcher, 17*(7), 17–21.

Plummer, K. (1983). *Documents of life: An introduction to the problems and literature of a humanistic method.* London: Allen & Unwin.

Powdermaker, H. (1966). *Stranger and friend: The way of an anthropologist.* New York: W. W Norton.

Reinharz, S. (1979). *On becoming a social scientist: From survey research and participant observation to experiential analysis.* San Francisco: Jossey-Bass.

Robertson, C. (1983). In pursuit of life histories: The problem of bias. *Frontiers, 7*(2), 63–69.

Roman, L. G. (1989, April). *Double exposure: The politics of feminist materialist ethnography.* Paper presented at the American Educational Research Association, San Francisco, CA.

Roman, L. G., & Apple, M. W. (1990). Is naturalism a move away from positivism?: Materialist and feminist approaches to subjectivity in ethnographic research. In A. Peshkin & E. Eisner (Eds.), *Qualitative inquiry in education: The continuing debate* (pp. 38–74). New York: Teachers College Press.

Ruby, J. (Ed.). (1982). *A crack in the mirror: Reflexive perspectives in anthropology.* Philadelphia: University of Pennsylvania Press.

Sheridan, M., & Salaff, J. W. (1984). *Lives: Chinese working women.* Bloomington: Indiana University Press.

Shostak, M. (1981). *Nisa.* New York: Vintage Books.

Smith, S. (1987). *A poetics of women's autobiography.* Bloomington: Indiana University Press.

Smith, S. (1993). Who's talking/Who's talking back?: The subject of personal narrative. *Signs,*
    *18*(2), 392–407.

Sparkes, A. (1994). Life histories and the issue of voice: Reflection on an emerging relationship.
    *Qualitative Studies in Education, 7*(2), 165–183.

Stacey, J. (1988). Can there be a feminist ethnography? *Women's Studies International Forum,*
    *11*(1), 21–27.

Strathern, M. (1987). An acquired relationship: The case of feminism and anthropology. *Signs,*
    *12*(2), 276–292.

Van Maanen, J. (1988). *Tales of the field.* Chicago: University of Chicago Press.

Visweswaran, K. (1988). Defining feminist ethnography. *Inscriptions,* (3 & 4), 27–44.

Watson, L., & Watson-Sparks, F. (1985). *Interpreting life histories: An anthropological inquiry.*
    New Brunswick, NJ: Rutgers University Press.

Wolcott, H. (1990). On seeking—and rejecting—validity in qualitative research. In A. Peshkin
    & E. Eisner (Eds.), *Qualitative inquiry in education: The continuing debate* (pp. 121–153).
    New York: Teachers College Press.

# CHAPTER 7

# Is Collaborative Research Collaborative?
# Life History, Whose Life?

*Karen Froude Jones*

## SITUATING A LIFE

I have written so many introductions to this chapter that my computer has started eating my words—a not too subtle message to be brief and to the point. I call Gretchen and she, pressuring me (as close friends do) to be more forthcoming, says, "Karen, why don't you tell the readers who you are and let them engage in the collaborative and life-history processes with you?" "Which who?" I ask. The complexity of a life within the page-limiting boundaries of publication? I offer a montage.

How do I define myself? By culture? (Welsh, English, indigenous . . . ) By class? (downwardly mobile English landed gentry, upwardly mobile Welsh coal miner, nonenrolled indigenous . . . ) By geographic frame of reference? (Laguna Beach, Hawaii, La Jolla . . . summers surfing at San Onofre, about 2 weeks as a Beverly Hills debutante, I left to go live on a solar-dome commune in New Mexico and to teach skiing at Snowbird, Utah, high school dropout, bitterly cold winters and scorching hot summers on the "res" with my adopted Navajo grandmothers . . . ) By education and schooling? (Mills, Stanford, UC Berkeley, University of Oregon . . . ) By political affiliation? (after I turned 18, I always made sure that I wasn't caught . . . I'm still, despite the bullet holes in my 4 x 4, pretty cautious) By theoretical orientation? (I shy away from representation through academic voices, too many "dead" white males and women wanting equality with them) . . . Is this enough of a resume? Can you hear my voice? My identity has always come through family, actions, and community. I'm much more comfortable with a relational approach.

This chapter is about relationships; about lives, representation, authority, and voice. It is about my experiences trying to "make real" the narratives of women from diverse cultural backgrounds teaching in the public schools. It is about my struggle within the academy for recognition of the strength that relationships bring to process and for realization of process as more important than product.

## NOTES FROM MY PERSONAL JOURNAL: REFLECTIONS ON THE RESEARCH PROCESS

I sit, I sprawl, I slouch, I record, speculate, reflect, evaluate; I'm the observer, the researcher-scholar, anthropologist-educator, exhausted human being—trying, sometimes desperately, to capture the dynamic environment of this elementary school classroom. Trying to represent the often missing voices of the teachers (and of the children). My tools: yellow legal pad, tape recorder, eyes, ears, heart.

The document trail—agreements with Human Subjects, with the school district evaluation specialist, paperwork, and conversations: strokes and reality checks, misunderstandings, "wonderful idea, life history, collaborative interaction, synergistic processes, multiple voices—the recognition of the roles that language, community, culture, and gender play in the creation of elementary classroom environments—WOW . . . by the way, please don't interact with the children . . ." (How, I ask myself, do I write about curriculum, classroom context, and multiple voices without interacting with the children?).

In response to my incredulous look: "No, that's not decontextualization; that's valid research." However, I'm fortunate, I made it through those hoops; trying to blend into the setting—drawing fugitive glances from the children, my presence eliciting darting comments over their heads from the teacher; the neutral observer, the lens theoretically able to capture all nuance, the pure tool for transcription, the artist pulling strands of multidimensional reality into text—the ethnographer.

An omnipotent presence filtering, refining, and labeling people's lives, taking contextual realities, and condensing them into text—representation or imposition, liberation or oppression? A voyeuristic experience, trading short-term status and rhetorical friendship for supposedly "insider" information—a quick, clean exploration into an "other's" reality; a futuristic holograph, a legal, controllable mind-altering trip?

I reflect again, what is ethnography? We're told, those of us who train to be ethnographers, that it is about people, patterns, and presentation—about truths. This chapter asks: Whose truths?

The chapter is based on a study that examines collaborative interaction and ethnographic processes from a self-reflective stance. Five women, including the researcher, spent a year attempting to share their experiences as educators, as women, as members of diverse (and distinctly different) cultural communities, and as colleagues working for educational change in the public school system. The research reflects on the ways in which the system is designed to silence diverse voices and to suppress difference. The purpose of this chapter is to explore the undefined boundaries and unlimited possibilities of collaboration—to recognize the intersubjective realities of relationalism, emotion, and sentiment, and to acknowledge the affective in trust relationships developed through qualitative research. Interwoven throughout this chapter is the following concern: If we are truly to transform the rational, predictable formats of public schools and university systems, how can we foreground the critical recognition that collaboration and process are about relationships and trust? As researchers, we need to expand our formats in manners that are inclusive and that recognize the other "facts": the relationships that are the essence—the heart and voice—of qualitative research. It is the belief of the researcher that it is these unrecognized relationships, the multiple voices of culture and connection, that inspire and transform and that are revealed through collaborative narrative research. In this chapter, I attempt to illustrate how those multiple cultural voices came to be connected and remain interconnected, despite the deeply entrenched elements of exclusionality and the fiction of rigor, validity, and clarity one finds embedded in traditional research processes.

Researcher and collaborative reflections are based on observations and discussions that occurred with the participating teachers during a year-long study in their elementary school classrooms. The focus of the investigation was on how four women elementary school teachers, from diverse first- and second-generation immigrant backgrounds, relate their experiences through collaborative narrative description. The taped and transcribed narratives of these four women educators provide an opportunity for the examination of the interconnected relationships of race, class, gender, culture, language, and community in their processes of curriculum accommodation (adaptation), implementation (execution), and transformation (change). There were two intersecting dimensions to this study: (1) the examination of the ideology embedded within the public school curriculum, as experienced by four female elementary educators from diverse cultural backgrounds and (2) a consideration of the ethnographic and collaborative process of life-history narratives. My intention was to stimulate reflection regarding how the standard public school curriculum, through its content and process, limits our vision through the imposition of a limited number of recognized expressions of knowledge and how those same impositional and hierarchical processes are replicated in traditional anthropology.

In keeping with the spirit of collaboration and self-reflection, the four "informants" are called coparticipants. The backgrounds of these women include cultures from within the geopolitical boundaries of western Europe as well as the Mediterranean and the Caribbean. They are, by their own definitions, Moriah, a "Jewish, American woman"; Kathleen, an "Irish American woman"; Eva, an "international, Austrian American woman"; and Martha, a "Hispanic, Puerto Rican" woman. Their primary language backgrounds include French, English, German, and Spanish. As women, these educators provide an opportunity to examine some of the issues faced by females in the hierarchical and patriarchal structure of the public school system. As first- and second-generation women residing in the United States, these teachers provide an opportunity for examination of issues of racial, class, gender, cultural, and language awareness as expressed through their stories of family and community experiences as well as through their roles as educators in the public school system.

The data collection included a series of three formal interviews, three informal interviews, and seven participant observations. Initial interviews took place in September and October 1990. Participant observation, oral dialogue, and the opportunity for collaboration through discussion occurred, as schedules permitted, from September 1990 through August 1991. Throughout this process, the participants were asked to keep journals. These journals were to be tools for written dialogue and personal reflection. In February and March 1991, I met with each participant in order to review the life-history transcripts and collaboratively reflect on the process. We met again in July and August 1991 in order to critique the collaborative process and determine a form for presenting their narratives.

The ongoing integration within the journals, the directed and informal interviews, and the oral dialogue were designed to enhance the possibility of this study becoming a rigorously self-conscious collaborative project. I felt that these methods would support a holistic and self-reflective approach. A holistic approach acknowledges the intangible web of interaction between human beings and their surroundings. A self-reflective approach recognizes the concept that each strand within that web is part of an integrated whole. The ideal was a collaborative process in which the voices of the participants would create the context for communication. This form of research allows a sharing of knowledge which empowers the individuals and creates desired change (Kyle & Hovda, 1987; Lieberman, 1986). Analysis was reflective, relational, and collaborative.

I had hoped that the commitment of these women to the process of teaching, the recognition of their unique cultural backgrounds, their personal power as women, and the celebration of diversity through their work as educators would inform the study. As stated by Carol Edelsky (1990), in the *Educational Researcher*, in order to understand "educational paradigms, one must see the relationships among a web of beliefs, theory, values, research, practice, discourse, goals, and so on. . . . Such vision comes not from standing outside a paradigm . . . or moving to some nonexistent paradigm-free lookout point. . . . It comes from entering that educational community" (p. 7). I chose these four women in order to enter that community.

Throughout the ethnographic and collaborative processes several questions emerged: (1) What role does critical self-reflection play in each of these processes? (2) Does the life-history narrative process represent a life? and (3) Is collaborative research really collaborative? This chapter addresses each of these questions.

It is my belief that all ethnographic endeavors include self-reflection (Crapanzano, 1980; Elmendorf, 1976; Myerhoff, 1975; Rabinow, 1977; Watson & Watson-Frank, 1985). My motives for the study were a set of multidimensional frustrations: with the public school system, as child and adult; with mainstream societal values; and with what I perceive as the limited vision of politicians, industrialists, and technocrats. I wanted proactive transformation, a forum, a platform, a voice.

As a public school teacher, I had felt that I had become an active participant in what is for many people personal and cultural genocide through assimilation. My memories of my first year of teaching in rural Oregon, outside the "closed door" (before Drs. Proudfoot and Collay came to support), mostly consist of shepherding the children from one place to another under strict orders that they "walk on the fourth square [of the linoleum grid pattern in the corridors], do not talk, and keep your arms by your sides." Inevitably, during our transitions to lunch, gym, or music, we would pass a white male administrator, stopwatch in hand, carefully monitoring our progress. During these transitions, I found myself modeling, and requesting from the children, the submissive behavior that seemed to appeal to this particular administrator. What I perceived as my dualistic behavior resulted in my continually questioning my role, my values, and the integrity of my work. I questioned these issues even as I continued to work with the children behind the closed door of the classroom, encouraging them to use their critical-thinking skills, acknowledge alternative perspectives, and asking direct questions of themselves and others. I asked myself, is this socialization for survival, for subservience, or am I helping to create possibilities for emancipation and social transformation? I am still unsure.

I was not alone in these experiences. These painful processes of assimilation and socialization have been described by many women, representing diverse cultural and class experience: Maya Angelou (1988), Mary Crow Dog (1990), Louise Erdrich (1987), Gretchen Freed-Rowland (1991, 1992), Madeleine Grumet (1988), Zora Neale Hurston (1984), Petra Munro (1992), Leslie Marmon Silko (1977), Twila Souers (1992), and others. Maxine Hong Kingston (1989), in *The Woman Warrior*, writes that "when my second grade class did a play, the whole class went to the auditorium except the Chinese girls. . . . Our voices were too soft or nonexistent" (p. 167). She contrasts this with the education she received in the evening Chinese school: "There we chanted together, voices rising and falling, loud and soft, some boys shouting, everybody reading together, reciting together and not alone with one voice" (p. 167). Mary Tallmountain (1987), in "You Can Go Home Again: A Sequence," states that "the devastation began in Oregon. . . . I refused to go to school because my school-mates mocked my Indianness. . . . I hid away in closets and bit my hands in mute rage" (cited in Swann & Krupat, 1987a: 6).

As a student, I had expressed my rage by dropping out of school—at age 15. As a teacher and a researcher, I had, as Kozol (1980) states, learned to disbelieve that "the walls that stand around the unjust world in which the U.S. schools now toil, exist and thrive will . . . be leveled by the sound of trumpets or by another research project funded by the Carnegie Foundation" (p. 184). Earth First tactics were beginning to look very appealing. I was tired of jumping through hoops. I had my pedigree of intellectual competence and I wanted to do something "real"; I wanted to blend the theoretical with the practical. I felt that this study offered the possibility of becoming a forum for pedagogical transformation. There were voices that needed to be heard, "truths" that needed to be recognized, as suggested by Trinh Minh-ha (1987) in the following passage: "You who understand the dehumanization of forced removal-relocation-reeducation-redefinition, the humiliation of having to falsify your own reality, your voice—you know. And often cannot say it. You try to keep on trying to unsay it, for if you don't, they will not fail to fill in the blanks on your behalf, and you will be said" (p. 7). One rarely hears the voices of the practitioners and never those of the children. Their stories needed to be told, their perspectives deserved to be heard. Or was it my story, my perspective?

The second question asks: Does the life-history narrative process represent a life? I chose the life-history method because I agree with the premise of the Personal Narratives Group (1989), who write that: "personal narratives illuminate the course of a life over time and allow for its interpretation in its historical and cultural context" (p. 4). I chose four female coparticipants from diverse cultures because I also agree with Ellen Carol DuBois and Vicki Ruiz (1990), in *Unequal Sisters: A Multicultural Reader in U.S. Women's History,* when they state that the traditional history of women and women's studies in the United States reflects an artificial women's experience that is "defined in contrast to 'man's' history" (p. xi). While this dichotomy has resulted in a recognition of women in this society, it has also resulted in the continued marginalization of those women who do not meet the traditional model of "white and middle class" that has been the criterion for women's experiences, and it continues the denigration of the historical and cultural experiences of those women labeled "white."

As a woman who can trace most of her family to their Welsh, English, Bavarian, Dutch, and indigenous roots, and whose rich tapestry of ancestors includes strands of oppressed peoples, as well as oppressors, I find the predominant notion of "white" as "lacking" history and/or culture to be reactive and based on ignorance. Ellen Carol DuBois and Vicki Ruiz eloquently support their thesis in the following statement:

In this uniracial model, race and gender cannot be brought into the same theoretical field. White women appear "raceless," their historical experiences determined solely by gender. By contrast, the distinct historical experiences of women of color, to the degree they are acknowledged, are credited solely to race. We choose the term "multicultural" . . . because we seek to focus on the interplay of many races and cultures, because we acknowledge that not all white women's histories can be categorized under one label, and because we seek to assume that the term "race" needs to be theorized rather than assumed. (pp. xi–xii)

I chose four women from diverse racial and class backgrounds because I also agree with Mary Romero (1991) who states in "The Maid's Daughter: A Modern Version of Upstairs/Downstairs" that "descriptions of interactions in inter- and intra-ethnic settings demonstrate the way our intimate relationships are shaped by systems of race, class and gender domination" (p. 21).

I chose to work with four women from four different primary language backgrounds because I believe that we need to examine the power that language plays in our perceptions and interactions. I believe that the language we use is said to "speak who we are" (Whorf, 1956): Its metaphors, patterning, and syntax reflect the values and expectations within each culture. Paula Gunn Allen (1987), in "Bringing Home the Fact," suggests that "for as we perceive, so we behave; and as we behave, so we create" (cited in Swann & Krupat, 1987b: 570). Language has the power to nurture and expand as well as fragment and oppress a world view.

Leslie Marmon Silko, in *Ceremony* (1977), addresses this issue in a passage that describes how deeply embedded and intertwined are language, nature, and humankind. Through the voice of an elder Laguna Pueblo medicine man, she describes the world as "fragile":

The word he chose to express fragile was filled with the intricacies of a continuing process, and with a strength inherent in spider webs woven across paths through sand hills where early in the morning the sun becomes entangled in each filament of web. It took a long time to explain the fragility and intricacy because no word exists alone, and the reason for choosing each word had to be explained with a story about why it must be said this certain way. That was the responsibility that went with being human, old Ku'oosh said, the story behind each word must be told so there could be no mistake in the meaning of what had been said; and this demanded great patience and love. (pp. 35–36)

I was worried that I had forgotten how to hear, that I had become insensitive to words, that I was about to perish, as N. Scott Momaday (1968) suggests in *House Made of Dawn*, in the "commonplace . . . [the] unending succession of pamphlets and papers, letters and books, bills and bulletins, commentaries and conversations" (p. 89). I often wondered: Why am I running this gauntlet?

It was language, stories, and context, rather than text, that drew me to the life-history process. My background—as a weaver, a teacher-learner, and a woman from cultures shared through oral traditions—emphasizes the necessity of allowing people to create their realities through whatever means they choose in which to share those stories. I was being drawn back to my cultures, to my communities.

I had been raised to look for patterns. I had been told that personal and cultural realities are revealed through patterns of interaction. I had also been told that the intent of ethnography is the illumination of these patterns. Harry Wolcott states that "cultural interpretation is not an ethnographic 'requirement,' it is the essence of the ethnographic endeavor" (personal communication, 1989). Paul Rabinow (1977), in *Reflections on Fieldwork in Morocco*, suggests that "culture is a human thing—it is human beings that create it, interpret it, and change it" (p. x). Life-history narrative focuses on the human element within that pattern. It offers the researcher a chance to see "how the person copes with society, rather than how society copes with a stream of individuals" (Mandelbaum, 1973: 177). It reveals "what is essential about the human condition" (Langness & Frank, 1981: 136). Watson and Watson-Frank (1985) suggest that "a return to the life history is really a return to the individual in the fullness of his (or her) social and unique humanness" (p. ix).

I had been taught that life-history narrative is a methodological technique that recognizes the element of process and introduces a multiplex of possibilities and impossibilities. It felt like a challenging process because it seemed to require continual academic and conceptual reevaluation and application. It also felt like a powerful process because it seemed to require dialogue, trust, compassion, and honesty. I felt that it would require human beings to speak and hear from their hearts—that it would be frighteningly revealing, perilously intriguing, and refreshingly transformative. I felt that because it does not promote the "scientific" process, it would celebrate the "human" process—the collective symphony in multiple voices. It offers what Harry Wolcott (1990) refers to as "the opportunities—and challenges— . . . to regard ourselves as humans who conduct our research *among* rather than *on*" (p. 19) other humans.

I was enamored of this ethnographic technique because it seemed to allow people to speak "for themselves as they speak of themselves" (Swann & Krupat, 1987b: xiv). I was supported in these beliefs by the work of men and women who recognize ethnographically informed techniques as a means for exploring language, race, class, gender, and cultural diversity and the narrative process as one requiring self-reflectivity. In Rob Proudfoot's (1990) first book, *Even the Birds Don't Sound the Same Here: The Laotian Refugees' Search for Heart in American Culture*, he relies on the life-history process to record the immigration and acculturation of Laotian refugees into the United States. He notes: "The results of this experience are not at an end. . . . They are part of the greater continuum which constitutes the learning process. One changes, one is changed through the act of compromising and attempting to understand. Empathy and objectivity are forged into a new tool. One explores, one is explored" (pp. 237–238).

Barbara Myerhoff explores the voices within the traditional Jewish culture in Los Angeles, California. She describes the life-history approach as "a research tool that holds tremendous power. . . . You can never dismiss people again. . . . It is a transformational experience" (cited in Langness & Frank, 1988: 155). In *Nine Mayan Women: A Village Faces Change*, Mary Elmendorf (1976) explores culture change through the descriptive narratives of contemporary Mayan women. She describes her role as an ethnographer in the following terms: "I could not remain a completely passive observer. . . . I found that I learned most when the women led the conversation" (pp. 7–8). Each of these researcher-scholars includes the elements of reflexivity and collaboration as necessary components of ethnography.

The third question asked: Is collaborative research really collaborative? Embedded within this question are concerns regarding power relations, ethics, and representation. Also addressed is the dilemma of textual representation and cross-cultural communication. In other words, whose "truths" are being told; whose voice are we hearing?

In each of the works cited in this paper, the ethnographic label informs us that the voices of the participants propel the research process. Theoretically, the ethnographic method "is always a delicate and complicated *collaborative* venture" (Langness & Frank, 1981: 61). In the process of creation "facts are made, fabricated, constructed . . . the ethnologist and his (or her) informants are collaborators in a work of interpretation" (Pierre Bourdieu, cited in Rabinow, 1977: 164–165). Richardson (1975) states that the life-history process is an illumination of the reality which is human myth, storytelling. Kluckhohn (1962) notes that "autobiographies" are in many cases biographies. In other words, the informant may be telling the ethnographer simply what he or she may think that person wants to hear. Aberle (1951) in his analysis of Simmon's *Sun Chief* (1942) reflects on the possibility that that work is one man's story, not the story of the Hopi people. Rob Proudfoot (1990) notes that in working with human beings one must always be aware of "interacting contextual considerations." Joan Acker, Kate Barry, and Joke Esseveld (1983) ask, "How do we explain the lives of others without violating their reality?" (p. 429).

The concept of talking about "self" is itself culturally constructed (Crapanzano, 1980; Minh-ha, 1988; Rabinow, 1977) and generally encouraged in cross-cultural contexts by "traditionally" trained male anthropologists. Frances Mascia-Lees, Patricia Sharpe, and Colleen Cohen (1989) caution us, in "The Postmodernist Turn in Anthropology: Cautions from a Feminist Perspective," that all data may also reflect projected expectation on the part of the "subject," perceived as an "exotic Other." As Barbara Christian (1988) states, "Many of us have never conceived of ourselves only as somebody's other" (p. 70). Trinh Minh-ha (1988) supports this concern when she suggests that "what the outsider expects from the insider is, in fact, a projection of an all-knowing subject that this outsider usually attributes to himself and to his own kind" (p. 75). Throughout this study, I continually asked myself: How can one achieve communication among women in a cross-cultural context? Can the life-history process be collaborative? Is there a form that can adequately represent this dialogue? Whose story are we hearing?

These statements are reminders that if the intent of ethnography is the illumination of "truths," then we must be self-reflective and continually examine the process in which personal stories are transposed into text. We must heed Judith Stacey's (1988) warning that while "ethnographic method appears to (and often does) place the researcher and her informants in a collaborative, reciprocal quest for understanding . . . the research product is ultimately that of the researcher" (p. 23). We must honestly ask ourselves whose story is ultimately being rendered "valid" through manuscript, article, presentation, and publication.

The following passage addresses these concerns. It offers the reader a glimpse of the research process through the self-reflective lens of the researcher.

## THE RESEARCH PROCESS

Notes from my field journal: It is mid-December 1990, vibrantly clear, unseasonably cold. I am spending the afternoon in a fifth-grade bilingual classroom in which Moriah is teaching. The room is rectangular, windowless, a repository for the school lunch odors drifting up from the cafeteria. What is it about the uniform smell of institutional food, how many years ahead of time is it manufactured, do they still serve "pups in a roll" and popsicles on Friday—is some child eating the lunch I refused to touch in third grade? The 26 children sit in individual desks grouped into sets of four. The desks are all at one end of the room, near the chalkboard. The large room is broken into two equal areas by a 3-foot bookcase and the teacher's desk, which extend about halfway out from one of the side walls. In the end of the room opposite the chalkboard is a circular "small-group" table and a large rectangular table, for projects. The walls are covered with glossy posters, mostly of locations in France. Along one wall, up near the ceiling, is a row of masks. There is a uniformity that implies an art or social studies unit project. I assume that they are supposed to be Native American Indian: physical evidence, artifacts of the "new sensitivities," multicultural perspectives, hopefully integrated into this classroom more than the only-at-Thanksgiving obligatory inclusion of the Native American Indian. I see no evidence of winter celebrations, Samhain, Christmas, Hanukkah, although I hear the class being reminded of an all-school assembly for the "winter

festival." The children tumble out of the classroom for recess and my coparticipant and I schedule a time for us to deconstruct and reconstruct my observations and her perceptions of the afternoon.

Later, we talk as we walk to a quiet room. I plug in the tape recorder, adjust
the volume, listen to Moriah:

> I carry this idea that all inclusivity is not something new—it's in the earth,
> it's part of the universe . . . and what has to happen is that language has to
> live up to the creation; the creation is all-inclusive, the language is not
> translated creation . . .

I interrupt, asking/stating, "And by not using inclusive language we're replicating a thought pattern that calls for exclusive behavior." I wonder, is this for
my own clarification? Am I trying to paraphrase, or am I overwhelmed by her
language, her presence? Am I perhaps wanting to assert my power in this
relationship, perhaps wanting to acknowledge the relationship, the element of
reciprocity I idealize in collaborative work?

"Exactly," she reassures me, "and it results in disastrous behaviors." Ah, I
think, I had better just be quiet and listen, and learn from this teacher. Moriah
is clearly needing this opportunity to talk. She goes on, expressing her frustration with the manner in which the school has approached the winter holidays
and in the process clarifying many of my observations from that afternoon and
raising issues that had not occurred to me:

> Today, it was very clear at the assembly that gender was at issue; there
> could have been a teachable moment. For the last six weeks they've been
> going through the issues of Christmas at that school, and with not the
> best results. They [the teachers] taught songs [for the assembly] in
> three languages, [but] in all three languages, there was no conscious-
> ness of gender issues. "Hello My Friends"—never thinking that the
> song refers only to boys and not to girls. . . . You start with third graders
> that way, where are you going?

Moriah had been called into this school as a guest teacher, an appropriate
model for this time of the year. She is a rabbi's wife, fluent in five languages,
from an extremely poor, extraordinarily distinguished line of scholars and poets
from a region near Morocco. She has mentioned that she feels like they had hired
her to fit an image; I wonder if they had counted on her insight and honesty.
She continued:

> They call it a winter festival, they said that they had peace in their heart,
> they said that they were not going to celebrate Christmas—which just isn't
> true because they sang "Silent Night" and to me that's the ultimate. . . .

They thought that by adding "Oh Dreidel, Dreidel" they had balanced it . . . which they didn't because we don't like to celebrate that way. . . . Even the kids know that it's fake.

At this point, I did need clarification; I wasn't sure of the appropriate context for "Oh Dreidel, Dreidel." I was told "it's not sung in assemblies, not even in Israel. . . . That's not how you celebrate the holiday." When I asked her what curriculum should be incorporated into the public schools, particularly during the so-called holiday season, she responded with the following statement:

> First of all, it's not their job to teach the Jewish faith; the schools should not represent any faith. What I saw was a system, [something] that functions as a system with multiple patterns . . . just incorporating within their tenants a foreign element . . . molding it in their patterns . . . decontextualizing and also simplifying. . . . There are many Jewish traditions . . . there are many different kinds of Jews, and they were all consumed in the dreidel song.

Moriah then talked about growing up in a family of 12 children, what it was like to be schooled by French nuns, and how her family eventually made their way to Israel. She calls the public school curriculum a simplification of culture and bourgeois elitism. She states that whether or not Americans want to admit it, there is an American culture, and it is not necessarily a good thing. She describes the decontextualized language of the public school curriculum, a reflection of the attitudes of "Christian colonialism," by elaborating on what she saw at the "winter festival" assembly in the following terms:

> Certain kinds of words make it as close to Christmas as much as possible, so the Christians won't be frightened and Jews will be absorbed.

We talked a bit longer, about personalities within the local school district, the politics of curriculum, and how we are each trying to survive. Toward the end of the conversation, Moriah stated that "in terms of language and gender, today . . . maybe because you called me . . . I was totally tuned in." I was forced once more to reflect on my role. Had my call changed her perceptions, her actions, because she expected to see me? Was she meeting my needs, or her needs, or were we creating something new? During our next interview I asked her how I could support her in her work. What I was trying to say, without using what Wolcott (personal communication, 1990) calls "the backed-into-a-corner 'Why' question," was why are you here, what are your motives, what is your agenda? Her response:

I need more knowledge, I need a community of people. . . . As I'm learning more about the public school I know that I need to seek soul sisters and brothers. . . . I am seeking allies.

I believe that she meant exactly what she said. I am as much her means to a forum, a platform, a voice, as she is for me—is that collaboration or, in the current jargon, codependence? Although I hold the pen, transcribe the tapes, and we tend to schedule interviews and observations around my other responsibilities and obligations, the study hinges on the final approval of each of the participants—or does it?

## Another Glimpse into Another Elementary School Classroom

Notes from my personal journal: It is 10 a.m., February 1, 1991. Four days ago faculty and students were informed that the Division of Teacher Education was going to be eliminated from the University of Oregon. I have not slept in 4 days, and it is beginning to show.

Observations from my field journal: I am curled up on a couch in the back of the room; sitting alongside of me are Pooh Bear, Piglet, and Roo. I'm drinking coffee and taking notes, my stuffed companions appear to be resting. The 21 children are in orderly rows seated cross-legged on the rug up near the chalkboard, basal texts in their laps. My coparticipant, Kathleen, is seated on a low stool, facing them while she has them take turns reading aloud. This is a gift to me, their favorite story, and they are reading for expression. I take one more deep sip of coffee, hoping that it will kick in soon, feeling a need to respond to their level of energy. I move nearer to them, perch on another stool off to one side, one child loans me her book, and I follow along with the others.

Later, as Kathleen and I walk to the staff room, we talk about recent events in Oregon and wonder how they will affect the public schools. Kathleen offers a long-term perspective; she has been teaching in the Oregon schools for over 30 years, and she has decided to take early retirement. I reflect back on when I first met this woman. Eleven years ago, she was my cooperating teacher during my student teaching experience. I found her to be a "traditional" teacher who demanded and received superlative work from her students. She was also warm, caring, and compassionate. Her days were filled with hugs from the children, and every afternoon older students would drop by to say hello. We had a wonderful time together. In the mornings, she covered phonics, math, and handwriting, and during the afternoons I took the children on grand adventures with plants, painting, storytelling, and cooperative learning. Her statement regarding her retirement made me feel as though I had stumbled onto a rare treasure, the chance to be a part of her last year as a public school teacher.

I think back to when I approached her about being a part of this project. She was not sure she could meet my needs. This concern is illustrated through a verbal-exchange pattern during our formal taped interviews. Within the first few minutes, she states, "Now I feel like I'm not really answering the question you asked." To which I respond, "It's your question. Once I put it out you can answer it any way you choose to." Seemingly reassured, Kathleen continues. We also close with a similar verbal ritual. I state, "Is there something that I haven't asked you that you would like included in this particular interview?" She responds with, "I think I covered myself." In reflecting back on these interactions I wonder how much her comments are indications of Kathleen's generosity, her strong Irish-Catholic background, her status as an older sister in a close, large family, or her desire to please me, help me with this project. When she states that she has "covered" herself, does that mean that she has said it completely or successfully cloaked herself? Am I presuming, as did Nancy Lurie (1966) with Mountain Wolf Woman, on my relationship with Kathleen, relying on her familial support as I did when she was my cooperating teacher 11 years ago? Am I working with her in order to re-create a pleasurable experience? Or am I assuming, as does Daphne Patai (1989) in *Brazilian Women Speak: Contemporary Life Stories*, that there is "some sort of bond with other women . . . despite differences in race, class, nationality, and much else" (p. 4)? Is this project partly an excuse for us to validate each other, as educators and as women? Once more I ask myself, how honest is the expressed intent of ethnographic collaboration? The Personal Narratives Group (1989) cautions: "In order to understand the configuration of the story—what it emphasizes, what it omits, what it may exaggerate—the interpreter must be sensitive to the narrator's purposes for telling the story. . . . Interpreters need to look for the reasons why narrators tell their stories" (pp. 202–203).

Narrators must also examine their own needs, their relationship to both the participants and the narrative process—the context of the ethnographic endeavor. Mary Elmendorf's work was published in New York, not in the Mayan village, and it was initially a dissertation project. Can any textual form represent human voice? How accurate is an English version of Mayan realities?

Aihwa Ong (1988) suggests, in a critique of feminist methodology, that lack of reflexivity, unacknowledged power relations, and Eurocentric elitism result in ethnographic works in which researchers "frequently seek to establish their authority on the backs of non-Western women, determining for them the meanings and goals of their lives" (p. 80). Barbara Christian (1988) states that "when theory is not rooted in practice, it becomes prescriptive, exclusive, elitist" (p. 54). She warns that without this critical perspective, the researcher overlooks the need for reflexivity, the ability to "distinguish the desire for power from the need to become empowered" (p. 57). Trinh Minh-ha advocates the multidimensionality available through film, while she also cautions us to be aware of power relationships within any form of cross-cultural communication.

Does the life-history process diminish human interaction, decontextualize what Barbara Myerhoff (1975) refers to as "ecological context" by hiding it behind the subject–object relationship of the English language, the ideology of the ethnographic endeavor, and the abstractly constructed and confining walls of the printed word? In *Shadows on the Grass*, Isak Dinesen (1960) describes an experience that resonates with these feelings:

> Once I shot an Iguana. I thought that I should be able to make some pretty things from his skin. A strange thing happened then, that I have never afterwards forgotten. As I went up to him, where he was lying dead upon his stone, and actually while I was walking the few steps, he faded and grew pale, all colour died out of him as in one long sigh, and by the time that I touched him he was grey and dull like a lump of concrete.
>
> It was the live impetuous blood pulsating within the animal, which had radiated out all that glow and splendour. Now that the flame was put out, and the soul had flown, the Iguana was as dead as a sandbag. (p. 267)

I worried that the life-history narratives were actually portraits riddled with such bullets; context and collaboration fragmented by agendas, motives, subjective and unacknowledged realities—another study destined to gather dust. Had I provided an opportunity for dialogue, a chance to really hear reactions, responses, voices, framed but not portrayed by my textual interpretation? Did the fact that my name was on the project, while each of my coparticipants had chosen pseudonyms, reflect the illusionary nature of this work? Whose truths did these stories contain? Whose stories were being heard?

The study formally ended in August 1991, with that "writ" of passage, the oral defense. I chose to maintain my emphasis on the relational throughout this ritualistic experience. I invited my coparticipants to be actively involved—to verbally represent their reflections on the dissertation to my doctoral committee during my defense. This unconventional approach not only raised the eyebrows of my dear Dr. Harry Wolcott as well as those of my esteemed faculty-colleagues Drs. Diane Dunlop and Mary Romero, but genuinely upset Jan, which was not my intention. I had hoped to illustrate the relational. What I ended up doing was severing my connections to the formal dissertation process—removing the institutionalized experiences from my resume and my life—while I strengthened my relationships with the community. The bridge between the two worlds is so fragile.

## REFLECTIONS ON THE PROCESS

During each of the final collaborative sessions central themes emerged that related to the collaborative narrative process. Most of these concerns revolved around issues of imposition and representation. While the narratives were accepted by the coparticipants, we all realized that these stories existed within the context of particular relationships and that each story's presentation was ultimately determined by institutionally imposed time lines and textual formats.

What I discovered during this research experience was that the imposed format of the study was a consideration that was difficult to overcome. Throughout all of our conversations, I was continually taking notes and mentally re-creating each of the narrative descriptions. I was continually motivated by the thrilling richness of narrative description and inspired by the textual portrayal. While I tried to acknowledge the diversity within the narrative and collaborative processes by creating different textual styles and calling the portraits by different labels, those styles and labels were ultimately determined by my dissertation committee and myself. After the first few months, particularly after the first collaborative discussion—after I began to know Eva, Martha, Moriah, and Kathleen as colleagues and friends—the experience began to feel impositional and inappropriate, voyeuristic and discourteous.

Concerns expressed by the coparticipants regarding the collaborative process addressed opportunities for collaboration and interpersonal "reorientation" as relationships moved beyond that of researcher and "informant." Implicit within this expressed concern is the fact that our relationships did move beyond that of "scholar" and "subject." The elements of self-reflection and collaboration, woven throughout this project (a study dedicated to hearing the voices of practitioners), resulted in an experience that was transformational for each of us.

What I believe may save this study from becoming an exploitative device is that I have returned the descriptive portrayals to the coparticipants, I am contributing one chapter on my doctoral research process to this book, and I am letting the relationships with the coparticipants continue through synergistic human processes rather than textual needs.

## CONCLUSION

Collaborative narrative description was a research process that emerged as a result both of the concerns expressed in this chapter and of my discomfort with traditional forms of anthropological inquiry. The research process evolved from academic studies in life history, ethnography, and anthropology as well as from personal experiences in collaborative, participatory, and action research. The result of these personal and academic experiences is a belief in collaborative, interactive, and self-reflective dialogue and a recognition that the multiple voices of the researcher-practitioners, of women, are necessary for educational and social transformation. In August 1991, after the oral defense, I had decided that "this is not a technique I will ever again attempt to use in this manner." Given the time for reflection and continued interaction with the coparticipants,

I suspect that my response was as much a statement of resistance against the imposition of the university system as it was regarding this methodology.

Rather than asking questions, I am now listening. What I am hearing is support for this collaborative process. As Moriah stated during one collaborative discussion, "You've given me a new consciousness of myself." She later reaffirmed her stated need for community and said, "Because of our conversations, I'm able to connect with more people." When I last spoke with her on the phone, she insisted that I mark my calendar for Passover and for her youngest child's Bat Mitzvah because "you're a member of this family whether you want it or not." In July 1991, during the last collaborative critique with Kathleen, she gave me a hug, tossed the narrative in her bag, ordered drinks for both of us, and insisted that we "never lose touch with each other." In January 1992, she called and reminded me that her birthday is the day after St. Patrick's Day: "Isn't it about time the Welsh and the Irish got together? The least we can do is celebrate my birthday." In August 1994, she informed me that she really had retired this time and would have lots of "opportunities for fun." Eva quietly assured me that "her extended family had just grown by one more member," and Martha asked in August 1991 and again in August 1992, "When are we going out dancing?" In August 1994, she invited me to "come meet her new beautiful baby girl so our children can grow up knowing each other" and informed me that because of our work together she now consciously brings her cultural heritage to the curriculum process: "I am much more aware of who I am, and therefore I look more at the whole person." The inclusion of the elements of self-reflection and collaboration transformed the potential imposition of narrative description because inherent within these elements is the acknowledgment of interactive and relational processes based on mutual respect and trust. The study became the responsibility of all of us as our awareness of and respect for one another grew.

What has become apparent to me through this research process is how rare and how fragile are the opportunities to see and hear the voices of women. This study offered an opportunity to hear four more stories, four additional perspectives. I offer it as a small beginning in a world in which there are many voices waiting to be heard, stories to be shared. When I informed Moriah of this publication, she said, "I must write something for your epilogue." I feel that it is only fitting that this documentation process end with words other than my own.

MORIAH: My collaboration with Karen Jones strengthens the strands in my own fibers as well as all my cultural ties as I co-midwife the birth of our society as multicultural. This process gave me courage to hear the voice within, and to hear other voices . . .

# REFERENCES

Aberle, D. (1951). The psychosocial analysis of a Hopi life-history. *Comparative Psychology Monograph, 21*(1), 59–73.

Acker, J., Barry, K., & Esseveld, J. (1983). Objectivity and truth: Problems in doing feminist research. *Women's Studies International Forum, 6*(4), 423–435.

Allen, P. G. (1987). Bringing home the fact: Tradition and continuity in the imagination. In B. Swann & A. Krupat (Eds.), *Recovering the word: Essays on Native American literature* (pp. 563–579). Berkeley: University of California Press.

Angelou, M. (1988). *I know why the caged bird sings.* New York: Bantam Books.

Christian, B. (1988). The race for theory. *Feminist Studies, 14*(1), 68–79.

Crapanzano, V. (1980). *Tuhami: Portrait of a Moroccan.* Chicago: University of Chicago Press.

Crow Dog, M. (1990). *Lakota woman.* New York: HarperCollins.

Dinesen, I. (1960). *Shadows on the grass.* New York: Random House.

DuBois, E., & Ruiz, V. (Eds.). (1990). *Unequal sisters: A multicultural reader in U.S. women's history.* London: Routledge.

Edelsky, C. (1990). Whose agenda is this anyway?: A response to McKenna, Robinson and Miller. *Educational Researcher, 19*(8), 7–11.

Elmendorf, M. L. (1976). *Nine Mayan women: A village faces change.* Cambridge, MA: Schenkman.

Erdrich, L. (1987). *The beet queen.* New York: Bantam Books.

Freed-Rowland, G. (1991, March). *Valuing diversity.* Paper presented at the International Institute on Peace Studies, Kah-Nee-Tah, OR.

Freed-Rowland, G. (1992, April). *Native-American-Indian women: Our own voices, our own songs, our own landscapes.* Paper presented at the annual meeting of the American Educational Research Association, San Francisco, CA.

Grumet, M. (1988). *Bitter milk: Women and teaching.* Amherst: University of Massachusetts Press.

Hurston, Z. N. (1984). *Dust tracks on a road: An autobiography* (R. Hemingway, Ed.). Chicago: University of Illinois Press.

Kingston, M. (1989). *The woman warrior.* New York: Vintage Books.

Kluckhohn, C. (1962). *Culture and behavior: Collected essays.* New York: Free Press of Glencoe.

Kozol, J. (1980). *The night is dark and I am far from home.* New York: Continuum.

Kyle, D., & Hovda, R. (1987). Teachers as action researchers: A discussion of developmental, organizational, and policy issues. *Peabody Journal of Education, 64*(2), 80–95.

Langness, L., & Frank, G. (1981). *Lives: An anthropological approach to biography.* Novato, CA: Chandler & Sharp.

Lieberman, A. (1986, February). Collaborative research: Working with, not working on. . . . *Educational Leadership, 43*(5), 28–33.

Lurie, N. (1966). *Mountain Wolf Woman, sister of Crashing Thunder: The autobiography of a Winnebago Indian.* Ann Arbor: University of Michigan Press.

Mandelbaum, D. (1973). The study of life history: Gandhi. *Current Anthropology, 14*(3), 177–206.

Mascia-Lees, F., Sharpe, P., & Cohen, C. (1989). The postmodernist turn in anthropology: Cautions from a feminist perspective. *Signs, 15*(1), 7–34.

Minh-ha, T. (1987). Difference: A special third world women issue. *Feminist Review, 25*(1), 5–22.

Minh-ha, T. (1988). Not you/like you: Post colonial women and the interlocking questions of identity and difference. *Inscriptions, 3/4,* 71–77.

Momaday, N. S. (1968). *House made of dawn.* New York: Harper & Row.

Munro, P. (1992, April). *Teaching as women's work: A century of resistant voices.* Paper presented at the annual meeting of the American Educational Research Association, San Francisco, CA.

Myerhoff, B. (1975). *Symbol and politics in communal ideology: Cases and questions.* Ithaca, NY: Cornell University Press.

Ong, A. (1988). Colonialism and modernity: Feminist re-presentations of women in non-western societies. *Inscriptions, 3/4,* 79–93.

Patai, D. (1989). *Brazilian women speak: Contemporary life stories.* New Brunswick, NJ: Rutgers University Press.

Personal Narratives Group. (1989). *Interpreting women's lives: Feminist theory and personal narratives.* Bloomington: Indiana University Press.

Proudfoot, R. (1990). *Even the birds don't sound the same here: The Laotian refugees' search for heart in American culture.* New York: Peter Lang.

Rabinow, P. (1977). *Reflections on field work in Morocco.* Berkeley: University of California Press.

Richardson, M. (1975). Anthropologist—the myth teller. *American Ethnologist, 2*(3), 517–533.

Romero, M. (1991, April). *The maid's daughter: A modern version of upstairs/downstairs.* Paper presented to the Center for the Study of Women in Society, University of Oregon, Eugene.

Silko, L. M. (1977). *Ceremony.* New York: Penguin Books.

Simmon, L. W. (1942). *Sun chief: The autobiography of a Hopi Indian.* New Haven: Yale University Press.

Souers, T. (1992, April). *Circles of power: Native American Indian women in education.* Paper presented at the annual meeting of the American Educational Research Association, San Francisco, CA.

Stacey, J. (1988). Can there be a feminist ethnography? *Women's Studies International Forum, 11*(1), pp. 21–27.

Swann, B., & Krupat, A. (Eds.). (1987a). *I tell you now: Autobiographical essays by Native American writers.* Lincoln: University of Nebraska Press.

Swann, B., & Krupat, A. (Eds.). (1987b). *Recovering the word: Essays on Native American literature.* Los Angeles: University of California Press.

Tallmountain, M. (1987). You can go home again: A sequence. In B. Swann & A. Krupat (Eds.), *I tell you now: Autobiographical essays by Native American writers* (pp. 1–13). Lincoln: University of Nebraska Press.

Watson, L., & Watson-Sparks, F. (1985). *Interpreting life histories: An anthropological inquiry.* New Brunswick, NJ: Rutgers University Press.

Whorf, B. (1956). *Language, thought and reality* (J. Carroll, Ed.). Cambridge, MA: MIT Press.

Wolcott, H. (1990). *Writing up qualitative research.* Newbury Park, CA: Sage.

# CHAPTER 8

# "I Felt Like We Were Rats or Something":
# The Problem of Imposition in Participatory Research

*Susan Victor*

Rachel's comment, coming at the end of the first in a series of interviews, evoked images for me of the basement of Tolman Hall, the psychology building at U.C. Berkeley where I did my undergraduate work in psychology, a basement floor filled with rat mazes, Skinner boxes, cages with wire- and cloth-covered monkeys, and other artifacts of experimental research. I could smell that smell which emanated throughout the building, and wondered why Pine's words, "the straight-jacket of experimental research," kept running through my mind (Pine, 1986).

In one sentence, Rachel, one of several adolescent mothers and coresearchers in this study, conveys the message that even seemingly collaborative participatory research can be experienced by "subjects" as impositional. My goal was to engage in research which was "emancipatory" (Lather, 1986) and to avoid those qualitative methods highlighted by Stacey (1988) and Munro (1993) as exploitative. My belief—that in order to be personally ethical and socially meaningful, research must be of a collaborative nature—embraced several requirements: First, the research process must generate research which is least impositional. Second, the goal of research should be to foster personal and social change. Third, the researcher–researched relationship must be nonexploitative. Fourth and finally, the study must be ethical and meaningful in process and product for all participants.

Despite or perhaps due to my beliefs, problems of imposition can and do exist in participatory research, as the study which is the focus of this chapter demonstrates. In sharing brief anecdotes of interviews from a retrospective participatory research project which involved a group of adolescent mothers, I highlight problems of imposition by reflecting on the following questions: Whose interests were protected or served by this project? To what degree did the project compound oppression or exploitation, or foster emancipation and empowerment of a group marginalized by peers, family, and society? What was the sponsoring agency's role as it imposed its needs on me (as the staff member-turned-researcher) and on the participants in this study? How did my changing role and relationship to the participants (i.e., from group counselor or facilitator to researcher) affect the process and outcome of the study? And, ultimately, what did it mean to be a participant?

## PARTICIPATORY RESEARCH, OR RESEARCH WHICH IS LEAST IMPOSITIONAL

Cancian (1989) describes the participatory research process as a "dialogue" in which researchers learn to identify specific ways in which they are oppressed. Such knowledge is produced through democratic, interactive relationships (Cancian, 1989). Knowledge is viewed as power, and all participants are viewed as holding expertise (Hall, 1988). The participatory research process involves a mutual sharing of perceptions and a collaborative production of knowledge. The product of participatory research is knowledge which is tied to the "daily struggles of ordinary people" (Gaventa, 1988).

Participatory research differs from action research in the degree of collaboration. Action research is applied research; it involves change, but the choice of method and the process itself are not necessarily collaborative (McKernan, 1988). The goal still is change in the lives of those considered socially "less powerful," by producing knowledge of their oppression. Research can still be participatory, according to Tandon (1988), even though the researcher chooses the initial problem—if she makes her ideology explicit, the method becomes participatory investigation, and the outcome leads to social change.

Participatory research allows for the emergence of problems in participant interactions and reflects the reality that curriculum, as suggested by Grumet (1988) and others, is a process; it cannot be a finite package. For the context of this study, participatory research served as a model for curriculum development and evaluation; it was through the research process that I hoped to allow for the emergence of a curriculum formed by the lives of adolescent mothers, not one created by an outsider. Alternatives to the unequal power in developing knowledge in the form of curriculum parallel the goals of participatory research as an alternative to the often unequal research relationship. Chitra Naik's study of young working girls in Pune, India, is one example of such a model (Naik, 1987). Naik and her colleagues engaged 400 working girls in a participatory research project in order to create curriculum which would fulfill their immediate needs and be congruent with their experience, that is, an experience which forces them to leave school at age 7 or 8 in order to support the family. The process and outcome of that study reinforced my desire to create curriculum for the adolescent mothers which reflected their identity and their needs.

In order to connect the methodology under question here with the context and purpose of the study, I will briefly summarize where my choice of participatory research as a methodology and as a model for curriculum development merges with my philosophy that curriculum be emergent and thus meaningful, process-oriented, and socially constructed. First, both share the same underlying phenomenological philosophy. Second, both processes "empower" the participants by shared control over decision making and construction of knowledge. The relationships between researcher and researched, and between curriculum developer and recipient, become democratic, interactive, and, one hopes, more egalitarian. Third and following this, the participants are just that—active participants. Fourth, both are clearly political processes in that they resist a hierarchical nature and imply social change. Finally, and especially important to me, each process is the least impositional because efforts are collaborative and ultimately (I hope) in the best interests (in process and product) of the participants.

The participatory research method seemed to fit my goal because the participants were to be included and the process seemed congruent with the outcome. I saw curriculum, especially in this context, as an ongoing process and saw my role to make explicit the adolescent mothers' implicit, socially constructed, emergent curriculum. My goal was to foster the emergence of their curriculum.

## THE RESEARCHER AS SUBJECT

Lather (1986) suggests that in emancipatory research, data are generated from people within relationships. The researcher's "self-disclosure" is essential, as she joins the participants in what is essentially a collaborative process of self-analysis. Interviews, when conducted in an interactive dialogic manner, require self-disclosure on the part of the researcher. The goal of such research is to encourage self-reflection or what Campbell (1990) refers to as reflexivity— to be reflective and sensitive to all forms of communication, in order to understand both "knower and known."

Chevigny (1984) describes what happens in the process of women researching women: "I suppose that it is nearly inevitable that women writing about women will symbolically reflect their internalized relationships with their others, and in some measure, re-create them" (p. 358). Through the process of projecting one's own experience onto "subjects," the researcher (unconsciously) identifies with the subjects' experience. Chevigny (1984) highlights this identification with the subjects as a risk as well as an opportunity; the understanding of the subjects is enhanced by an awareness of their effects on the self of the researcher. The relationship may allow for a "deeper and clearer appreciation of the subject than usually accompanies objectivity" (Chevigny, 1984: 359). The subject serves a "mirroring function," allowing the researcher to satisfy her needs for self-knowledge without abusing the subject.

Levesque-Lopman (1990) is critical of the tendency to view subjectivity as "suspicious" and to fear that it will contaminate data. What is needed, she argues, is an acknowledgment of the researcher's stance or place in relation to the subjects. The researcher's "direct experience of the world" must be acknowledged as the primary ground of her research. The definitions of "subject" and "object" change when women research women and especially when the focus or the curriculum of the research encompasses experiences shared only by women, for example, pregnancy and childbirth (Levesque-Lopman, 1990).

It is my belief that research is at its core a search for self-knowledge, a wish to see ourselves in the "data," affirmed in the experiences of the "subjects." My political motive in this study—to foster the voices of adolescent mothers—is fueled not only by my desire to be an advocate for marginalized adolescents, but also by a personal wish that someone had spoken up for my parents and their relatives during the Holocaust. Moreover, at a level of understanding which came into awareness only at the end of my time with the young mothers, I realized that in our connection and disconnection were reflections of my relationship with my own (teenage) mother. To that extent, the subjects served a "mirroring function" for me.

## THE BIRTH OF A RELATIONAL CURRICULUM

After 19 months and 70 meetings, I attempted, with this retrospective study, to present the experiences (the emergent, relational curriculum) of adolescent mothers as reflected in the discussions, among the voices of, the 38 women in a teenage parent education/support group. For the purposes of this study, the group served as the context for an examination of the developmental issues of adolescent girls and mothers. Through a self-reflective analysis of my journals, a critical examination of curriculum materials and agency expectations, and most important, the verbal reflections of the young mothers who directly participated in the analysis phase of this study, I attempted to answer questions about the meaning of pregnancy and mothering, adolescent relationships, and the life experiences of adolescent mothers in a particular social-economic context. This study brought together assumptions I hold in regard to the development of girls/women, to definitions of curriculum, to an understanding of human interaction, to the meaning of mothering, and, as I have shared above, to ethical and meaningful research.

The women who participated in this study formed the core of the group for 19 months. At the time of this study, all were 20 or 21. Most were European American, one was Native American, and most were unaffiliated Christians. Of the five who received high school diplomas, three completed requirements at a special school (a self-contained classroom housed in a church) for adolescent parents. Two attended college; one was in her third year at a university. The average length of membership in the program while it was the focus of this analysis was 15.2 months, with a range of 9–19 months.

The primary sources for analysis were my journals or field notes of the 70 group sessions with a total of 38 adolescent mothers; curriculum and agency materials were also included. Four group interviews served as the tool with which we all reflected on the group experience. I asked open-ended questions from four perspectives: the emergent curriculum; the participants' relationships with me and each other; their development as girls, women, and mothers in this context; and their participation in this research. The first two group interviews were more directed, with a focus on the first three items listed above; the second two were used to share the ongoing analysis of my journals and to gather their reactions to the collaborative nature of this study. In addition, I interviewed the two participants who had been members of the group for the entire 19-month period, asking questions regarding their participation in the group, their relationship with me, personally relevant themes in the curriculum, and beliefs about self, mothering, and group support.

## DATA AS CONTENT AND PROCESS

The first group interview was scheduled for the normal meeting time for the group. Although this mutual scheduling decision was based, at least overtly, on convenience, it became clear to me that other dynamics informed the decision. It was a clue when Mariah called me to say, "I heard you were coming back for a month," that the 2-month period in between my departure as the facilitator and my return as the researcher had not diminished the need to keep me in the facilitator role. Her comment served as a warning to me that the transition, whether real or illusory, would not occur without difficulty.

The five women present reacted initially to the tape recorder and stack of consent forms with quiet glances of suspicion and several minutes of sharing reactions to the transition. They commented that it "did not feel the same" and that they were "afraid of another good-bye." At the close of the interview, they voiced their preference for another meeting time (different from the normal group meeting time) and, in a symbolic gesture of participation, insisted on changing the pseudonyms I had given them.

In between the first and second group interviews, I interviewed two participants, Carly and Shaina, individually. Carly was, at the time, a 21-year-old college student and single mother of Amy, 5. Carly had given birth to Amy in the summer between her sophomore and junior years in high school. A serious A student, bound for college and a career as an elementary school teacher, Carly shocked friends and family (especially her religious mother) with her relationship and the pregnancy. Amy's birth father, Drew (a "deli-rat"), seemingly represented everything Carly disdained. At the time of Amy's birth, Carly wrote "unknown" next to "father," preferring that Amy have no legal father rather than one with whom neither she nor Amy would have a future relationship. Drew died in a car accident several months after Amy's birth.

Shaina, a close friend of Carly's from high school, became pregnant with Damon, her 2½ year old, early in her senior year. Unsure about the relationship but determined to be a mother, Shaina convinced Rick, her boyfriend, that his remaining in the relationship would have no impact on her decision to keep the baby. Despite the fact that most teachers denied her opportunities to participate, Shaina graduated 3 months before her due date. She and Rick married shortly after Damon's birth.

Carly's and Shaina's responses to questions similar to those in the first two group interviews provided, to some extent, areas of direction for the subsequent group interviews. In this sense, they served as key informants, although I did not acknowledge them as such. These interviews, more importantly, brought into focus two aspects of the facilitator-turned-researcher dilemma, one a problem, the other a possible advantage. Carly's questions during the interview about the extent of group friendships represented an important process issue in group development.

> It's like we're all best friends in group, but when we're outside, it's totally different, because I don't talk to anyone until someone calls to ask if I'm coming to group. . . . I feel close enough to share, but not close enough to call to share or chat or whatever. . . . I could be taking up their time for chores, as they could be taking up my study time.

Carly describes the relationships among group members as those of "adult friends," who gather to share once per week but resist "intruding" on each other's separate lives. I struggled with the recognition of this issue in the group process and the urge to become involved in facilitating it, but knowing I could not. I had a similar reaction to Shaina's description of shifting alliances in the group and to the implicit leadership of another participant, Rachel. My struggles were reminiscent of the dilemma faced by Leslie Roman in her study of young punk women. Roman recognized the abusive relationships her subjects were in, but knew that the limitations of the researcher role prevented her from intervening (Roman, 1989). For me, the struggle was intensified because I knew the members individually as well as the group as a whole and had served in the formal role of group facilitator. Did my responsibilities as a counselor end because I had made myself the researcher?

Similarly, Carly's emotional vulnerability during the interview made it difficult to continue to ask questions and to seek information, when, as a counselor, I knew she needed to explore the feelings. The advantage of our relationship, however, became clear in her comments:

If you had been a stranger, I wouldn't talk about the same things. I'd be superficial, with less detail. . . . I would have had more self-control, question-answer type thing, not all the grisly details.

She implies she would not have shared the "grisly details," the in-depth descriptions or the accompanying feelings, had she not had a relationship with me. This raises a question about conducting research with adolescents who are typically reluctant to share without the trust familiarity brings. It raised a larger question for me, one I will revisit, as to whether I could engage in ethical and meaningful research without a prior relationship with the "subjects."

The second group interview took place at what became our regular time—2 hours prior to their group meeting time. Due to the very real imposition of unreliable child care, we were forced to meet in the nursery and attempt to record over the noise of the children playing. Despite their obvious frustration with the interruptions, the participants became involved in the interview immediately. I experienced that same struggle of facilitator/researcher, as I could not always resist the urge to "process" their reactions to the children in the room. The awkwardness resulted in several periods of silence; questions about individual roles in the group prompted, however, enthusiastic and affectionate responses. The interview ended with a comparison or rather a contrast to the first one. They described it as "easier" or "better" or "almost like group"; Rachel commented, "I know where you're coming from." I attributed their reactions to three possibilities: the presence of the children, the absence of paperwork, and perhaps, a less than conscious recognition of my struggle with the role.

Two related events occurred during the 3-week interval between the second and third interviews which represent further problems of imposition in the research process. The first was that the present staff facilitator left suddenly to attend to her dying mother in another state. The second event was that Shaina assumed responsibility for organizing the three subsequent interviews; this included calling each participant and arranging child care. Although the latter on the surface facilitated the process, both events posed additional dilemmas for me in this role. The coordinator of the program, rightfully concerned about Shaina's ability to sustain the group through the facilitator's absence, asked me to be available to her as a backup. Moreover, she and other members of the staff minimized concerns about the group by noting that I would "be there" a few times, in reference to the scheduled interviews. The underlying assumption was that, regardless of the boundaries I was attempting to maintain around the researcher role, I should (and could) be available as the facilitator. It placed me in a bind, especially when Mariah asked me pointedly at the next interview if I planned to stay for the group. I did not.

I will digress here briefly to describe the relationship between myself and Shaina. At 21, Shaina was the oldest in the group. As her 21st birthday approached in May 1990, the tension surrounding her seemingly inevitable departure increased. (The provision that the program served only parents through age 21 loomed over the heads of these young women. My reassurances notwithstanding, they seemed to feel tremendous concern over the impending separation.) Although I was sure I could find a way to keep Shaina in the group until the others turned 21, she did not feel reassured until she approached me with the idea of being a "cofacilitator." (This is an aspect of the adult parent program, in which a "mentor" is chosen to lead the group, in order to allow the group to become autonomous.) The arrangement satisfied the program coordinator and Shaina. Although she remained clearly a participant, she became anxious to help; she took over buying the snacks, making a few reminder calls, and helping to arrange child care or rides. The role provided Shaina with an experience she had never had before—"feeling special."

> What I'm told is that they look up to me. I have a hard time understanding why. I never had . . . why? I'm nothing special but group makes me feel special. That's what I like. I really like that. . . . I'm that special person I've never been. It feels good.

Providing snacks and some telephone contact led to greater responsibilities for Shaina after my departure as the facilitator in October 1990. Although the agency provided a new facilitator—as I mentioned earlier—this person missed several early group sessions, leaving Shaina the responsibility of "holding group together." She reflects:

> Now, I could be wrong, but I think people think, Shaina's going to hold us together. I feel like if I left, then everybody else would leave. I don't want to sound conceited or anything. I'm not trying to; I just felt like, after you left, I would have left, it would have fell apart. So, I kind of felt like I held it together; you know, by calling them, calling new members, reassuring them I'm not going to leave.

Shaina's leadership in the research process could be interpreted in a number of ways. I question whether it was a channel for continued approval from and connection with me by, in a sense, taking care of me. Through the relationship, she could continue to feel "special." On an explicit level, she may have perceived her responsibilities as a cofacilitator to extend to the research context. I allowed her to do so, colluded with her. Should I have surfaced our mutual motives?

The third group interview began with a discussion of the facilitator's absence, comparisons with me, and a recognition of their reliance on Shaina during the transition. Erica and Denisa joined this interview. It was revealing to watch how the others initiated them into the interview process by telling them they needed a "new name" and by sharing their perceptions of the responses made in the first two interviews. The tone of this interview reflected a recognition of collaboration on some thing and a recognition that this "thing" was not group. In a brief digression, Rachel asked Mariah about the status of her relationship, but was interrupted by Carly, who said, "Wait until the next group." The others obliged quickly and turned to me, awaiting the next question! Although Carly continued to use the word "group" to describe both meetings, she (and, it seems, the others) made a distinction between the two contexts.

Denisa's presence prompted a brief return to the issue of my leaving. Having not seen me prior to this for 3 months, she explained her absence as a reluctance to return because she had never said good-bye to me. Others took this as a cue to share their reactions and their efforts to remain a cohesive group. This was one of several moments again in which I did not know how to facilitate their reactions while continuing with the research and negotiating my own guilt.

Although she knew she could call me during the intervening week in the event of a crisis, Shaina did not. I experienced a sense of relief, although I could not pretend I was not concerned about the group. The fourth interview began slowly, but was ultimately the most productive in deconstructing my analysis of the group content and process. Using the analysis of my journals to prompt their recollections seemed effective. By the last half-hour of the interview, an example from me prompted Mariah or another participant to supply the question as well as the response. The extent of their responses reflected the importance of the particular issue in their experience of the group. This time, they did not ask if I planned to stay for the group session which followed. As I left with a mental image of Shaina organizing snacks, child care, and other aspects of the group, I realized in my own sense of abandonment that my relationship with the group had indeed changed.

In hindsight, I attribute my lack of sensitivity to the underlying tone of the final interview to my horrible cold or maybe to my final transition to researcher. The process of the final interview revealed almost more than the content, in regard at least to problems in participation. The interview began with short responses to my analysis and a review of some pertinent issues and how these affected the overall group content, as well as an extension of the discussion of group roles. Coming to the end of close to 5 weeks without a facilitator, Shaina and the other members were beginning to feel the burden and to realize the difficulty in Shaina's attempting to be both participant and facilitator. They began to question whether it is possible to be a participant and a facilitator simultaneously. This exchange provided Shaina with an opportunity to express her discomfort at being put on a "facilitator pedestal when [she has] the same problems as the others do." As Shaina struggled to understand her ambivalence about the role, Erica jumped in:

If you're a facilitator, you feel like you're supposed to listen more than put in your opinion, your ideas, how you feel, what upset you last week. Oh, I shouldn't be saying that. I'm supposed to be listening to them, because that's what you and Connie have always done.

Shaina then pointed to the distinction that they (the group members) knew "everything" about each other but nothing about the facilitators (myself and Connie, my replacement), alluding to the difficulty of being both inside and outside the group.

At the close of the interview, I inquired about their overall experience with the research process. Several highlighted how it differed from group in that I asked "too many questions," and they could not "get into a topic" which interested them because "we're doing this." Some resentment underlying these comments was reflected also in the way I perceived they took control of this last interview; their responses to the final analysis were short, and they kept returning to an issue of concern to them in that moment (i.e., the facilitator's prolonged absence). Rachel's question on why I had left them for another group" startled me, though it should not have. I grasped for explanations, emphasizing, as they had just done, how the role of researcher conflicts with the role of facilitator. As I left, Rachel shared that she was expressing feelings "others" had had, especially Shaina.

In a telephone conversation with Shaina that evening, she shared that seeing my words in the agency's newsletter about the "other group" had saddened her. (At the time, I was serving as a trainer and consultant for another group.) The issue was not the research directly, but the fact that I had left "for another group." She also explained to me that the tone of the last interview reflected the members' concern that it was the last one and that they would have to say good-bye again. I had neglected to address this, being focused on completing the interview. Moreover, I had not perceived the interview as an end to our collaboration.

## POSTPARTUM REFLECTIONS

The misunderstandings described above point to a dilemma throughout this process, a dilemma represented in the terms "subject" and "object." For the purposes of this research, I needed these seven women to be "subjects"; did they in the end feel like "objects"? Did they feel imposed upon or symbolically used or exploited? Was the research a recapitulation of earlier exploitation, abuse, or abandonment? Or was it a channel for their voices, their private knowledge? If my goal was (and continues to be) to surface the discrimination, oppression, and neglect of adolescent mothers, was I in some sense furthering oppression? In the group context, in the language of object relations theory, they needed me to be (and to remain) the "object." I, however, increasingly became the "subject," the maternal figure who experienced the countertransference of abandonment and the urge to take care of others, as well as a very conscious desire to complete this study. Like Shaina, I struggled with being inside and outside the group.

In defining who I was in relationship to the young mothers, I found it necessary to reconcile the researcher role with the service provider role. As I discovered in my attempts to be both advocate and service provider, these roles bring with them contradictory agendas. In the case of the latter (and really in both cases), sustaining social stereotypes of adolescent mothers as "at risk" was necessary from the agency's perspective because funding is contingent upon maintaining this group's "at-risk" status. However, sustaining stereotypes is the opposite of empowerment and certainly contradicts the goals of participatory research. Perhaps it is not possible to be simultaneously an advocate and a service provider when, at least in this case, the functions seem to be at cross-purposes. The participatory research context, however, allowed me to continue to be their advocate, by engaging their voices. Yet I arrive at only one conclusion that feels like a conclusion: I cannot do research on or even with anyone without a relationship in which I give something back, be it emotional support or an opportunity for self-knowledge and voice. Ultimately, the relationship becomes the data but the relationship only exists for me in my ability to provide something. With this realization, the three roles—researcher, advocate, service provider—blur into one because it is less important to know who I am than how I am in relationship to the young mothers.

Is the goal of participatory research—to foster recognition of the ways in which a group is oppressed and to facilitate action—in itself an imposition? In the final 3 weeks of this study, several women began to speak publicly about their experiences with discrimination. Invited to speak to the media on behalf of the agency, they spoke instead of frustrations with doctors and prevailing social stereotypes. Beneath the administration's acerbic comment to me, "They talked about doctors," seemed to be the question, "What have you been teaching them?" At a conference of a state early childhood organization, at which several participants and I presented the preliminary analysis of the group's experience, they were asked not to speak at the agency's presentation. As the participants followed me into the buffet lunch for presenters, an official approached them, insisting they did not belong in the "presenters only" section. As Rachel pointed to their name tags, I reflected that the result of "emancipation" and "empowerment" was the message they should remain not seen and not heard. Physically and symbolically, they were in places where they should not be. In response to these events, Shaina expressed an urge to hide, to retreat into silence if their voices were "causing trouble." As I affirmed how hard she had worked to overcome her "shyness," I saw the agency as a domineering father, myself trying to be the good mother, and the participants as children who knew the truth, but should be neither seen nor heard. I wondered, if the participatory research process had indeed given them "voice," did prevailing stereotypes and contradictory agendas threaten to take it away?

Finally, there is a danger in assuming that adolescent mothers do not hear what research says. Lesko points out that most studies of adolescent mothers focus on sexual irresponsibility, bad mothering, and hopelessness (Lesko, 1990). Researchers convey a sense of blame and hopelessness by emphasizing the inevitability that the children of adolescent mothers will be dysfunctional or disadvantaged. The tendency in research on adolescent parenting is not only to blame the mother (the victim), but also to ignore her as a young woman with her own developmental tasks and as a subject with her own voice.

## A POSTSCRIPT

As I sit at my desk with a draft of this chapter, wondering how best to conclude it when I really am left with questions at the end similar to those I had at the beginning, the mail comes and with it a postcard from Shaina, and with the postcard, an answer to my questions.

> I have six weeks left [of a second pregnancy] and it's going slowly. Everything is fine except I'm tired a lot and grouchy. I wish you could be here. I really need a friend to talk to. Rick doesn't seem interested in this baby. It feels lonely, it hurts, and I don't know what to do.

## REFERENCES

Campbell, J. K. (1990). Inside lives: The quality of biography. In R. R. Sherman & R. B. Webb (Eds.), *Qualitative research in education: Focus and methods* (pp. 59–75). London: Falmer.

Cancian, F. (1989). Feminism and participatory research. *CSWS Review* (pp. 29–32). Center for the Study of Women in Society, University of Oregon, Eugene.

Chevigny, B. G. (1984). Daughters writing: Toward a theory of women's biography. In C. Ascher, L. DeSalvo, & S. Ruddick (Eds.), *Between women* (pp. 357–381). Boston: Beacon Press.

Gaventa, J. (1988). Participatory research in North America. *Convergence, 21*(2/3), 19–26.

Grumet, M. (1988). *Bitter milk: Women and teaching.* Amherst: University of Massachusetts Press.

Hall, B. L. (1988). Participatory research, popular knowledge and power: A personal reflection. *Convergence, 21*(2/3), 6–15.

Lather, P. (1986). Research as praxis. *Harvard Educational Review, 56*(3), 257–277.

Lesko, N. (1990, April). *Social context and the "problem" of teenage pregnancy.* Paper presented at the American Educational Research Association, Boston, MA.

Levesque-Lopman, J. (1990). *Claiming reality: Phenomenology and women's experience.* New York: Rowman & Littlefield.

McKernan, J. (1988). Dialogue . . . dialogue . . . dialogue: Teacher as researcher: Paradigm and praxis. *Contemporary Education, 59*(3), 154–157.

Munro, P. (1993). Continuing dilemmas of life history research: A reflexive account of feminist qualitative inquiry. In D. Flinders & G. Mills (Eds.), *Theory and concepts in qualitative research: Perspectives from the field* (pp. 163–177). New York: Teachers College Press.

Naik, C. (1987). Educating rural girls: A review of an action-research project. *International Review of Education, 33,* 495–501.

Pine, G. (1986). Collaborative action research and staff development in the middle school. *Middle School Journal, 18*(1), 33–35.

Roman, L. G. (1989, April). *Double exposure: The politics of feminist materialist ethnography.* Paper presented at the American Educational Research Association, San Francisco, CA.

Stacey, J. (1988). Can there be a feminist ethnography? *Women's Studies International Forum, 11*(1), 21–27.

Tandon, R. (1988). Social transformation and participatory research. *Convergence, 21*(2/3), 5–14.

# CHAPTER 9

## Research as Autobiography: Imposition/Life

*Janice Jipson*

*I construct a biography of my own identity, the strengths, the crises, the shattered myths. What I learn from research, I learn from myself.*

&#x223D;

My plane is somewhere over Idaho—flying into the sunset, orange and then blue over the top of the thunderheads—going back, to the West Coast. My thoughts drift, seeking the metaphor to connect my experiences and my work to the events of the past few months. Weaving? No, there are no separate threads, no points of connection that I can discern. A symphony? Too complicated—I could never pick out the patterns in the seemingly discordant cacophony. A story or a play? Writing suggests an impending climax which is frightening in its deliberativeness. I am tempted to believe that the closing of the University of Oregon Teacher Education Program was an unexpected catastrophe, the accidental result of the chaos of our universe—and that my colleagues and I were the undeserving victims. That, of course, is not true.

&#x223D;

*To understand what has happened is inconceivable without metaphor. The real stories are too painful. So to search my memory for understanding, I settle, temporarily perhaps, on a travel narrative, an itinerary—not the adventuresome and purposeful trip across the Oregon Trail that I fantasized about as a child, but rather something reminiscent of an old Jim Croce song: "I've been up and down and round about and back again. Been so many places, I don't remember who or when . . . And I found myself right back where I started again." A grand tour through a looking glass, back.*

&#x223D;

I never thought of being a researcher, growing up in northern Wisconsin. In fact, I probably had no idea that such a role existed. Girls of my generation, if they were ambitious, could become teachers or nurses. There were no women's clubs in Glen Flora except for the Mission Circles and Ladies Aid Society of the Protestant churches. Not to work outside the home, for most of the women in my community, still meant a life of outdoor work, in the fields, the barns, the farmyards. My positioning had been rural, Baptist, working class. I did not realize what I had not learned until I got to college—that a whole other cultural experience was part of other people's lives. Classical music, dance, theater, museums became the curricular content for my first crash course in doing research. I wanted to know how other people lived. Years of curriculum and research courses later, I realize that my early personal experiences frame the only things I can ever know for sure.

༄

*I struggle with the idea of "doing research" right. The multiple regressions which I perform seem to be in my own imagination. I resist the imposition of proper research design, the imperatives of objectivity, validity, and subject–object opposi-tions, and I play with the fleeting, provisional nature of meaning and voice, the multiple forms of testimony and confession, the devices of self-representation and critical/personal narrative. Petra sends me Patti Lather's (1993) article on a reconceptualized validity "that is grounded in theorizing our practice" (p. 674), a "'rhizomatic validity' that undermines stability, subverts and unsettles from within" (p. 680), on an authority that "comes from engagement and self-reflexivity, not distanced 'objectivity'" (p. 682). And then, sometimes, I succumb to the conventions, insert the parentheses and the attributions, as I struggle to identify the soul of my inquiry. My only area of expertise seems to be myself.*

## BEGINNINGS

My birth family lived, surrounded by grandparents, aunts, uncles, and cous-ins, in a small rural town in northern Wisconsin where my great-grandparents had settled when they immigrated from Scandinavia and Germany. Although they were primarily farmers, the family tradition to teach and serve was strong. My great-grandmother had come from Sweden to be a missionary in North Dakota. My grandfather kept store in a logging camp and, when the trees were finally gone, became a farmer and a lay preacher. My great-aunt began teaching in a one-room country school when she was 16 and later became a nurse.

༄

*So, how to start. Leigh Gilmore (1994) begins* Autobiographics: A Feminist Theory of Women's Self-Representation *with an introduction entitled "Getting Lost" (p. 1), describing how "autobiography wraps up the interrupted and frag-mentary discourse of identity, those stories we tell ourselves and are told, which hold us together as persons" (p. 17). Even in her articulate context, however, making sense of my own life seems a potentially narcissistic endeavor—deciding which stories to tell, imposing them on others.*

∽

My childhood was spent within the extended families of my parents. Although my father served as a medic in the Pacific islands during World War II, he returned home after the war and worked in a lumberyard, a concrete plant, and as a carpenter. My mother also taught in a one-room country school and finally completed her college degree in elementary education when I was 14 years old. She continued to teach throughout my childhood while my sisters and brother and I were left in the care of our grandmothers. I did not realize while growing up that it was unusual for a mother of the 1950s to have a full-time teaching career. Observing the work of my friends' mothers who were farm wives, I felt my mother was fortunate to be able to teach.

∽

*Cynthia Cohen (1991) states that when we tell our stories, we construct a biography of our own cultural identity, our strengths, our crises . . . the shattered myths we live by. I consider her words. They fit my own messy and intuitive beliefs about how human beings should learn from each other, about how none of us have the right to deliberately impose our perspectives on any experience other than our own. I am also reminded of Elizabeth Ellsworth (1989), who suggests that the relation "between teachers/students becomes voyeuristic when the voice of the pedagogue . . . goes unexamined" (p. 312). My colleagues struggle with the ethical issues, in doing life-history research, of power and representation that arise in action research projects. My quest is to invent an autobiographic inquiry: a methodology through which to explore my own life as an academic; a methodology with which to find the patterns for understanding what has happened to me as a teacher and as a woman; a method for imposing meaning on my own life.*

∽

I grew up with family stories and with the expectation that I, too, would contribute to my community and to those who were "less fortunate" than I. The stories were shared mostly by my grandmother and mother to teach my sisters and me of our responsibility to others. My mother told of my grandmother giving her mother's cherry wood bedroom set to a new family in the community and of how my grandfather would always turn over the contents of the Sunday church collection plate to poorer families in the congregation. Tithing was strictly practiced, and outgrown clothes were sent to the missions in Africa and China. Obligation and sharing were taken for granted.

I thought of my childhood as ordinary. We lived on the edge of town and I was free to roam the countryside, the big sister taking care of younger sisters and cousins. I believe I was fortunate. My normal school–trained teachers had been primarily influenced by John Dewey and the project method of education. We built twig forts, learned Central American songs and dances, and went on field trips to sketch trees and streams. I read constantly and daydreamed about living alone on a mountain top and writing poetry. In seventh grade, my mother was my teacher and I learned to be polite, always well prepared, and silent—to truly be a "good girl."

The lessons of my girlhood were accumulating—I vowed I would live a life of kindness, silence, and, above all, work. If I did these things well enough, I would be rewarded with the respect and security of my family and community that my mother, grandmothers, and aunts had enjoyed. The predictable liturgy of "happily ever after" was seductive. I did not question its virtue.

∾

*While recognizing that I had been culturally positioned to be a traditional female, I find I do not always mind the essentialism inherent in that identity. I know that it is more complicated than a simple maternal pedagogy, with my need to nurture tied inextricably to my need to create change. Jane Roland Martin (1994) writes: "In our determinations to honor diversity among women, we told one another to restrict our ambitions, limit our sights, beat a retreat from certain topics, refrain from using a rather long list of categories or concepts, and eschew generalization" (p. 631). She adds that "no trap is more dangerous for women than the self-made trap of false difference" (p. 646).*

∾

After high school, I entered the state university on a scholarship, majored in English and psychology, and discovered John Donne, T. S. Eliot, Emerson, and Thoreau, the first "great white masters" to influence my life. I stopped writing my own poetry to read theirs, spending long evenings in pubs and coffeehouses with my new friends discussing what these poets had to say about "our" lives. My mother insisted I become a teacher so I could "support myself" and be independent—her insurance, perhaps, that I would continue the traditions of work and service practiced by the women in my family but also avoid the drudgery of the many farm women in our community. Responding to my own frustration as well as her logic and pressure, I abandoned my planned graduate program in comparative literature and took a position as a high school English teacher.

∾

*But why would I want to tell the story of my own experiences? As Sidonie Smith (1993) reminds her readers, "Autobiographical writing is always a gesture towards publicity, displaying toward an impersonal public an individual's interpretation of experience" (p. 159). What is the impetus behind my self-disclosures? Does my story mean anything to anyone but me? Will it count as knowledge? Or is it again just a narcissistic indulgence?*

∾

I began teaching, at 20, in a southern Wisconsin small town. During the day, I taught literature and composition. Two evenings each week, I tutored Spanish-speaking migrant workers in a nearby camp. Although I enjoyed working with the high schoolers, I felt much more effective as a teacher at the camp. I had increasing difficulty making my senior class study hall be quiet during the last period of the day. I was puzzled that my "remedial" sophomore English class hated *Macbeth* so intensely and that, after teaching the play, I also began to dislike it. I did not understand why the chair of the English department criticized my playing a record of Simon and Garfunkel's popular song, "I Am a Rock" to help these same students understand John Donne's "Meditation 17," which says, "no man is an island."

Believing that the problem was mine, an inadequate understanding of adolescent development and of appropriate pedagogical strategies, I quit my job at the end of the year and returned to graduate school to study psychology. Once again, I silenced my teaching self in deference to the judgments of the school masters, thereby abandoning the high school students and Hispanic families with whom I had built connections.

〰

*The necessities of methodology plague me—there should be themes, interpretations, tensions to explore, or questions at least, I remind myself. How do I interrupt this rushing story to make sense of it, or does it carry a sense of its own? Why do I sense that the story is telling itself?*

〰

I returned to the public schools in 1969 to work in a small rural district as a school psychologist. Although I was no longer teaching English, I recognized the same issues from my earlier teaching experience. I questioned why the self-contained classrooms for the mentally retarded had so many bright and verbal settled migrant children in them. I became involved in an intensive assessment program to re-place these children in regular classrooms. I also joined the elementary staff in their curriculum planning meetings and began to consider the possibilities of open classrooms and child-centered education.

As my interest in younger children grew, I volunteered to teach summer school in a reading enrichment program for migrant children in the community. Once again, I saw the formal curriculum fail. I discovered that the stories we wrote about our personal, everyday experiences such as fishing expeditions, trips to the beach, and playground picnics were much more relevant and effective reading materials for the children than the direct instruction materials the district provided.

I began to think more directly about what I knew about child development and diversity and about how the instructional materials, basal readers, and teaching experiences used in classrooms did not represent, in any way, the life experiences of the poor, rural, and migrant children with whom I worked. Although we had created a strong core of staff committed to transforming elementary education, the school board and superintendent did not agree. They replaced our principal with an advocate of more traditional education, and within a year six of us had resigned in discouragement. Once again, I reluctantly left the "kids" behind and moved on, wondering why I never seemed to be able to "fit in" with the educational systems in which I worked, why I was always attracted to the marginal, the experimental.

～

*Sue Middleton (1993) writes about how her research did not start with her career in the university but "had [its] origins in the conscious and subconscious tensions of a lifetime" (p. 62). I read her words and am somehow relieved, almost comforted by the idea of anticipatory meaning-making.*

～

In 1971, I moved to a teacher preparation position at a small private college in southern Wisconsin and began to learn to be a college teacher. My expanding interest in early childhood education coincided with the birth of my two daughters, and I became involved in the planning and opening of a parent cooperative day care center on the campus. Consistent with the trends of the early '70s, my colleagues and I read Kozol, Dennison, Berne, and Kohl and plotted the transformation of our program into one aimed at "humanizing education." We took our student teachers and cooperating teachers on retreats, taught workshops on active listening, and experimented with using holistic grading. Predictably, the college trustees brought in a new, more conservative dean, and once again, after several years of intense pressure and pain, I left.

The pattern seemed well established: Innovation led inevitably to trouble; good programs were eventually closed; and if one worked very hard, it seemed, and stayed alert, one could figure out when it was time to move on. I still did not get it. I fixated on my bad luck and did not yet recognize the multiple impositions and manipulations of my life by the institutions for which I worked.

～

*I pause to reflect on the repeated issues that seem to be emerging in my story and my complicity in constructing their meaning. I recall reading that "we bring biases and more than biases. We bring idiosyncratic patterns of recognition. We are not, in fact, ever capable of achieving the analytic 'distance' we have long been schooled to seek" (Krieger, 1991: 167).*

～

After working for 2 years in another "dream" program—Head Start—and once again experiencing the frustration of being unable to support my children on the meager salary I earned, I returned to Madison, where my daughters could attend a public school open classroom program and I could go back to school myself. The summer of 1976 was a critical period of intellectual and personal transition for me. Michael Apple's seminar on elementary curriculum introduced me to the idea of "hidden curriculum," which I immediately recognized as providing a framework to account for many of the difficulties I had observed children experiencing in public school. The things that children were best learning in their classrooms frequently were not the curriculum that teachers believed they were teaching. I looked back at my experiences with *Macbeth* and the high school sophomores, at the white houses with picket fences from the basal readers of the migrant students who lived in field shanties, at the Alpha-time letter puppets and Peabody Kit circus posters for the 4-year-old children in the Head Start classrooms who had never been to a shopping center or ridden an elevator. Reflecting on the developmental and cultural disparities between the children with whom I worked and the curriculum I tried to use, I became convinced that creating options for resistance and change was essential.

A second experience that summer helped put what I was learning into a new perspective. The partner of one of my colleagues killed himself. He had just been served with papers for nonsupport of his former wife and children and could not, according to my friend, stand the humiliation of being taken to court and possibly jailed. I completed an assignment for my social issues seminar in the form of a journal where I wrote about his life and connected it to T. S. Eliot's "Love Song of J. Alfred Prufrock," focusing on how he, too, had found himself "pinned and wiggling on the wall," trying to understand the hopelessness he had experienced. "All of these things I'm learning," I wrote, "what do they really have to do with George and Mary and her kids and with me and my kids, too?" I had named the problem but, ironically, still within the patriarchal frame. I was still identifying the problem as happening to "others" but beginning also to recognize myself on that same wall, wriggling to get free.

∽

*I recently read Shoshana Felman and Dori Laub's (1992) consideration of the issues involved with witnessing and testimony and particularly noted their point that "as readers we are witnesses . . . to these questions we do not own and do not yet understand, but which summon and beseech us from within the literary texts" (p. xiii). I wonder, did I anticipate then, in the experiences of those days, the questions of privilege and oppression that now haunt me?*

∽

Graduate school had become a blur: classes, a day job at the university, evening teaching in the local technical college day care apprenticeship program, two children to support. I began reading poems, autobiography, and novels again, this time discovering the feminists Doris Lessing, Nadine Gordimer, Marge Piercy, Adrienne Rich, May Sarton, and later Tillie Olsen. Their stories spoke to my experience in a way that traditional educational texts and my favorite male poets never had. I began to view my work through my life experience as a woman. Reading, I identified my alienation from the elite world of the university and my reality as a mother and teacher. In 1979, I dropped to part-time status as a doctoral student and accepted a teaching position at a local private college, hoping to regain balance in my life.

My new job provided me with a haven in which to reflect upon what I wanted to do. The Dominican nuns shared my social commitment and supported me in integrating the campus preschool with Head Start children and in starting a campus day care center for faculty and students. After finishing my degree, however, I took a much better paying position in the public university system.

Once again, I realize now, I had sacrificed a position where I believe transformation was possible for a more comfortable job and the convenience of an adequate salary. A new baby and a lovely Victorian house did not, however, distract me for long from the basic philosophical discontinuities between my child-centered approach to education and the behavioral psychology of my direct instruction–oriented colleagues. Although appreciating the need for ideological diversity in academe, I chose to move once again, this time to a position at the University of Oregon, where I felt the faculty and programs were consistent with my strongly held personal beliefs.

## MIDDLES

*Writing the rest of this story is even more difficult. There is the fear of inadequately representing the multiple dimensions of personal experience tangled with the complexities of economic and political issues. It is no longer just my story. But is it still autobiography? A case study? Action research? I reread Patti Lather's (1993) article where she asks, "How does a researcher work to not see so easily in telling stories that belong to others?" (p. 684).*

∾

I had joined an elementary faculty which shared my commitment to implementing progressive education: whole-language instruction, integrated curriculum, constructivist teaching, and multicultural education. Several of my colleagues had prior experience with the alternative educational models of the '70s and shared my commitment to multicultural, critical, and collaborative perspectives.

We began to explore the design of a new program for teacher preparation. The process was often frustrating and difficult, but simultaneously exciting and empowering, presenting opportunities we had not expected to address the curricular impositions of the past: What could or should public schools teach in the years to come? How could we best facilitate the development of elementary practitioners in a manner that empowers both teachers and students? How could our teacher education curriculum both model and teach to the interrelationships between content areas, between teacher and learner, between school, families, and community? How could we construct a program that reflects a pluralistic society? How could we really put education that is multicultural into our practice?

The issues, for us, were not neutral. The goal was, simply, radical change in our teacher education program. We were influenced by a complex array of personal historical, political, economic, cultural, and philosophical considerations as well as by personal values. Several of my colleagues had also experienced the hope and betrayal of the civil and equal rights movements and alternative programs of the 1960s and 1970s. We had all shared the disillusionment of the Vietnam War years. We committed ourselves to change, to addressing issues of oppression and institutional racism through our teacher education program.

∽

*Shouldn't there be replicable results, or at least generalizable findings—I recall reading that point in some formal source, but I also remember Patti Lather's (1991) discussion of a "conceptualization of knowledge as constructed, contested, incessantly perspectival and polyphonic," of the process of thinking and acting within an uncertain framework, of her assertion that "reflexive practice is privileged as the site where we can learn how to turn critical thought into emancipatory action" (p. 13).*

∽

As a faculty, we raised concerns about the seriously fragmented existing model of teacher education, which included multiple foundations and methods courses representing both "traditional" and "direct instruction" strands, and a variety of unrelated practica. The resultant decontextualization of theory from practice and teaching from learning, we believed, contributed significantly to the dissatisfaction expressed by experienced teachers and teachers-in-training alike.

We identified as essential elements of the curriculum the focus on a relational model of education and the creation of an educational context that acknowledged and validated the contributions and participation of diverse members of the community; the development and integration of subject matter; the selection of teaching methods that enhance active pupil participation and construction of their own knowledge; the use of diverse instructional strategies including inquiry, cooperative learning, and problem solving; the encouragement of prospective teachers as reflective practitioners; and the continual need to critique and reflect upon these processes through a multicultural perspective.

Ignoring institutional signals of dissatisfaction, we negotiated our way through the myriad details of course approval processes, the politics of practicum placement, and the inevitable discussions of the knowledge base until we reached a tentative idea of what our teacher preparation program would be. Suggestions by others that we "stop talking about it and just do it" were countered with concerns for "getting it right," working out the details of the plan so that it consistently represented the philosophy on which it was based.

The process of curriculum reform was energized by our ongoing discussion of what we knew teacher education programs could be. Out of the discussion came the idea for how an integrated, emergent curriculum based on a relational education model might look. As one faculty member said, "Why don't we dream of what we think could be the best elementary program we can?" Our new teacher education program emerged through ongoing reflection on our current practices and our struggle to integrate new understandings about teaching and learning.

Ironically, in our passion for the democratic, multicultural principles of our new program, we failed to notice the apparent undermining of our program by our colleagues from other departments in the College of Education and from the "hard right" political groups in the community. When the local consortium of public school educators failed to approve our model, we sought, and received, direct approval at the state level. We did not, however, discern the increasingly well organized resistance to our changes which came from within our own institution.

The program designed, we began our first year of implementation. And then, halfway through the first year, our associate dean announced that our teacher education program was being eliminated, ostensibly because of budget cuts at the state level. Only the federal grant-enriched special education program and educational administration were to be retained. The masters had once again asserted their right to impose their priorities, and our plans for educational reform were squelched.

The impact was experienced not only by faculty but by students as well. Of my 13 female doctoral advisees, 7 of the 9 who were able to finish were Euro-American women. Three of the 4 who dropped out were women of color. In addition, neither of my two male doctoral students, both men of color, was able to complete his doctoral degree at Oregon. Ironically, while the doctoral students were given 2 years to finish their programs, we, their faculty advisors, were fired after 1 year. Many of us returned the next summer, at our own expense, to support the learning communities we had created and see the students through to the completion of their degrees.

My colleagues and I resisted the university's decision, protested, and generated support from our constituent communities, the students, local feminists, Head Start teachers, day care workers, men and women of color, all of those people willing to join in our plea for survival, all of those people seldom heard or affirmed in academic environments. But it was hopeless.

Two images pervade my memories of that time. The glass ceiling had created a professional pit from which none of us escaped. The ground seemed to open and swallow us up. We lost our positions and our programs and scattered, in desperation, across the country to different jobs in different places. Once again, subdued, confused, I found myself back where I started—at the edge, teetering, looking into the ever widening chasm, and sensing the bottomless depth. The image reminded me of a recurrent dream from my childhood. I stand at the edge of the vortex and then helplessly slip in, and am carried down to the point which I know signifies the beginning of nothing.

Twice last summer I had another dream. I was in front of my class, teaching, but no one could hear me. My voice had no sound. Inattentive, my students drifted away and I stood there alone, wondering what to do next, staring into an empty field. The silence of my adolescent years still haunting me, I hear the shattering cracks no longer just at the margins of my life, but criss-crossing the length of my experience until I cannot tell which distortion came first.

༄

*Kamala Visweswaran in* Fictions of Feminist Ethnography *(1994) suggests that "ethnography, like fiction, constructs existing or possible worlds . . . [and] no matter its pretense to present a self-contained narrative or cultural whole remains incomplete and detached from the realms to which it points. . . . We have yet to fully understand the relationship of the novel to the practice of anthropology" (pp. 1–2). And to dreams, too?*

∽

What of the chaos that was created in my life? In the lives of the others? We are the fragments left lying about even as we thought we could escape. We were not just at the margins. We were, and continue to be, systematically swallowed up. I have gone on to yet another institution with new rules and rituals, with yet other ways to impose its power. I find myself even more reluctant, vulnerable—my voice even more tentative, hushed. I have once again been taught the lessons of the dominator culture. What I have learned is to be angry and afraid, to recognize once again the pattern of hope enacted with good heart and of ultimate silencing. I have realized that it will happen again. And I've also learned that it is not, and has never entirely been, my fault.

∽

*I tell my story and, eventually, the questions emerge. "Is this not just sentimental, romanticized gibberish?" "How can this be real research? Where's your data?" And most stinging, "What does this have to do with the rest of us? With children? With schooling?" I shudder to think that I have imposed my personal meaning on an uninterested world.*

*And yet, I see other researchers also challenging the imposing cultural universals of research; critiquing familiar, totalizing systems of methodology; creating opportunities for new methods for doing and displaying research; making spaces for new ways of knowing and doing. Kamala Visweswaran (1994), discussing the role of confessional field literature, asks: "What would experimental ethnography's concern with the constitution of subjectivities, the politics of identity, look like if it addressed a politics of identification? If it addressed the dynamics of autobiography and community, rather than authority and disaffection?" (p. 32). I wonder, can they ever be separated?*

∽

So where has my journey led me, and what have I found? I have sought answers and have discovered the power of narrative in my life to map for me the connections between my life experiences. I have found a way to relate my own personal passion for stories and history with "research" and realized that the knowledge I generate is not from findings or interpretation but from recognition and understanding. And I have learned that I cannot cease seeking to understand the world as I find it.

∽

*Chris Weedon (1987) has suggested that we need a theory which can explain how and why people oppress each other, a theory of subjectivity, a theory of unconscious as well as conscious thoughts and emotions, a theory which can account for relationships between the individual and the social, a theory respectful*

*of people's experiences and their lived narratives. She insists that we need to be*
*critically aware of how the knowledge to make choices leads either to social*
*transformation or to the reinforcement of existing values. She argues that we must*
*bridge our theories, our experiences, our histories, by allowing for multiple, differ-*
*ing, and yet acknowledged, respected, and shared perspectives and that we must*
*create collaborative, multivocal research through which we can construct new*
*understandings of ourselves, our work, and our worlds.*

∽

I return to the Oregon campus in the autumn. They are painting my old
building, remodeling the offices, getting ready for the new regime. I turn away,
seeing in the beautification efforts the repudiation of my work, of the programs
we created.

∽

*I take comfort in Deborah Britzman's (1994) idea of making a "non-narrative*
*narrativity" and in Miles Richardson's (1991) statement that "to be human is to*
*be in a story. . . . Our task is to speak the text, to inscribe it through our acts, the*
*acts of everyday life, so that those who come after us may read and marvel that here*
*once we strode, authors of our own story" (p. 214).*

∽

And I realize the importance of story, of never letting fade the testimonies of
who we were and what we did.

No endings . . .

## REFERENCES

Britzman, D. (1994, April). *On refusing explication: A non-narrative narrativity.* Paper presented
    at the annual meeting of the American Educational Research Association, New Orleans,
    LA.
Cohen, C. (1991, November). *Are we willing to bear the pain? Adult learners addressing issues of*
    *oppression.* Keynote remark at the 17th annual conference of Research on Women in
    Education, San Jose, CA.
Ellsworth, E. (1989). Why doesn't this feel empowering? Working through the repressive myths
    of critical pedagogy. *Harvard Educational Review, 59*(3), 297–324.
Felman, S., and Laub, D. (1992). *Testimony: Crises of witnessing in literature, psychoanalysis, and*
    *history.* New York: Routledge.
Gilmore, L. (1994). *Autobiographics: A feminist theory of women's self-representation.* Ithaca, NY:
    Cornell University Press.
Krieger, S. (1991). *Social science and the self: Personal essays on an art form.* New Brunswick, NJ:
    Rutgers University Press.
Lather, P. (1991). *Getting smart: Feminist research and pedagogy with/in the postmodern.* New
    York: Routledge.
Lather, P. (1993). Fertile obsession: Validity after poststructuralism. *Sociological Quarterly, 34*(4),
    673–693.

Martin, J. (1994). Methodological essentialism, false difference, and other dangerous traps. *Signs, 19*(3), 630–657.

Middleton, S. (1993). *Educating feminists: Life histories and pedagogy.* New York: Teachers College Press.

Richardson, M. (1991). *Point of view in anthropological discourse: The ethnographer as Gilgamesh.* In I. Brady (Ed.), *Anthropological Poetics* (pp. 207–214). Savage, MD: Rowman & Littlefield.

Smith, S. (1993). *Subjectivity, identity and the body: Women's autobiographical practices in the twentieth century.* Bloomington: Indiana University Press.

Visweswaran, K. (1994). *Fictions of feminist ethnography.* Minneapolis: University of Minnesota Press.

Weedon, C. (1987). *Feminist practice and poststructuralist theory.* Oxford, England: Basil Blackwell.

# CHAPTER 10

## Words! Words! Words!

*Gretchen Freed-Rowland*

MINAKUTSIK

POEM-STORY

WINTER 1992

Winter Solstice is approaching. . .
as is Hanukkah. . .
as is Ramadan. . .
as is Christmas, the day of the whiteman's forgotten Jesus
as is. . . ????

I replay vignettes—fragments of my life
ragged at the edges—still
I feel the weight of sadness
at what I have lost or had taken away.

Yet life is full
too full
so many pulls
so many tugs

This life
This "civilized" Native American Indian/Indigenous woman
of the First Nations-life.

The propaganda of "upward mobility," with which to wash away
the sins of "caste"
of race—the colors of skin

the cant of throwaway consumerism
the metaphors, the images that inevitably
strip away
each pound of flesh,
and leave us naked
of all that has kept us human
through those thousands of "dark age" years.

The psychic pain of that eternal trying to strip away,
wash, bleach, vomit, starve out who we are
and become the Barbies and the Kens of this "conquering" culture.

The "play the game" or lose face,
lose membership in this whiteman's civilization
believe
in the propaganda of the schools,
their communities

The government,
corporate America
needs "talking heads,"
numb,
brain dead,
to the socialization process of becoming

*American*

Which in retrospect
was like the careful peeling away of American Indigenous peoples' skin
for ornaments in the early days of settlement.

It has been no different
from the Nazis' use of Jews' skin for lampshades in Germany, or the shooting of
Indigenous people in Paraguay like "vermin rabbits"
in the middle of the 20th century.

Then there was use of taxpayers' money
to pay the bounty hunters
in Oregon and Washington
for our people's scalps
as proof.
Scalps of women, children and men
It did not matter.

In many places,
It still does not matter.
Our useless land to which we often were moved
from our Sacred places and our Memories
is once more valuable.

They want
Mother Earth's valuables
underlaying her skin—
to peel away her skin and take them
They want to rest their nuclear wastes
with us.
They pollute our mothers' milk
in the name of progress
and their god.

Why do we still hold to our faith with Creator and Mother Earth?
Our sacred places are targeted and defiled,
one by one,
as if
on purpose, and not
for the resources only that they hold.

How is it that we each are brought back to what is left of our old ways,
That we hold up and cherish the ragged remnants of our families, our cultures,
and our spiritual connections
with all that is,
Even
the whiteman? . . .

Forgive him Creator, he knows not what he does. . .

How is it we keep on,
captive and dying
in our own land,
in our own history
and in truths denied us then
and denied us now?

We are appropriated and marketed
as other people's ideas, design, knowledge.

Hunger.
Hunger for who we are and who we were
hunger for our stories
our humor
our food
our warmth

We share it with good heart.

Fear.
Fear for our children
the hunger and poverty
that grinds us all down

keeps us at their treadmills
like everybody else.

It separates us from each other
We ignore each other's pain and suffering.

*School* taught us what we have to be
to feed our children
to be a Good Indian

We must become the Apple,
the BIA Indian—

Do what others had to learn to do
to make it in their world
to be "legit"
Emulate "The Man."

Go tell your poor relations and brethren
how to live, how to be
just like you.
It is not your fault if they don't make it then.
You tried.

Just like the history of the immigrants
who had to sell their language and cultural souls,
lose their sons and daughters
to affluent neighborhoods
and restaurants where they don't fit.

Lose yourself to commodified numbness
Just follow the lead of our great leaders
in the Euro-American culture. . .

So here we are. . .
1992 drawing winter down around it
The winter holiday season upon us,
Hope in a new president *and* his wife, Hillary
of "our, my" era,

Hope in the new and greater numbers of congresswomen
Hope in our first elected Native American Indian/Indigenous Senator
who doesn't appear to follow in the footsteps of Ross Swinger,
who liked it in Reagan's pocket (so says the "Moccasin Telegraph")

Yes, the suicides, accidents, old wounds will fester.
Pushing, as well as pulling at families
keeping us together
in spite of everything.

Money is supposed to be spent
in this Western tradition of overindulgence.
Commodities, products purchased.
Overindulgence in human and cultural frailties.

Yet,
it is the season of
Earth, our Mother, of Father sky, and Creator.

It is the time to reflect on "whiteman's" control
through our own excesses.

Their Jesus was a village man in his prime.
He also experienced the urban excesses.
he called all to remember who they were
how none of us is without fault.

He prayed for a renewed understanding of community.

As in all historical records,
the context
the living dynamic
the fiber of the cultural biospheric marriage becomes abstracted
distorted,
privileged in its written form

So how
can we reconnect
living in an alien artificial world
which is spinning away from us
faster and faster?

We no longer even have control over what we have begot
at the technological secular altar.
We cannot even maintain control over what it is we have to know
just to stay in work.
we know how to survive
how to be a part of a community
as it was in the beginning. . .

It is so overwhelming

At what point will *we* begin to riot?

In the time from March 1993, when this chapter was originally put together from different pieces, until now, I have been reminded of how my passion, writing, and speaking impose on the space of some men and women. I am especially reminded of the common usage in Indian country of the word "whiteman" and the response: "Her words are so angry. It makes me shut down.

. . . It won't solve anything." Others have responded to me with cries, smiles, and comments such as "YES!" telling me how they were brought back into things they too experienced.

When I wrote the first draft of this chapter, I was in the middle of my dissertation field work and transcriptions, financially and personally stressed, trying not to impose on the already stressed lives of the Native American Indian women in my life-history study, recognizing the lie of it (Freed-Rowland, 1993). I had been in their personal spaces before, but as friend, as sister, as relative. With the dissertation, our relationships and positions had altered. Now the criteria and requirements of the university to get my degree meant I must take away their words and my understanding of them and write them down in a certain way. My participants and I knew the importance of our degrees; with them we would be better able to help our peoples and others. We knew we served as role models—that Native American Indian women can do these things. But without meaning to, we had agreed to do something that ended up feeling dangerous. The other women now felt vulnerable about things we had shared in friendship and about the questions I was asking. Now, my presence was a painful imposition on their space, an unwilling juggling of their time. We were not prepared, and as one of the women said, "I find myself sharing with you memories I thought I had safely locked away." We became aware of the university and academic requirements as extensions of stories and memories of missionaries, colonizers, bureaucrats, educators, and "cutting" doctors[1]—"for our own good" (Altbach & Lomotey, 1991; Gunn Allen, 1989). We have lived with "their" versions of us, of our experiences, and of the meaning of our lives. I almost walked away, finding myself in the footprints of the "whiteman" anthropologists and other social scientists, using their expertise "to frame our work together." I was responsible for "writing culture" about my own relatives, but not on our terms (Clifford, 1988; Merleau-Ponty, 1988; Said, 1989).

As a consequence, I turn to forms of narrative, to poetry. The two poems included in this chapter are used as a vehicle to illustrate how the reader, the hearer, can phenomenologically experience the positionality of the "other." Thus, poetry exposes the audience to the physiology of language and context and to historical, social, and personal "fact"—of cultural and personal interpretation. It breaks down the barriers of formality which often pass for the lived experience of the studied, observed, reflected on, and which are "written" with a particular cultural audience—or clientele—in mind. Poetry is a shortcut to a life-history experience, and it highlights how research is more about the researcher and the cultural nature of her or his institutions and her or his cultural lens. It also expresses how the stories and memories of our own peoples and our cultures become our own. It colors the lens with which we see, hear, read, and otherwise make meaning of our everyday world and our lives.

March 1993: I am in that "liminal space" within my dissertation process, wondering, as in Doris Lessing's (1988) *The Fifth Child*, what I am birthing. Or am I part of a process that our Native American Indian tribal history tells us is a means to appropriation? I am agonizing over how to be most fair and truthful, yet protect the six Native American Indian women in this study. It is therefore an autobiographical life history, an "experimental" and "personal" representation, attempting to be collaborative within the difficult limitations of the dissertation process. It is a fiction in the best sense of the word, as sociologists of knowledge, linguists, literary critics, and social scientists use it to critique modernity and hegemony in their various guises. It is a journey through the landscapes of Indian country; Euro-anthropocentric scholarship and requirements; feminist, women of color, and Third World scholarship; and six Native American Indian women's testimony. Each of them had been academically successful at the university level.

I cannot offer the data and the themes that are emerging in the context of this book, for that would, once again, abstract our stories from the larger story, which is the context for the telling. What I offer instead is setting a context for the work with which I am struggling. I am faced with features of landscape that are familiar to one community and not the other. This project attempts a dialogue/conversation among different ways of being in the world. These include the following three interacting entities in voice and story—in Indian country, academia, and myself, as (Anishinabe) Ojibwa-(Hatcanjgara) Winnebago woman/educator/researcher. These processes are the action of voice and story. How do the women in the story see themselves, act out their relationships with the other two—me and academia? What is said; how is it said; by whom? How are these problematic for the other entities and their way of understanding being in the world? The text emerges as an attempt to bring together such multiple voices and to explore the implications of the relationships among a host of cultural phenomena. Critical issues in this are about cultural meanings—the underlying assumptions and expectations in language and representation. How are schooling, education, individuality, identity, family, community, spirituality, ritual, ceremony, and authority/power experienced? How do these manifest themselves in very different cultural contexts (Minh-ha, 1987, 1989; Mohanty, Russo, & Lourdes, 1990; Spivak, 1987)? As major questions and challenges emerge, they shape the context for this endeavor. This context and process are characterized by storytelling in a methodological manner ideally more culturally congruent for the Native American Indian women participating in this study (Fernandez & Tandon 1981/1983; Ong, 1988; Vizenor, 1989). Its significance is also readable to the non-Indian reader through setting a larger context, grounded in issues that arise in the mainstream, feminist, and Third World literature, and how that also intersects with the history and lives of the Native American Indian women. This study is also about how the criteria and agendas of higher education, explicit and implicit, conflict with the values and lives of these women (Altbach & Lomotey, 1991; La Croix, 1993; Souers, 1993).

It is important to bring to the surface the recognition of conflicts in cultural values and assumptions in the gendered languages and form considered appropriate for formal research (Gluck & Patai, 1991). The challenges are to reach beyond the culture of academia and yet, through the languages of academia, to encourage Western and Euro-American keepers of the discourse and the canon to expand traditional monocultural processes, rituals, and structures (Bowers, 1993a). My work questions the fragmenting, reducing, and isolating nature of current academic practices, their underlying assumptions and expectations, and how these distort what is knowledge. As one deconstructs the underlying assumptions and expectations of ethnographic research theory, praxis/methodology, and their epistemology and pedagogy, questions arise as to the credibility and validity of what is sanctioned as knowledge, discourse, curriculum development, and instruction. Who are the cultural legitimating agencies of voice and story? For whom? (Said, 1989, 1993a, 1993b). Who should be the cultural legitimating agencies, and in what context? Where are the voices of us, the women, sisters, daughters, mothers, grandmothers, community members and educators, who represent the diverse long-lived world views of this land? Why are the voices that are heard as the call goes out for the vision and restructuring for the 21st century still framed by machine/tool metaphors and dualistic language instead of the language of "relationship with"? (Berger & Luckmann, 1967; Bowers, 1993a, 1993b). These broader challenges manifest specifically through voice and story in Indian country, and in academia through myself, as catalyst, as part of the two communities. It was and is my task to translate and mediate my interpretations of the voices of the other five Native American Indian women speakers, the academy, and Indian communities and to examine what happened as we engaged in the mandated academic process. Questions are framed by my experiences and assumptions embedded in my reading of the two above mentioned communities. For example, differences emerged in these women's meaning of community, individuality, freedom, equality, spirituality, and the means of knowing and doing from that of the dominant Euro-American culture as framed in academia. Issues arose differently for the six women involving their tribal identity retention, representation, and transiting higher education. The structures and epistemology of research and discourse in the academy are broadened by the process ventured in this study. It has been difficult but necessary, therefore, to discuss the barriers in meeting the requirements of a scholarly research project and yet to avoid delegitimizing or overgeneralizing. It is culturally inappropriate to appear the "expert" based upon what I know from the stories and the voices of both communities. I encourage the reader to engage in the complexity and importance of these issues.

In addition, I have attempted to engage in a dialogue across a chasm of misunderstanding and misinformation. Even the academic "public" has had little experience with what is available about the magnitude and complexities of the Western or Euro-American cultural and governmental relationships with Native American Indian peoples or with Native American Indian literature. Nor have they reflected to any degree upon their lack of that knowledge or the general involvement and use of academic knowledge in government policies and practices, and how that shapes relationships between Euro-American communities and Native American Indian or other indigenous peoples and their communities.

Because of the climate of paradigmatic shift and the current deconstruction of the Western and Euro-American cultures and languages, it is possible to more broadly address and implicate the underlying particularized anthropocentric and gendered asymmetry of privilege and power in the dominant Western and Euro-American cultural world view. This perspective underpins the oppressive colonial and genocidal attitudes and practices in the historical and contemporary relationships between indigenous/aboriginal peoples, tribes, and communities and their labor and resources, and the dominant Eurocentric communities, governments, and corporate and economic leadership. Schooling in schools of the dominant culture has been about defining literacy very narrowly, as only learning how to speak, read, and write in a linear/rational model of education that assumes and expects expertise toward unlocking categories of meaning which will fit neatly into hierarchical structures leading to universal, absolutist/essentialist truths. Therefore, the very nature of the exercise denies the multicultural and organic holistic world in which we live. It denies Native American Indian people their historical understanding of being in the world, their languages, arts, and literature; and it devalues and changes the meanings and purposes of the oral tradition. These difficult and complex topics must be discussed to create a framing more sensitive to Native American Indian peoples' history and issues and more congruent for Native American Indian tribal women telling their life histories. Many paths appear to lead in many directions, but they are interwoven parts of the whole; they are our heritage; they constitute our stories. They inform where we are going, not just where we think we are going. The signposts are there. Yet the Eurocentric academic expectation is of a rationally informed outline that clearly delineates the next stop or detour in a progressive forward movement. The metaphorical illusion of such a movement comprises a particular way of linguistically and phenomenologically experiencing and understanding being in the world and meaning-making which is different from that of many other cultures, including Native American Indian cultures. Thus I use anthropology as cultural critique (Marcus & Fischer, 1986). Whose purposes have been served and whose have not by the Eurocentric definitions and uses of cultures, languages, education, literacy, story, poetics, and the arts? How can Native American Indian women's voices be heard when we have been delegitimized as "other"? How can we be heard when we must speak in those objectifying languages and voices of the "other's" fictions to be considered legitimate? This creates but another distortion because the stories are decontextualized from their oral telling and meanings in tribal and community locations. Just "writing down" the stories changes them, and further, "writing culture" (Clifford & Marcus, 1986), which has been the ethnographic task of anthropologists and other social scientists, again privileges a certain framing of literacy (Manganaro, 1990).

I too am caught in the Cartesian box of metaphors on "his" terms. It is not even a clean cedar box, but one of hammered metal, with sharp edges, sullied through centuries of misuse, appropriation, and denial. All the surfaces are sticky with his male metaphors of domination and superiority—his, as in the image of "godness." The box represents both war and sport, and I, as the overeducated Pocahontas, represent the open vessel into which he poured both his beneficence and his violence. I continue to refuse to give up my identity as "other," as Anishinabe-Hatcanjgara-half-breed woman. My otherness is my self and my pride. It gives me freedom. I recognize how it is supposed to be—how it was—I can make sense of how I fit into the larger organic whole of this life on Mother Earth.

I am saddened and angry at how we must all live in order to survive in this Euro-anthropocentric language and illusions of reality. I am shocked and amazed at the power of this colonial fascist (concerned with academic, racial, and religious purity) language to control all our "dusky" minds in oh so many taken-for-granted ways in the rules of the academy and scholarship. But because of the stories of my family, my friends, our peoples of the First Nations, I am not surprised. Other sisters who are framed in other collective metaphors of "otherness"—as white, middle class, or color, or Third World, or sexual preference or disabled, talk of being change agents for emancipation from the prison of his defining and his terms of normalcy and excellence. Too often, such talk is still trapped in metaphors of war and dichotomous illusions, by "his" defining of deviance, validity, rigor, and excellence.

I was an ABD doctoral candidate in a university education department which had already begun deconstructing. Jan, first my friend and then colleague, professor, and mentor, Petra, Susan, and Karen, and the members and friends in the larger women's writing support group were gone, dispersed to the next stage in their lives. The halls were full of boxes of files shifted, furniture piled in corners, and gaping bookshelves, the rooms empty, in spite of the warm bodies that may still be there. The professors and secretaries that I knew for so long, with whom I shared laughter, real flights of "what if we could create our ideal elementary and secondary programs—what would they look like?" are all gone from these halls and rooms. The shock reverberates endlessly of the cultural and political reality of moving too fast with an egalitarian, relational model of collaborative integrated education—no add-ons, no take-aways, no sending children into special places where they will be labeled as trouble, slow, not good enough, or too good for the rest of us. Gossip has it that the president of our prestigious university does not believe we need to do research with teachers about the situatedness of teaching, context, praxis, and curriculum theory and development. Perhaps he is right, on some levels. The management (read "control"), behavior-efficiency model which is based on the rationally defined logic of economic theories and corporate needs assumes a nonexistent neutrality. The underlying cultural assumptions and expectations of "manifest destiny" are alive and well. "Western civilization" has no intention to redeem what it has taken away. We are still stuck with numbers and tests that measure quantities which according to Gregory Bateson (1979) are unmeasurable and logic that is mistaken.

Can we remake society, as Chet Bowers (1993a, 1993b) and others imagine? Can we take lessons from other cultures which have existed for much, much longer than Western civilization and whose memory has not been totally erased by the colonial imperialistic pollution, rape, and extinction policy (Minh-ha, 1989; Mohanty, Russo, & Lourdes, 1990; Said, 1989, 1993a, 1993b; Spivak, 1987)? Can we teach the maleness of the Euro-American culture, relations, and institutions of power (Smith, 1989) what they have forgotten or are afraid of remembering within themselves? Are the stakes finally high enough or is the game play still too addictive, the emptiness of their souls seen in their morning mirrors as they shave still too scary? What would six Native American Indian tribal women in their 30s, 40s, and 50s, who persevered and who were academically successful at the baccalaureate and graduate level, be allowed to tell? And in what language? Or is it still too dangerous? What games am I as the researcher/participant required to play?

In reading through the essays in Sherna Berger Gluck's and Daphne Patai's (1991) *Women's Words, Women's Words, Women's Words: The Feminist Practice of Oral History*, I heard voiced my anguish and issues in the real world of attempting to use and reform the life-history, narrative, autobiographical, and biographical theories and methodologies into a form and process more sensitive and culturally congruent to the lives and concerns of the six tribal women in my study. I am facing the question, Is what I had hoped to achieve in this project, and with the integrity I believed necessary, even possible as a dissertation? Will we, as coparticipants, be able to achieve our title, "North American indigenous Women: Our own voices, our own songs, our own landscapes," even as a postdoctoral project?

Given the circumstances, the dissertation was co-opted by financial and time constraints, my lack of experience (and time) to write grants, and the necessity of finishing my project after supportive members of my committee had left for other universities and before the end of the designated time for finishing a curriculum and instruction degree. It was so hard for me to separate myself, the intention of my work with the five other women—what I consider the basis of its integrity—and objectify my predicament using "his" rules of scholarship. I was constantly reminded of what could happen by my taking away the "data," decontextualizing the words of my friends, their stories, their beliefs and experiences, and the enormous imposition of my ideal collaboration as a dissertation. How could I protect their integrity and give of their honesty? What purpose is served by proving I know how to find cultural categories and label and analyze according to what I have learned from recognized experts in the field except to prepare my work so that it can be replicated? What am I forced to leave out?

The dissertation process was explained to me by one professor recently as an exercise, not the real research. It is to prove that I am capable of doing scholarly research in a manner approved by the academy and capable of adding something of significance to the canon and the discourse. If I was to get that piece of paper, I must go through the rites of passage and prove "I know how to do *it*." I cannot help but be reminded of the other times I was told by a bunch of boys/men that they got to determine the rules and the meaning of knowing how to do it. Until the age of 14 that meant that I got to punch *them* out. In college, and as a faculty member, however, I was *allowed* to pretend I did not hear them or feel the pat on my behind. I must remember that if I want to play *in* the sandbox, I must do what I am told. I must behave appropriately. I am promised certain academic freedoms as Dr. Freed-Rowland, but will they allow me alternatives which for me have integrity?

POEM
AFTER 3 YEARS
(AT THAT POINT)
OF UNIVERSITY TEACHING
IN MULTICULTURAL EDUCATION

Undoing racism is not an intellectual exercise.
Change in this instance
cannot occur comfortably

Change cannot occur until
enough
somebodies
*know,*

can feel

what it is like

to be the fattest,
the dumbest,
the ugliest,
the weakest,

the blackest,
or
the whitest

Until YOU know
what it feels like
when "THEY" make jokes
or call out to you
slant eyes,
nigger,
jiggaboo,
Jap,
Gook,
Chink,
Squaw,
Tonto,
dirty Indian,
Geronimo,
Pocahontass,
Hey, honey,
wanna little?
Great tits
I'd like a piece of that!
Jew,
Yid,
Kike,
Polack,
Wet Back,
"homo,"
lesbo,
dirty queer,
queenie,
stupid fucking cunt

dirty American . . .

Until somebody else KNOWS what that does to your insides . . .

Until enough somebodies know

the relentlessness
of such
little
thoughtless
incidents

the helplessness,
the impotence,
the inner rage—

*that it never stops*

Until enough someones understand
what it's like to be always
looking over your shoulder,
"checking people out,"
looking at eyes *very* carefully,
but oh so casually
every day,
every time you go out the door,
out of your space,

that being a good person
comfortable in your own space
means
"nothin's happen'n"
means
"nothin's chang'n"
it's
"jus goin undergroun"
and gettin
more vicious
in a sneaky sort of way

Until enough somebodies look to what they say and do
and take for granted. . .
and ask
"the others"
and listen
listen real hard

Until enough somebodies begin to *feeel* it
feel it
creep up in them
from their back
and
from their toes
and *feeel* it
twist and knot their guts
feel it take over
as they listen

as they begin to-hear
things-they-never-heard-before
in the same-ole-con-versions
and see-things-they-never-saw-before
in the *same*-ole-situations

then. . .

nothing
can change. . .

The dark underside will continue to eat away,
sucking out the
humanity
of being human
THEY
will continue
to bribe
those of us who won't fight
who don't understand. . .

There but for the grace of the Great Spirit and Mother Earth

or a roll of the dice

go I

or my daughter
or my son
or someone else
I CARE ABOUT. . .
Mother Earth and all her beings. . .

SHUT UP!

Have another drink
another puff,
buy another dress
buy a bigger dress
a faster car
another toy
pop another pill,
waste . . . kill . . . poison . . . plunder
go to confession

WHO THE FUCK CARES?

Yet "writing culture" is my academic task. As a Native American Indian woman, I struggle with the inappropriateness of it all. It is a dilemma for those of us who respect and understand how we live as being about cultural identity and relationships. As Native American Indian women, we are only too well aware of the dangers in writing it down, but we are also aware of how it has always been the "Others" writing culture about us. Above all, we are aware that none of us speaks for any other Native American Indian person or for her or his cultural interpretation of knowing and doing. We recognize expertise as temporally and contextually bound. We value and listen to each other's personal points of view for what they can teach us. We offer these as our testimony. We can only offer our interpretations of our work and our willingness to listen.

I was the last posted oral defense in curriculum and instruction on the last possible day for my degree. The minutes ticked down as the doors of education, as we had known it, were closing forever. It was 10:00 a.m., Friday, August 13, 1993. . .

## NOTE

1. "Cutting" doctors is a term used by native women in Phoenix, AZ, to refer to obstetricians with Indian Health Services who sterilized native women without their knowledge.

## REFERENCES

Altbach, P., & Lomotey, K. (1991). *The racial crisis in American higher education.* Albany: State University of New York Press.

Bateson, G. (1979). *Mind and nature: A necessary unity.* New York: Dutton.

Berger, P., & Luckmann, T. (1967). *The social construction of reality: A treatise in the sociology of knowledge.* Garden City, NY: Anchor Books.

Bowers, C. (1993a). *Critical essays on education, modernity, and the recovery of the ecological imperative.* New York: Teachers College Press.

Bowers, C. (1993b). *Education, cultural myths, and the ecological crisis: Toward deep changes.* Albany: State University of New York Press.

Clifford, J. (1988). *The predicament of culture: Twentieth century ethnography, literature, and art.* Cambridge, MA: Harvard University Press.

Clifford, J., & Marcus, G. (1986). *Writing culture: The poetics and politics of ethnography.* Berkeley: University of California Press.

Fernandez, W., & Tandon, R. (Eds.). (1983). *Participatory research and evaluation: Experiments in research as process of liberation.* New Delhi, India: Aruna Printing Press. (Original work published 1981)

Freed-Rowland, G. (1993). *North American indigenous women of the First Nations: Our own voices, our own songs, our own landscapes.* Unpublished doctoral dissertation, University of Oregon, Eugene.

Gluck, S., & Patai, D. (1991). *Women's words, women's words, women's words: The feminist practice of oral history.* New York: Routledge.

Gunn Allen, P. (1989). *The sacred hoop: Recovering the feminine in American Indian traditions.* Boston: Beacon Press.

La Croix, D. (1993). *Indian boarding school daughters coming home: Survival stories as oral history of Native American women.* Unpublished doctoral dissertation, University of Oregon, Eugene.

Lessing, D. (1988). *The fifth child.* New York: Random House.

Manganaro, M. (Ed.). (1990). *Modernist anthropology.* Princeton, NJ: Princeton University Press.

Marcus, G., & Fischer, M. (1986). *Anthropology as cultural critique.* Chicago: University of Chicago Press.

Merleau-Ponty, M. (Ed.). (1988). *Consciousness and the acquisition of language* (H. Silverman, Trans.). Evanston, IL: Northwestern University Press.

Minh-ha, T. (1987). Difference: A special third world women issue. *Feminist Review, 25*(1), 5–22.

Minh-ha, T. (1989). *Woman, native, other*. Bloomington: Indiana University Press.

Mohanty, C., Russo, A., & Lourdes, L. (Eds.). (1990). *Third world women and the politics of feminism*. Bloomington: Indiana University Press.

Ong, A. (1988). Colonialism and modernity: Feminist re-presentations of women in non-western societies. *Inscriptions, 3/4,* 79–93.

Said, E. (1989). Representing the colonized: Anthropology's interlocutors. *Critical Inquiry, 15,* 205–225.

Said, E. (1993a). *Culture and imperialism*. New York: Alfred A. Knopf.

Said, E. (1993b). *Orientalism*. New York: Random House. (Original work published 1978)

Smith, D. (1989). *The conceptual practices of power: A feminist sociology of knowledge*. Boston: Northeastern University Press.

Souers, T. (1993). *Circles of power: Life histories of native American Indian women elders in education*. Unpublished doctoral dissertation, University of Oregon, Eugene.

Spivak, G. (1987). *In other worlds: Essays in cultural politics*. New York: Routledge.

Vizenor, G. (1989). *Narrative chance: Postmodern discourse on Native American Indian literatures*. Albuquerque: University of New Mexico Press.

# PART IV

## RECONSTRUCTING REALITY: DECONSTRUCTING THE COLLABORATIVE PROCESS

*Each day is a tapestry, threads of broccoli, promotion, couches, children, politics, shopping, building, planting, thinking interweave in intimate connection with insistent cycles of birth, existence, and death.*

This part of our book shares our reflections on the ongoing group process that began 4 years ago with an exploration of the implications of "imposition" in our educational experience. Facing now the final imposition, that of being told we must leave, go on, because the institution no longer values or desires our work, we mourn. As educators, we have faced the challenge of trying to work together without violating each other's rights to live within her own reality and the inevitability of being unable to do so.

In this, our conclusion, we examine the emergence of our identity as a work group and our continuing struggle to validate and support each other. We acknowledge the commonalities that brought us to this project but also the diversity and tensions between us that have seemed insurmountable at times and have always provided us with the chance to grow. In presenting our collective project and our ongoing reflections on our experiences with each other as teacher-learners, we have confronted several core questions:

1. How is a process of collaboration achieved and maintained by a diverse group of women representing very different ideological perspectives and cultural realities?

2. How can individual identity and difference be acknowledged and validated while we maintain commitment to shared purposes?

3. How can we continue to support and empower each other while confronting external obstacles to our project?

We offer our narratives and the collaborative stories of our experiences of the past years working together. In their contradictions and affirmations we believe they blend together as a response to the questions we posed. But they are also incomplete, and the story has not ended.

∽

PETRA: *It is fall 1990. I am in a cafe/bookstore in Milwaukee, scanning the shelves of the women's studies section in search of the newest, the undiscovered, perhaps even the seminal work which will illuminate "the answers." A title catches my eye: The Sound of Our Own Voices. It is poetic, like the music our group creates as each voice enters the conversation, a new instrument, each clamoring over the others, challenging the others to be heard. It is a rhythm, a harmony that is unique and in some ways unfamiliar to me, for it is the sound of women's voices.*

*As I take the book from the shelf and open its cover, I am reminded again of the beauty of inspirational moments. The title page reads, The Sound of Our Own Voices: Women's Study Clubs, 1860–1910, by Theodora Penny Martin (1987). I can hardly contain myself as I race over to Jan and show her my new find. I feel like the child filled with delight at discovering some new hidden treasure. The author describes these study groups, which were also known as the "light seekers," as "clubs that filled that gap between society's formal institutions and the stirrings of intellectual independence—an awareness of and confidence in themselves and in their sex which they had not been able to accomplish alone" (p. 3).*

*These words evoke romantic visions of women engaged in stormy, intellectual dialogue, pouring over books, debating until late into the night. Certainly this was my hope as our study group formed 2 years ago. I sought the confirmation and validation of other women in a world which still values male over female ways of knowing and being. I just assumed that was the reason others had been drawn to the group.*

*We had been in Milwaukee to present a paper on our work over the preceding year and a half. We had struggled to understand our relationships, our identity as a group, and the seemingly illusive hold "the group" has on us all despite the many differences we have. These differences in style, our varying needs for control, our multiple understandings of what it means to be cared for and what it means to care, emerge even moments before we are to do our presentation.*

*As my fingers page through the book, I sense a bond. The descriptions and pictures of women clad in Victorian dress of times gone by, of other women's study groups, seem to connect me to some lost relative. I wonder if there are clues hidden within this work that will help me to understand the complexity of our group. I need to understand. I sense a continuity of experience, a connection to a broader phenomenon, a context for understanding our group's work. As I read the opening quote of the book, written in 1899, my sense of connection is confirmed:*

*We dreamed still more of larger possibilities; of the chance to think to the best advantage by working together; for it is a strange thing but true, when people are in earnest that, given a certain number of human souls, the result of their coalescence is not as the sum of their units, but something larger and other. It sometimes happens that, to quote our poet Browning, "out of three sounds we frame not a fourth sound, but a star." And that is the bottom reason why we women desired to combine. (p. vi)*

*Again, romantic illusions soothe over the sometimes painful memories of our work together. I am compelled to ask, what did bring us together? What were we seeking? What has kept us together?*

∽

JAN: *Why have we been unable to get it together? In many ways, this has been the hardest project I have ever undertaken, as well as the most difficult challenge our group has ever faced. The deconstruction of a process that has become so central to our lives seems a travesty, a declaration that the group is over and that we have gathered for the last rites, the final wake that marks the end of our time together. And in a way that is true. Most of us have completed our academic work at the University of Oregon, finishing dissertations or, with the closing of the Curriculum and Instruction program, moving on to other places. Some of us suspect that what Arnowitz and Giroux (1991: 36) have suggested is true, that "what women, minorities, and working class students have always known [is] the precincts of higher learning are not for them, and the educational system is meant to train a new mandarin class."*

*And yet, we treasure the experiences we have had together, regret seeing them change, letting go. We fear that the geographic separations inevitably to come will somehow fracture the relationships we have formed and the work we have been able to do during the past 4 years. The separation is difficult. The reconstruction of new relationships with each other has barely been envisioned. But perhaps this is the place to start.*

∽

SUSAN: *It's February 27, 1991, 3:25 p.m. Oregon time, and I am attempting to re-create reality as it applies to this paper. I have lost count; how many times have I addressed the ever present, ever befuddling issues in our group process, whether in the form of written drafts, in the mental confusion of persevering thoughts, or in long, sticky telephone calls which usually end with my rhetorical "I don't know . . . "?*

*Recently, the conversation has enlarged; we met the last time, stared at each other, and wondered who would start. Once we did, the struggles with this "deconstructing thing" became clearer to me; the definitions of work, commitment, group process, power, friendship, and difference held by each of us brought to the surface a mass of conflicting beliefs and expectations. This particular meeting represented, for me, a milestone in OUR development in the same way that an earlier conference in*

*Milwaukee did. Collaboration is a developmental process. To gather the experience of our collaboration over the past 2 years into a neat conference presentation implies a finiteness to this PROCESS which could only be artificial and romantically misleading.*

◌◡

KAREN: *As I think about our group process over the last 3 years, the phrase that keeps running through my mind is "shifting images and shattered mirrors." It appears to me that the university relishes linear configurations, predictable patterns, and dispassionate discourse—values and assumptions relished also by the mainstream middle class. I joined the group because I thought it offered an opportunity to create a different context. I had assumed that it offered an opportunity for women to cherish other women—to recognize our strengths from what I perceive of as relational and interactive experiences—experiences in which the divisive effects of fear, jealousy, and competition can be confronted. In my idealism, I believed that it offered a chance to teach and learn through reflective processes, to explore possibilities. In short, it offered an experience rare in mainstream society and virtually nonexistent in academe.*

*As we each address the issues of commitment, power, trust, and friendship, I realize that we did learn a great deal from each other. We began to know each other, to read discomforts, and know when and how to support each other. We started to share our lives, slowly building a new place, a space that blended the academic and personal. We started to rely on each other, and we also started to draw strength from our membership with the group and use our voices with assurance and conviction. With our "knowing" there also developed an impatience, with ourselves and with each other, that could, given the time and circumstances, I believe, have led to understanding.*

*Over the last 4 years, I have learned that what these women expected and deserved was what they gave and that the struggle was just as painful a process for each of them. I worked to learn to trust this group process, and now I struggle with cynicism as unresolved issues arise and we are constrained by both geographical distance and fear of vulnerability; yet the issues need that same care—the precious time and space we were once able to create.*

*The frustrations of our different styles and expectations have been illuminating. I still cannot ignore the fact that every time we create another agenda, set another deadline, and project another conference presentation 8 months ahead of time, inwardly I scream from what feels like ropes, however gently placed, stuffing me into yet another box. I also cannot ignore the needs of others in the group to do these things. Working with these women offered me a place from which to view doctoral socialization with a sense of whimsy, to see it as one small part of a greater whole. I had initially perceived the group process as a shelter, and for a season it was.*

◌◡

GRETCHEN: *The hardest for me was to say what I needed from the group or to even need because of how I was brought up. In my family, we were brought up to be brave, do our best, and never lie because the Great Spirit could see inside our souls. We were to take care of each other out there in "the whiteman's world" where we went to school. We were told, in the end, never to fully trust "them." "Trust only your own kind, only your own blood." We were taught we were different, but to carry that with pride. At the same time we were taught not to be prejudiced against any human being, animal, or plant life. We were to be of good heart and trust our sense of when others were also of good heart. It was confusing.*

*When our group went to Milwaukee during the fall of 1990 to present, I realized, afterward, that we had shared a grown-up equivalent of a girls' slumber party in the interest of graduate student and junior faculty economics. I had never done that before, except to a lesser extent last year in Boston, with Karen and two other women. In Boston we each went our separate ways for the most part. In Wisconsin, we really did things together. In fact, when I was invited by new acquaintances "of color" to go with them, I felt I needed to be loyal to our group and go with them. I didn't ask, but I felt that they would have minded, and I again felt my invisible difference. How to explain it, where are the words? (What have I projected now?)*

∾

SUSAN: *What do these things—commitment, power, difference, and other internal obstacles—mean for our group process?*

*The meaning of our group is closely connected to the question of commitment. How can I commit to something when (1) I am not clear what the "something" is; (2) we have never explicitly agreed on the meaning or conscious function of the group; and (3) we clearly have different definitions of "commitment."*

*It was different to come together initially to create our imposition project, our first conference presentation as a group. The focus was clear; I felt enlivened by the members' faith in my writing, excited by the collaborative effort, and comforted by the distraction of work at a difficult time in my life. Yet that was several months— close to a year—ago, and our focus has become increasingly ambiguous. On one level, we continue to meet to prepare another AERA presentation. The resistance is obvious: people physically or emotionally not present, drafts missing or late, competing and absent perspectives. Are these symptoms of a "lack of commitment" or symptoms of something larger, more vital, to which we should attend?*

*It was easier to commit explicitly to the imposition project because the topic was distant enough, separate from the group process, and the individual papers reflected individual interests, struggles, and resolutions with teaching, supervision, and curriculum development. This deconstruction of the group process cannot be written comfortably from an academic distance because the anecdotal data are ourselves. Each time I begin to write, I find myself thinking, yes, this is it, this is the overriding issue (power, commitment, difference), the explanation I have searched for, for why our group functions, and just as frequently, dysfunctions.*

*I look back on my reflections of fall 1990: "I withdraw from the group psycho-logically as **words** which lack meaning for me and **labels** which did not adequately reflect my experience dart back and forth. How personal are the voices here? If we* *do not hear each other's voice clearly, are all voices being heard? Is this collaboration about change? If so, is the change on a conscious level only?" Can we call our process a collaboration if we do not look at the unspoken, the barely perceptible processes in our interactions with each other? The salient learning experiences for me in this collaborative endeavor have been the psychological ones—those encompassing the dynamics intertwining the relationship I have with each participant.*

*Perhaps it speaks to cultural differences and personal needs. In earlier and other relationships with women close to me, the internal dynamics of our relationships with each other, with our mothers, with our partners and our ongoing desire to be self-analytical consumed our discussions. Still, I find myself spending hours and money on long-distance telephone calls to Berkeley, deconstructing my ego with a close friend. The intellectual dimension of this group, I have outgrown. In the length of time we have known each other, I expect we would have begun at least to speak on another level, to share another domain of ourselves, to recognize that unilateral commitment cannot occur without trust and mutual interests. Moreover, it seems that these AERA papers/presentations are the only legitimate, I dare say safe, channel for expression of the feelings of perhaps loss or abandonment elicited by the absence of commitment.*

 ～

**PETRA:** *We meet at Susan's. We are gathering to begin our papers for AERA. I wonder how we have managed to stay together for almost 2 years. At times our group feels like a family. We have known each other so long and have weathered so much together that there is a level of comfort—a level of comfort that allows me to love them, but also to get angry with them. I know I can say things to them and they won't run away.*

*I think back on the various times when one or another of the group's members has had to step back, what I perceived as putting her needs first and the group's second. Last spring, when Gretchen's crisis drew her away, I experienced a tempered anger and confusion. Karen's competing commitments to community activities also raised questions for me about loyalty and commitment to the group.*

*I struggle to understand the deep feelings that these moments of separation evoke in me. On a rational level, I understand that we each lead complex and multiple lives. Sometimes we have to prioritize. On the other hand, the placing of other needs above the group's makes me question the depth of our original commitment. Is our work together only valued when it is convenient? Is my anger a result of the disappointment that others do not value the group as much as I do, that they do not value the political, emotional, and intellectual dimensions of the group as I do?*

*I see the group as work, a commitment of women to work together despite all the difficulties and competing demands because those are the diversions that have been created to divide us. For me work is staying together, and work always comes first. For others, work comes second, only after relationships have been nurtured and maintained. And for some, "work" is avoided at all costs. Sometimes it seemed we all did want the same thing, we just called it something different.*

*I understood that our original commitment was to learn the language of feminist theory, become fluent in the jargon which I thought defined our lives. We were focused on feminist readings, deconstructing theory and finding our way through the maze of hermeneutics, phenomenology, and postmodernism. We were trying to understand voices, those voices whose words we did not understand but whose language seemed essential to our survival. In the process, some members even violated their resolve not to submit to the elitism of a language which excluded their voices and experiences, in order to help others of us learn the dominant language so we would no longer feel threatened by words we did not understand.*

∽

**JAN:** *It was obvious from the beginning that our needs, our histories, were different. My assumptions about our common commitment to feminist theory quickly eroded as members of the group announced they were not feminists and did not want to be. If this was not to be the common connection, something else had obviously taken its place, for we did not dissolve, disintegrate, and fade away.*

∽

**PETRA:** *For Karen, our intellectual debates had never been central; it had been the individual relationships. For Jan, as "leader" in the group, commitment to relationships seemed to conflict with her need to maintain a distinct boundary to protect and preserve the faculty–student relationship. The need to be "fair" and treat us equally seemed to conflict with Jan's understanding of commitment as identification. Since her identification with each of us was different, how could she be equally committed? For Susan, the papers and products were secondary to her commitment to group process. Our varied and multiple connections, identifications, and needs seemed to pose a constant threat to our collaboration, our commitment to the group.*

*In some sense my understanding of commitment has been confused with sameness, that we all needed to be feminists, to share equal enthusiasm, to put the same level of energy into "our" work. Perhaps my need for sameness stemmed from the fear that if we were different we would no longer be connected, have nothing in common, that I would be abandoned. The simultaneous joy and fear I have experienced in this group echo the complexity of so many of my relationships with women.*

*My assumption was that as women we would be committed to empowering ourselves by creating new forms of organization which did not re-create the hierarchical and oppressive structures usually designed to disempower us. I sought a safe space in which I could be myself, away from the male gazes which left me unsettled, unsure, and convinced that I was not thinking about the "right" questions. I hoped that working together collaboratively would allow each of our voices and experiences to be validated and honored. I looked forward to renegotiating the decision-making process so that "power over" would be reconceived as "empowerment."*

∽

JAN: *How could I "stay real" as a teacher-learner and yet present the authority and stability my students seemed to need? Staying real, for me, is living out my values as honestly and clearly as I can, in my teaching, my writing, and my relationships. As part of this, then, I think about my commitment to commitment. Loyalty has always been one of my most highly held values. My very existence, at times, seems based on my identification with others for a common purpose. Working with this group, I discovered that commitment for me had two meanings—both necessary to constitute the full commitment I sought with this group. What I first sought was other women who would take themselves seriously, want to learn, and share their ideas and energy with intensity. My experience as a student had been one of forming liaisons and friendships with men because women I knew did not want to be intellectual, to argue theory, to discuss meanings. I suppose this has to do with growing up knowing that the only "true" value was to be taken seriously for what you knew and how you thought. Class became the issue that overshadowed gender for me. Working-class women are not taken seriously as thinkers or doers in the public sphere. I worked hard to ensure that would not be my fate. My commitment has continued, then, to those who also took themselves seriously as thinkers, who "worked" at it all of the time.*

*Commitment, and the work that accompanied it with this group, meant full participation—being there physically, to acknowledge the importance of the work but also with energy and a sense of being "on." I also acknowledge my need for stimulation. For whatever reason, I get bored easily with small talk, shopping—the stuff done by women who had no need to work to support their family or to affirm their value. I needed this group to share my values of work and commitment, to be intense, with fierce debates and arguments where I was not responsible for facilitating and teaching but could participate fully and thereby learn. The early months with these women, their commitment in putting themselves out, engaging with us all, responding, were among the most exciting of my teaching experiences.*

*Staying real also took support. It took longer for me to recognize the gentler but equally needed commitment of Susan, who eased into the verbal fray and also seemed a co-conspirator around personal issues—her commitment to the relationships helped me understand and accept the other part of what the group meant to us all—companionship, friends, and trust. This commitment meant taking the time to carefully consider the others' work as well as their needs—being there emotionally for each other but also putting in the time to help with projects; appreciating each other's moods and honoring needs for space and privacy; offering those little "helps" of proofing, photocopying, and sharing articles, references, and books but also the companionship and support of time to talk, listen, ventilate, complain, and tease; and finally, sharing the catharsis that comes with a chance to say "it" whatever it was. Commitment, in this case, meant being a good listener, without judgment, and honoring whatever was said. I realized how the isolation of my role caused me to need the friendship of these women but be unsure of how much I could trust them. Sometimes I felt used. I wanted to share what I really thought but didn't feel free to do so with everyone—I wanted to reinvent a few close friends from my past experience at another university.*

∽

KAREN: *As I write this, once more I realize that I may not have been able to survive the last few years in higher education without these women. We came together for a variety of reasons, a plethora of expressed personal agendas and academic expectations. In retrospect, it feels as though what we were all seeking was a place for our voices to be heard. A place of trust, respect, and integrity—a place to share and to grow. I now find it both amazing and comforting that we sought this space within the realm of academe. I am amazed because of my own disillusionment with "higher" education. I am comforted because we somehow found each other—five women willing to take a proactive stance for educational transformation and struggling to work within the system.*

*I wonder what really drew us together and I wonder in what form we'll survive the current chaos. I have no doubt that we will survive—as individuals, richer for the group experience, if not as members of this group. I know we will survive because in this society, simply being women is to continually risk the fire. I worry that we have become tempered steel and are taking out our frustrations, differences, dissonance, on each other. It is a scary thought because we have learned enough about each other to harm, if not enough to heal, and we have learned to recognize our strength by working together. I wonder if we have also acquired wisdom and compassion.*

∽

GRETCHEN: *Our collaborative process and what we have learned about learning and our taken-for-granted cultural framing have been irreplaceable. It has been a time of growth, of learning to appreciate and develop our own strengths in the willingness to struggle with each other's difference: difference in style of participation and writing, difference in needs from each other, and difference in sensed responsibilities beyond the group and beyond the academy. We have been willing to move beyond the writing and critiquing purpose of our group's formation and to take the risk of honest reflection and dialogue, to look at our process as data. Not only has it been a way of informing ourselves and each other of our cultural, class, and personal, psychological selves, but it has opened up our learned and taken-for-granted cultural, gendered, verbal, and nonverbal attitudes, assumptions, and expectations.*

*Several things have helped to shape our friendships that have to do directly with the dynamic of forming the collaborative process. We are similar enough in the sense of job responsibility and meeting final deadlines, yet we have been willing to consciously negotiate how to be supportive and tolerant of differences in how we prepare and collaborate for those final dates. That is not to say these areas haven't been problematic; they have, but we have been willing to talk about them, at the time or after the fact, and it has always been illuminating. Interestingly enough, most often what we had thought as the reason for one of the other participants not meeting our or my expectations, the reasons for conflict, turned out to be something different from what we expected; and we learned something very valuable about another way of being in the world. Staying in the group has been a constant reminder of how much we take for granted in our use of language, our conceptualization and reading of others' behavior, of what we have set ourselves to do as part of the collaborative effort, of our compulsive "should do's." It has been a reminder of how much we assume "they" are like "us" or are not like "us." It is a reminder of the subtleties that have to be explained and talked about over and over in human relationships, let alone across more obvious issues of difference.*

*Although the women in our collaborative research group have all grown up within the mainstream culture of the United States, we understand ourselves to have diverse cultural and religious lenses and different conceptualizations of the same important words and meanings. Yet, obviously, we have found things in common which continue to hold us together. Sometimes, it seems we have different words for these shared meanings. Through these almost 4 years of intensive work together, it is my sense that we held our working relationship together through our separately formed friendships—the outside things we share. Otherwise, as work-oriented overachievers, would we have stayed together only for the specific purpose of the seminar on feminist theory and pedagogy, to learn about proposal writing, and then gone our separate ways? We all have enormous pulls in other directions. We each have other agendas to deal with both in our academic and in our personal lives. We are all on a different step toward our professional goals. We all value teaching not as a separate job, but as a way of life, as part of who we are, what we believe.*

*Even in the beginning, our group began with heated discussions over the language we used to interpret our roles as practitioners, over the meaning and use of imposition and expert knowledge, over the meaning and practice of commitment. What is an individual's responsibility and from where does it come? What is power and empowering? I argued and found out that my sense of individuality comes from and resides in a different place from theirs. I find my sense of sharing, of the appropriateness of certain things, is different from theirs. I make assumptions that what feels awkward for me is not so for them.*

*How much have we been taught to project and assume it is easier for someone else, for the mythical "them"? Sometimes, at such moments, I feel my own prejudice through these women, as "white women" and not as who I know they are as part of my support group, as my friends. But then we have all felt the dissonance of this whole academic journey. It has proved to be about trying to "stay alive" and helping others to "stay alive," and to do it with integrity through gendered, racist, and class-determined rites of passage.*

∽

**KAREN:** *I feel as though we are shadows, irritating presences, guilty reminders for those who believe in tidy carnage, who have perpetrated and implicitly supported,* *but never experienced, a massacre. As I watch this, am I part of this? I wonder about the role of the group in this time of chaos. I wonder **what** we are here to learn from one another. I wonder if we test one another because we want to know each other or if we do it in an attempt to prove that we do. Is collaboration so rare that we have to battle not only the institution but our own deeply ingrained patterns of interaction? Will we be capable of forging new bonds, or will the potential pain of separation be so great that we will not be able to risk touching one another?*

༄

**PETRA:** *Looking back, I wonder how naive I was to think that this would occur naturally, especially in light of the different roles we had in the group. How could we have ignored the fact that Jan was our professor, chaired our dissertation committees, was invested with powers bestowed on her by her position that were central to our relationship with her? The suspicion and distrust of outside forces have also threatened our group. The power and presence of women working together have been unsettling to those unaccustomed to hearing the sounds of women's voices.*

*As outside pressures mounted, my resolve to defeat the institutional structures which serve to divide and conquer and to impose autonomy and individualism was strengthened. The neat separation of work and family, school and home, teacher and mother, that results from these divisions clouds the complex processes of identification and differentiation that make up women's realities. The totality, the complexity, the multiplicity of our lives, our distinctly female consciousness, have been muted by the institutionalized subordination of women to men. To keep dislodged, to isolate, to deny the existence of a woman's culture, are to keep us disempowered.*

༄

**JAN:** *Imposition, for me, is all about control and power. What is most difficult for me is letting go of control. As the oldest in my family and the one who always had to get home, start dinner, be responsible for my sisters and brother, I have struggled, it seems forever, with my need to be in charge, so that unnamed disasters won't occur. I can remember being upset when some of you did not meet my expectations of the "good graduate student," didn't make it to our meetings, or seemed to dismiss my preoccupation with getting "the work" done. Also, I recall sensing that, as major professor, I should chide you to get your dissertations done, yet not wanting to be too active in assuming that role, which seemed so unpleasant and impositional. I had to remind myself that it was OK to let you have some space to create your own time line as long as you knew I was there to help when you needed it.*

*I get tired of continually being needed to be on! Petra, thank God, took over a lot—sometimes I wonder if it was because I hadn't been doing the leadership organization thing well enough—I wished we could share that responsibility more, and yet I felt it was primarily mine. It has been suggested that I have a high need for control. My belief is that I have trouble tolerating things not getting done or not getting done "well," so I take control and responsibility to ensure that things move on.*

*Growing up the oldest daughter in a working-class family, becoming the surrogate mother in my early 20s when my own mother died, I find my control issues very much tied up with class and gender expectations. I was raised to take care of people, and to take care meant to be in control, to ensure that nothing terrible would happen to the others. Living in a world which betrayed us and devalued us at every opportunity, we learned early to take control and thus protect ourselves as best we could. Within my family as well as within the group it almost seemed an issue of being indispensable—and I resist considering the questions of whether you really need me, whether our group has outlived its purpose, and whether continuing to meet is an even greater imposition.*

*Do Petra and I collude to control? Do we both impose our agendas on the group? Probably. Is it necessary that we do so? Probably. I believe, however, that Karen and Gretchen had the real control—they could choose to focus on and worry about their personal issues, ignoring the rest of us in the group and thus unraveling the edges of the group cohesiveness. It seemed like they took the liberty to be outrageous, to test our commitment and affection. And Susan, the peacemaker, her control is in understanding us too well—no one fools Susan.*

*In looking at our myriad impositions I am reminded of the metaphor of family—still. Petra, strong, confident, surrogate patriarch—sense of direction—I don't think she really wants to be cast in that role but she does it so well. Me—harried, distracted, sometimes crazy and overwhelmed mother—too many chirping open mouths, sometimes I resent it—wish I could just focus on our group—don't have the patience and energy for all the needy people. The group knows me, knows what I need, can treat me and seduce me with their generosity—who has the real control?*

*So what is control? That which we all wish to project—self-control, coolness, brilliance, polish—like Petra, like Susan (what she says is usually true), like Karen, who can absolutely demand that we pay attention, that we at least try to be honest to our values—is Karen our conscience? Like Gretchen, outside the circle, gone, acknowledging her earthy, bodily reality—able to be the friend, the cared about, the excused, because, in the end, it is not us that she really needs.*

*How did these dynamics play out? The power in the group is in the constant swinging to the loss of control and our commitment to come back, to continue to care, to place our work with each other at the center of our lives—will this continue? Can we preserve the group cohesion through the chaos of the double closing of this phase of our academic lives?*

∽

SUSAN: *Power has to do with control—implicit or explicit—and competition, dominance and submission, inclusion and exclusion, participation and resistance. Perhaps more than any of these, however, power has to do with need. Within any group, I think each member symbolically acts out a familiar way of demonstrating need. Maybe it is a desire to feel included, or to take care or to be taken care of, or to take control when things are perceived as out of control. What is my need? In this group, I am Alice Miller's (1981) "gifted child":*

> *This child had an amazing ability to perceive and respond intuitively, that is, unconsciously, to this need of the mother, or of both parents, for her to take on the role that had unconsciously been assigned to her. . . . She could sense that she was needed. . . . This ability is then extended and perfected. Later, these children . . . become mothers (i.e., confidantes, comforters, advisers, support- ers) . . . and eventually develop a special sensitivity to unconscious signals manifesting the needs of others. (p. 8)*

*Our perceptions of this experience differ, at times dramatically. In my image, Jan was the mother, the leader; we placed her in that role and she felt compelled to assume the responsibility. No matter how close I felt to her or how affectionate I always sensed our feelings for each other were, and regardless of the length and comfort of our working relationship, I always mentally held Jan in the mother/leader role. This manifested itself in imagining I was writing for her, anticipating her expectations, assuming she would set deadlines and "assign- ments." To a great extent, Jan fulfilled those functions; to what extent was that appropriate or fair? I still struggle with that question.*

*I often wondered if Jan was burdened, yet the ways in which I responded to her needs, nurtured her, did not include assuming or sharing a leadership role in the group. I listened to her, taught with her, complimented and supported her, and more than anything, identified with her overactive superego, her seemingly endless ability to give to and take care of others. Petra took care of Jan in another way; seeing Jan take on the burden of our group's work, Petra became slowly, but with certainty, what she calls the "taskmaster." Soon into our process, we began looking to Petra for leadership, deadlines, direction. Unfortunately, my truth was that Petra and Jan were running the show, and with Gretchen's gift for intellectual discussion, the three became the group, unintentionally leaving Karen and me on the mar- gins—quiet or preoccupied. Milwaukee in early November was a milestone in that we began, albeit only briefly, to address such internal dynamics.*

∽

GRETCHEN: *My sense is that our group struggles with these issues not only intellectually but in our lives. We have survived our group process, gained confi- dence in our very different styles, agendas, family and community needs and commitments. Because of our work together and through it, we have become friends. Yet the fabric of our union is both fragile and tough. Our needs, sometimes, seem overwhelming, both our own and each other's. The questions, the problems as they arise, our emotional involvement, the push and pull of our commitments, for which there is never enough time. The push-pull of guilt or frustration—how can we take time for the human, if a hug and "pregame locker talk" aren't enough?*

*We all have so much to do, to get done. What about the ongoing issue of unequal participation and doing one's fair share, not making excuses? How are colleagues, in these circumstances, supposed to carry someone who isn't jumping through the hoops as well as she is capable of doing or as quickly as she should? Whose criteria are really measuring these? The group gets larger. By popular demand, other women colleagues in our field who were not part of the original group form another group in which we are to be included—they also work with our mentor and advisor, and three of us choose not to be a part of the second group. What will happen to that fragile fabric of friendship and the incredible sense of finding our own voice, being supported and appreciated in those very differences when we have to keep finding time to hash out, to reach understanding, to reach consensus?*

*We have a previous history together; we took precious time, sometimes far into the night, to work, to sort out the dynamic of collaboration. We don't have time now. Will it have to be a more professional relationship now? What does that mean? Will it mean more of the deadlines and responsibilities for reading and giving feedback when I can't seem to get even my own work done? Otherwise, how will we get the work done which is the reason the other women want to join? It is an important shift because one of our underlying questions has been, how do we transfer this experience to other work areas, particularly our classrooms?*

ᴄᴡ

**JAN:** *How do I consider this group and my place with them? It is awkward; I call them my research group and my work group—is that a way of denying the power of the relationships, the friendships, and the occasional discomfort? While these people, different ones at different times, provided a major part of my social and emotional support system, I felt that I must maintain a distinct boundary to "protect and preserve" the faculty–student relationships. How can I really tell someone how I feel about her actions when I know it is important that I be there as her advisor; that I will support her, no matter what; that I will suspend, in fact, personal feelings to make things as fair for her as possible? It is in this way that the group really has made me look at commitment as a teacher and the ways institutional regulations and rituals have clouded the simplicity of human relations.*

*How could I be the fair and equitable mentor to all, yet maintain individual interpersonal relationships with each of the other participants? I seem to always have trouble with boundaries—we don't share with each other in all ways, and I don't understand the relationships. Has Petra become the stable center—the place where I should be if I didn't need to remain outside the circle to be fair, to keep it in place? Perhaps I am the maintainer of the boundaries, after all.*

*And what of the competition? Do I care who gets what favor? It seems that I am not allowed the uniqueness of relationship with each of these women that they have with each other. Do you give all of your children the same number and kinds of birthday presents? Can you ever love them all the same? And yet fairness, jealousy, competition, are the primary obstacles to group process, for me. Do I really want to be that accessible to all these people? Haven't maintaining slight distance and shifting the boundaries been a way of surviving? Don't we all need to keep our separate identities and relationships, too?*

*In the fall of 1990, I pull back, try not to exert leadership. Is this more fair? Will it work if I am more of an equal participant? I wait—what will happen? Nothing much in terms of my need for work—the relationships survive, but I find us back to the forsworn privatization of our complaints and interactions—unhealthy for the group. Why are the group pull and energy less, I ask; have we outlived our purpose? Or is it that I, once again, have chosen to lead in an unfair way, have pulled out the supports that perhaps they still need?*

*I feel like the arbitrator, peacemaker—I cannot be part of the group when my role is to maintain everyone's place both within and outside the group and everyone else's (false) sense of security. Trust, expectations, sharing—sometimes they are right there—why can't we hold them? The question becomes, for me, how can I be truly fair, or perceived as fair anyway, when we are all so different? The shifting balance as we negotiate our projects and selves plays out with the realities of our outside worlds and our connections to our personal cultures.*

∽

PETRA: *Despite the outside pressures and our internal reckoning, we have managed to survive for close to 4 years. Interestingly, we are no closer to having a common goal or commitment. In fact, I would suggest it has become more tenuous. Perhaps our ultimate commitment never was to any tangible goal or product in the first place. I wonder if our claim to be a "research study group" served to legitimize us in the eyes of others and among ourselves, since women who gather together are usually perceived of as merely "gossiping."*

*Perhaps our research group provided the guise under which we could tell our life stories, make some sense of our lives. I wonder if the exchange of our life stories provided a way in which we tested reality in order to modify our own perceptions. It was through the sharing of our stories that we saw ourselves in the reflections of others. As we transverse the multiple realities of our everyday lives, our under-standings of each other were in part determined by our gendered position and, consequently, I believed, our need to survive.*

*Bettina Aptheker (1989: 174) suggests that for women "survival has meant emotional connection." Perhaps that is what our commitment has been all about, to stay whole, to understand the multiple and contradictory strands of our lives, staying real in the process. Our multiple definitions of commitment, our changing needs for degrees of commitment, our different interpretations of what level of commitment each of us has, or had, or should have, are not insignificant. It does matter that we don't all agree, that we all don't interpret events the same, that we haven't come up with any single, right, absolute answer. In fact, I see this as part of our resistance to capitulate and give up a consciousness that we struggle to maintain and that is essential to our survival and identity. Our commitment has been a form of resistance; we have also resisted commitment. This contradiction seems to reflect the reality of our complex lives, which we struggle to claim and name, in our own voices.*

&#8766;

**KAREN:** *I wrote during the fall of 1990 that I felt that we had just experienced glimpses of what we are capable of becoming, individually and as a group. I wrote these things from the heart, in an environment which values only intellectualism—and I was, and am, deeply gratified that these women heard. I now feel that in this process of separation we are not only losing each other and a bit of ourselves, but that we are also losing the power in community, we are slowly unraveling the intangible relational threads that support a group. I am not sure there will be another opening in our lives to offer these gifts created through collaborative processes. These are the questions that working with this group has raised for me . . . and I have no answers.*

*I also wrote in 1990 that the differences, the dissonance, the diversity, have created a tension that is empowering, that strengthens all our voices. That I felt that we were more than the sum of parts. That we were alive with multiple possibilities, rich with multiple voices. That to harm one was to damage the others—to bring joy to one was to inspire the rest. That to walk away, to withdraw, was comparable to strangling in isolation—inconceivable in a group process where each thread has become an integral part of the whole. And now I watch us take the pressures and the angst of the university and allow those externals to shatter a fragile configuration. Some call death an end; I wait for transformation.*

&#8766;

**SUSAN:** *Cultural differences again. Our different perceptions of the group inform our expectations of its members. I did desire and expect elements of the "conscious-ness-raising" intimacy, the emotional connection, I have experienced in other groups of women (and also mentioned in Milwaukee). The work should come second, only after we collaborate to understand and see each other. I was mistaken in my belief that the group would eventually take that form.*

*There was clearly appreciation of some difference. The group appreciated my Jewishness, recognized my interest in adolescent girls, understood my struggle to be a practitioner and researcher. Gretchen is Gretchen, sometimes struggling, always able to participate in a discussion. Karen comes to meetings early and slices French bread into a straw basket. Petra is prepared. Jan is everything. The fondness for each other happens, exists without explicit expression; instead, we tease each other with myriad theoretical labels and engage in a never ending debate about who is or isn't a feminist.*

*This speaks again to a shared vision and commitment. We could probably agree that we share a desire to understand and enhance the experience of girls and women. How we do that, in what theoretical framework, differs. I wonder whether these differences should be reconcilable. We have not directly addressed most underlying differences to some sort of closure. Cultural differences are, like personal idiosyncrasies of style, appreciated. Gretchen's clothes, jewelry, way of speaking. Petra's organization, her beautiful tea parties. Karen nimbly jumps from one rock to the other among the waves; respects and knows the outdoors. Jan talks about farm animals, cooks Scandinavian dishes, reminds us to ask questions about class bias. And me? I am the group "shrink." I can be emotional and ask people to face themselves and each other because it is culturally and professionally appropriate. Worry about my family. At least joke about personal boundaries.*

*I do think we miss deeper "cultural" differences—in values, in voice, in comfort level. Petra used a phrase, "Midwestern love of intellectual debate," to describe a similarity between herself and Jan; I found the phrase useful for its contrast to me, its sense of not-me. I value emotional connection, above all else. I long for the "analytical," the real relational stuff, the long conversations about men, motivations, and mothers, to make the unconscious collaboration explicit.*

∽

**PETRA:** *A major issue throughout our work together has been the struggle to understand the relationship between our individual identity and that of the group. The tension that resulted from group members' need to retain their individuality while at the same time wanting to share a group identity has been a central dynamic of the group. The need for a common direction or goal has seemed necessary in keeping the group together. From the start a strong resistance to conformity or like-mindedness has provided the "difference" that seems to keep us coming back for more. It is the tension, the difference, which keeps me coming back and savoring the experience of our work together.*

*The initial resistance to feminism, or the question of whether we all needed to be feminists, provided me the impetus to requestion my basic assumptions about feminism, its language, its exclusionary possibilities, and its contradictions. My confusion as to why the others in the group didn't identify themselves as feminists also forced me to listen. I could not assume that I knew who they were, for they had no label with which I could identify.*

*Since we did not share a feminist world view, other connections formed. With Susan it was our common German heritage; with Gretchen, our love of books; with Karen, an interest in multicultural education; and with Jan, a similar Midwestern values system and love of intellectual debate. In this sense it was actually through my explorations of our differences that I connected with members of the group.*

*It took time for me to realize that gender was not necessarily the foremost factor in shaping others' lives as it was in mine. For Susan it was ethnicity, for Jan class, for Karen categorical assumptions about class and cultural identity, and for Gretchen an intertwined configuration of race, gender, and class. What I have come to understand is that difference is not static or absolute. That at different times in our lives certain factors are more prevalent than others. That to suggest that we can systematically identify, separate, and order the impact of variables like gender, class, and race betrays the complexity of our lived lives.*

∽

**JAN:** *I acknowledge the great differences in our cultural experiences, and yet, for me, ethnic identity is not the only great differentiator. We share being women, and* *having to be "good" academically, especially. For Gretchen and me, the culture of growing up in the 1950s, the work ethic, rural roots, undermined self-esteem. The cultures of class, race, gender—which was/is the most important?*

*In this group it is the sharing of our personal cultures that holds us together despite the difference—our commitment to and need for support and intellectual honesty—our abhorrence of oppression. Defining cultural differences by ethnic origins is hard for me with this group because I see Gretchen's Native American upbringing and values and Susan's German-Jewish identity as congruent with my second-generation immigrant experience. Despite our shared European roots, Karen and Petra represent, culturally, that which I might have liked but could never be—social class is everything. Sometimes I think we are radically diverse—other times I believe we are essentially similar, just manifesting it all differently! And yet each woman in the group reflects a different part of me.*

⌒∿

**GRETCHEN:** *How do I clarify for others what my feelings and thoughts were that came to light through our working together? Why do I feel so different? In my life, the historic and the political were never separate from the stories, from our lives and the lives of our relatives. Even as a child, I participated with my mother and my grandmother in peaceful sit-ins. My mother, her sisters, my grandmother, and my grandfather asked to be heard in the whiteman's language and in his manner. They were respectful. So, even now, I am caught between my anger and my hope, between trying to live as I believe, in some sort of ecological balance and a university career. How do I get my degree and find a university environment that will allow me to pursue what I believe I need to do and be? How can I help in the larger arena with issues of education for those marginalized, and not be untrue to my own Indian community and beliefs? I don't know if it is possible. What should I be doing as a person whose meaning lies in the meaning of the whole? Because the pieces don't fit anymore, I feel lost. I keep remembering what a Hopi elder once said when a reporter asked why the Indian people didn't rise up against the federal government's continual legal misappropriations and broken promises and treaties. The Hopi said, "In a thousand years, what does it matter?"*

*That, for me, speaks a world of difference in how some of us see our connections and importance in the larger meaning of our existence here on this planet. I see it as a sacred place, as our mother of all mothers. Native Americans have 40,000 and more years of stories and songs of our being here in this place. We have always welcomed others of good heart. We have always thought we had more to learn. We have always tried to respect ways we didn't always agree with or understand. The difference is in the kind of pride, perhaps. It is not and should not be the hubris of the Greeks that has dogged the Christian civilizations' warrior, racist, and ethnocentric mentality.*

*I can understand how class became part of the issue in translating a sense of difference for some of us in our research for the original imposition paper presented in Boston in 1990. I can also understand class as a part or the focus of the deconstructing of self and being a lens with which to name one's experience. But I suppose I have the same problem with class as my personal issue as Jan has with naming her issues as primarily related to her northern European cultural roots. If class is so overriding for her as the issue, how does it affect her relationship with all or each of us within the group? Is she, as someone suggested, too culturally embedded in the Cartesian gendered world view to see the issues as cultural? She said she found clarification in critical theory after not finding it in psychology. It is interesting that we all value the framing of our images enough to resist the pressure to revise those frames toward those preferred by others in our group. What keeps reoccurring is a sense of pressure around the language of feminist theory and pedagogy and what that means, given the languages with which we learned to name our personal and professional experience. Karen and I are still struggling with what feminist thought is about. We found the naming of our experiences more meaningful elsewhere. Petra and Jan seemed to find echoes of the voices through feminist writers. I, for one, have found support in what the feminists have accomplished, their process, what they have "dug up" historically, what they have chosen to deconstruct about language and culture. However, I have not found my Native American Indian voice, my place, among the majority of published mainstream feminists or among feminists of color.*

∽

SUSAN: *The holidays pass; we meet in early January, at the start of winter term, in my house. On one level: Petra and I complain softly to each other that "hosting" our group meetings is becoming a burden; it imposes on our partners; our mutual European upbringing demands that the house be CLEAN and we offer food— which gets costly; and probably more specific to me and my acute sensitivity to blurred psychological boundaries, a sense of control over and ownership of one's space and privacy is diminished. And there's time, or no time, I should say. We pour over our datebooks for the umpteenth time, looking for a gap, a space, a compromise. In this as with the other too-numerous-to-mention factions of my life, I am the limit setter, the busy one, the perpetually guilty one, the one labeled uncommitted or resistant, but I am really overwhelmed. Time. Entangled with commitment. With difference.*

*On another level. Space. Food. Time. Others. We each have a need for privacy and acceptance, nurturance and sustenance, understanding and flexibility, and faith and respect. I juggle so much and so many, and come close to cracking often. When I set limits, as I did at this particular meeting, try to take care of myself, to say honestly what I can and cannot do, Petra feels "abandoned"; Karen feels "annoyed"; Jan looks worried but I know understands. Unable to tolerate what Karen has earlier termed the "internal dissonance," the sense of being immobilized by too many conflicting demands, I withdraw, depressed, and sit in my rocking chair while the telephone rings repeatedly. No, I cannot turn on the answering machine; it may be someone who needs me: a client, a student, my mother.*

∽

PETRA: *Food. We must spend half our time talking about food, who brings what, how much, whose turn. What are the issues? Well, I am certainly invested in food; not only do I love food, but preparing it, serving it, and creating it are the avenues through which I can express my care and disguise my needs to nurture.*

*The carefully set table, flowers, and warm muffins, are safe ways to show affection. Yet sometimes I wonder if the formality of the tea, its high structure, keeps us at a distance after all. It is supposed to be our time to relax, to socialize, yet our teas, as well as other "social" activities, often tend to be awkward and contrived, at least for me. We don't know what to say to each other after all.*

*When and where to meet have become issues that allow us to work out other underlying tensions. The fact that I no longer wanted to meet at my house so often certainly had to do with the fact that Andreas was feeling displaced, but it also had to do with my anger that I wasn't being appreciated and that I felt taken advantage of. Every other week, I was providing food, drink, and my home. The money and the time I spent to do this I felt were taken for granted, to the point that people stopped bringing food or asking what they could bring. Of course, I didn't have to do all the work, but in part due to my European upbringing I would have felt uncomfortable not having food and a clean house. That people weren't sensitive to this or didn't know me well enough to understand this was disturbing.*

*I think it is really funny how the opening up of our calendars is the sign of closure of our meetings. Our obsession with organizing our time (or should I say my obsession) is perhaps symbolic of my need for control, but also my need to categorize and understand my relationships. By planning our interactions regularly I know what is expected of me, when it is expected. It is a way of maintaining boundaries so that I don't get too close and get hurt.*

∽

JAN: *I sit at my computer, trying to figure out why I am writing about food, settings, calendars—the part of the group process in which I have the least interest. I think back to the evening at the Glenwood when we talked of our analytic categories and decided who would do what, of how I really wanted to write about the issues of power and control but so did others, of how, as the good mentor-mother, I deferred and took what was left—the leftovers—so motherly. I reflect on that incident as symbolic of my participation in the group—neither in nor out—kind of an apartment house manager, musical score arranger, or student teacher placement person—charged with enormous responsibility for ensuring that things go "right" but needing to do it in such a way that everyone is taken care of unobtrusively. I see these women doing these things for other students, in other settings—why not here?*

*Perhaps it was my hesitation at taking on one additional responsibility for the group that made me resist making them completely part of my family; perhaps it was my own reluctance to share my personal space with work—or my dis-ease with being at home, with cooking, with all things domestic. I became annoyed that it was such a big deal—who cared where we were? Although I greatly enjoyed the comfort and hospitality of others' homes, I could not be bothered with those details myself. And me the mother? Ironic.*

*What then were the dynamics around these decisions? The emphasizing of difference, I believe, shattered the happy illusion I had built of a shared reality. It was hard to be at Gretchen's—cats, cold, transients living on her land—it made me confront the real Gretchen apart from the brilliant and witty academic scholar—I got too close to the rawness and chaos of her real life. In an equally odd way, Karen's generous offerings of beautifully prepared food and the cozy comfort of Susan's and Petra's homes were also disquieting. For me, it represented something that was almost too nice; I wanted to say, this is a fairy tale, people don't really live like this—but then, I thought, maybe they do? I dreaded the imposition of my disorganization on these others' lives, revealing my true lack of energy to cope with crumpets and tea, making me face the reality of Wendy's and Burger King and how my job had made my nice desired life too out of control. Stopping hurriedly at Humble Bagel to grab something—not wanting to admit that I had not honored my friends with preparation.*

～

GRETCHEN: *How did these logistics become, finally, so symbolic of why we could no longer do what we had done so well together? For me, logistics are about time and space and how it gets defined and used. We no longer have time right now to share space as a group. What has been going on in our work and our personal lives over our second year together has precluded that sharing. That means that logistics are also about powerful forces in our lives, our resistance or our commitment to those forces that determine how, when, and for what reason we will interact, negotiate, or resist.*

～

KAREN: *On January 29, 1991, the students and faculty in the Division of Teacher Education at the University of Oregon were informed that our program was scheduled to be eliminated. It is impossible to separate this unexpected and catastrophic event from a discussion of the experiences of this group, and of our collaborative process. It is a reality that is all-pervasive; it invades all our work and interactions. It is not the sole reason for our breaking apart, but it feels like the final burden, the force that shattered our fragile configuration.*

*In each of our academic and personal works we have expressed our beliefs in the power of interactive teaching and learning, qualitative and ethnographically informed research, and critical self-reflection. In our research, we each worry about the integrity of textual portrayal and the lack of respect inherent in what sometimes feels like divisive relationships.*

*While we continually discuss our concerns regarding our studies, we rarely leave time to discuss our concerns regarding each other. We do not seem able right now to look at each other. In simplistic terms, I wonder if we backed away from the images and the mirrors, our projections of each other, ourselves, or the reality that human interaction is much more complicated than the mainstream labels of "us"* and "other." I wonder, are we really being fragmented by externals or by internal conflicts we refuse, do not have the time, the energy, to face? What truly frightens me is that I am convinced that a world in which there is no room for this type of sharing is at best unstable, at worst destructive.

ᕯᕽ

PETRA: In the midst of the closing of the College of Education, each of us struggling to finish our dissertations, find jobs, and maintain some sense of sanity, we met to assemble our final presentation. In hindsight, it seems appropriate that at this, our last meeting, we should return to the question of why each of us chose to join the group. I thought a common direction or goal was necessary to keeping the group together. Yet, from the start, it seems our "difference" was really what drew us together time and time again.

ᕯᕽ

SUSAN: Yes, there are external obstacles to this process; yes, women collaborating for social change may be a romantic notion. Deconstructing the collaborative process does not represent a means to an end (a paper, a presentation, a book) but is, in and of itself, an end for me. To see the **internal** obstacles is more difficult; to surface them, more painful, but re-creating the reality of this group and the relationships within it is an impossible task without mutual willingness to do that. And, if not now, when? February 27, 1991, 11:05 p.m. I believe we have reached an impasse.

## REFERENCES

Aptheker, B. (1989). *Tapestries of life*. Amherst: University of Massachusetts Press.

Arnowitz, S., & Giroux, H. (1991). *Postmodern education*. Minneapolis: University of Minnesota Press.

Martin, T.P. (1987). *The sound of our own voices: Women's study clubs, 1860–1910*. Boston: Beacon Press.

Miller, A. (1981). *The drama of the gifted child*. New York: Basic Books.

# EPILOGUE

## 1994

With the closure of the School of Education at the University of Oregon, we scattered across the country, resuming previous work, creating new opportunities. Ironically, this book has become the imposition on our lives, the link that pulls us back to each other and our old issues, the opportunity that allows us to address them once again.

❧

JAN: *I left Eugene frantic, needing to escape the painful and oppressive atmosphere of the University of Oregon. Summer teaching in Wisconsin, surviving 6 depressing months of winter in Kalamazoo, and, finally, beginning to construct a new life, a new job in northern California. Yet I keep going back to Eugene, graduate students to see through their dissertation defenses, old friends to visit, and the inescapable lure of the place that afforded me several of the most rewarding years of my life. On the first trip back over the Siskyou Mountains, I reach the summit and can hardly go on. I stop in Ashland and the strong, rich Allan Brothers coffee reminds me of the goodness of life in Eugene. Later, I drive near campus, past the bookstore, the library, my old office. I'm anxious and angry, mourning the loss, missing my former home, realizing that nothing is the same.*

*Two years later, I relocated to Santa Rosa, bought a house, planted a garden, got my kids into California schools. When I finish this book project, I plan to make blackberry jam. It helps that Susan lives here, too, a comforting connection with the past. I am beginniing to understand my rural heritage and appreciate immensely the farms, gardens, and small towns of Sonoma County. Novelists like Dorothy Allison, Carolyn Chute, Jane Hamilton, and Jane Smiley remind me of the uniqueness of my early life in a small rural northern Wisconsin town. Are farm families working class? Are teachers? I read the stories and realize that somehow the experiences of growing up in rural North America precede and overlap the usual class distinctions.*

*I return to Eugene in August 1994 to finish this project. Eugene seems different, quieter, dustier. Favorite places have closed, and friends have moved on, too. I find our group has changed. In a way, we've become better colleagues, working together on new shared projects, enjoying "normal" life with each other, potluck dinners and trips to the beach or the neighborhood pool. The frantic desperation of finishing dissertations and finding jobs is mostly gone, and we don't seem to intrude on each other's lives as much. I listen to my coauthors' suggestions for the book and find myself saying "whatever," let's just get it done. The intensity of our interactions and the issues that had seemed so important remain real, but a psychological as well as physical distance has been created. I miss the closeness yet feel liberated, unburdened from the responsibilities I had earlier carried so seriously. We are mostly now friends, women with separate lives and responsibilities. We have repositioned ourselves and we must now go on.*

∼

PETRA: *To speak of epilogues is to speak of endings, to suggest closure. One of the profound things that I have learned since coming to Louisiana is the irony of separating past, present, and future. To suggest that I have moved beyond our collaborative group process, that I can now distill the essence of our experience, would be to impose a narrative structure that certainly does not resonate with my experiencing of our work. Too many questions remain, issues are not resolved, and there are more unknowns than knowns. I liken this process to that of my pedagogy, where I strive for questions, unresolved issues and disrupting knowns. My work with these women provided a space to experience this unquiet pedagogy. I carry that into my classroom as I continue teaching in a 5th-year teacher education program and work with graduate students teaching qualitative research and curriculum theory. As I sit each morning at my computer looking out at the dense, lush vegetation of southern Louisiana, trying to finish my own book in time for tenure, I breathe deep and remember that the most powerful aspect of my experiences with this group has been the recognition of the importance of process, of being in the story.*

∼

SUSAN: *I've been here before.*

*I moved home. Home to the familiar sights of suburban row houses and miles of freeway. Home to the sunshine and to my mother and grandmother. Home to teach teachers at a college where I became a teacher 12 years ago. I am a wife and a mother now. As I write this, pushing the stroller back and forth with my other hand, I can think of only one thing to say to Shaina, Carly, Rachel, and all the other young mothers: **Now I really understand.***

*I am in my 4th year as an instructor in a secondary teacher education program at San Francisco State University, a campus considered to be the most anti-Semitic in the country. I was welcomed here with a picture of Hitler on my office door and, at my first Yom Hashoah (Day of Remembrance of the Holocaust), Palestinian students holding up photographs of children in the Occupied Territories. I have tried to find a Jewish niche here—a place to be a culturally identified, political, nonreligious Jew. I met with groups of Jewish male professors, groups where I was often mistaken for someone's daughter or clerical assistant. I tried to start a Jewish Campus Relations Council, to connect Jewish faculty and students with members of the many other communities on campus—to form peaceful and productive alliances. I am involved in a collaboration with an Oakland teacher, an African American woman, Mary Murray; together we have created a curriculum/teaching exchange, teaching student teachers about the Holocaust as part of a "multicultural minicourse" Mary developed at at Fremont High School in Oakland. I am committed to continuing (as I have for 12 years) to teach about the Holocaust, within the context of racism and discrimination.*

*I love teaching the students here, yet struggle to find a niche in a department and institution where my way of working, with integrity (I hope) and relationally, are respected only by a few. My closest friend is a male mentor whom I have known for 12 years. Relationships with women are fraught with mistrust and competitiveness. I sit at meetings and keep waiting for things to be honest, for people to address the immediate problems in how we (don't) communicate, for the politics to get personal.*

*I've been here before.*

∾

**KAREN:** *It is September 1994 and I am reading another draft of this book, actively engaged in an exploration of multiple perspectives. As I read, I renew my appreciation for the power Petra, Susan, Gretchen, and Jan bring to this collaborative venture.*

*Like Gretchen, I have stayed in Oregon. I teach, mother, paint, weave, write grants, garden, collaborate on other books and many conference presentations, learn and find continual joy in my growing family and diverse communities. I remain in Oregon because I am stronger when I am with family, and in my small way, I continue trying to "make real" the experiences of the doctoral program in order to support the dreams of my students and the visions given me by my family and other teachers.*

*Emotionally, spiritually, and intellectually I am doing fine; however, I have found I am much more addicted to coffee and ice cream than I have been willing to recognize. Maybe they will come up with a new study that touts the vitamin and mineral strength of these two foods (no doubt sponsored by the coffee and dairy industries). In the meantime, I buy ice cream for my stepchildren, make industrial-strength coffee for my husband, and in the realm of nutrition, live vicariously, while I thrive personally and professionally from within my families and communities.*

∾

GRETCHEN: *Karen and I are still in Eugene. As I write, it's hard to believe that I defended my dissertation in 1993. The time since has been, as usual, overly full as I try to find a balance in what I believe and what nurtures me as an Anishinabe-Hatcanjgara (Ojibwa-Winnebago) person-woman-new grandmother, healthy being, member of multiple communities. I have published some poetry and been in several art shows featuring Native American Indian artists. I have been asked to contribute to other books and encouraged to get in touch with particular publishers for my work. I have been asked to contribute art work for the cover of the new edition of a friend's novel. I was an adjunct professor at the University of Oregon in ethnic studies, which reminded me of why I loved teaching and why I want to continue. I renewed my self through teaching art forms for the first time over the week-long annual Title Five Native American Kids Camp up in a beautiful lakeside setting near where I live in the foothills of the Cascades. I did some landscaping, house renovation, and interior decorating consulting. Sold some eggs, herbs, and fruit—it is so bountiful around here in August and September, and so much of it goes to waste.*

*In the summer of 1994, I was once again unemployed, with no safety net and no health insurance. I'm still waiting to hear the results of a recent job interview. At this point my education acts as a psychological shield. I knew it was temporary, the fallout from so many years in graduate school. The requirements of the job search, deferment on my school loans, and ongoing research and writing toward publishing represented both an opportunity and a cultural and academic imposition. What if I failed to find the position I yearned to find? I had alternatives, but I wanted to teach and do research in higher education. It is a site of amazing influence and power. It is the site where cultural canon and discourse are reified. As professors and scholars we interact with those who are leaders in their fields, and with the potential future leaders in the dominant culture, the students who are the ones we have traditionally counted on to make institutional change, according to their times. It is a powerful place from which to reach out to our communities and our governmental bodies to create new dialogues and build new bridges more collaboratively.*

*Our core women's support group has once again come together, in a manner of speaking. In rereading, updating, and editing with Karen, through telephone calls to Jan, Petra, and Susan, I feel how much I miss each of them. In the interim, each of us has found out how rare our experiences with each other, our special professors, staff, and other graduate students were. I still feel connected to those people. We each are making our way as members of our families and communities; some are old connections, some are new. I reflect on how, in the beginning, we tentatively reached out, learning to trust each other—learning to risk broaching and talking out small hurts or misunderstandings before they loomed large. These women are still my friends. Petra, Karen, and I talk about how we are again excited about how the book is emerging; and our "work," via technology, feels good.*

*As Petra said the other day, she carries us, and what she learned from us, into her work and classroom even now; so do I. I still believe we were given special gifts within our support for each other's emerging writing, and now, in the time we take to once again connect and reflect. I know it felt hard and bitter at times. But it forced us to learn more about ourselves and group process in important ways. It is there in the text. But it also was a heady experience to have the concerns and solutions we had come to as classroom teachers validated by others as we read, listened, and discussed.*

*I believe the greatest gift I received was confidence in my own writing, my own thinking and research. From my perspective, this group recognized each of our voices. We continue in pursuit of our dreams, more sensitive to when we too impose. And perhaps we are more aware of the frailties of "hubris"—of knowing "I am right," "I have the answers," which makes, by implication in the English language, those who disagree wrong. They bristle, as did we. We have been brought back to the cultural realities and the politics of attempting to move so quickly and too publicly. We have all now experienced, once again, the tenuousness of our positionality in relation to those who defend their positions of power in the status of the Cartesian paradigm of the dominant culture. At the same time, our voices continue to be affirmed as worthy of being heard.*

∾

It is the hope of each of us that our collaborative process will inspire you to create or re-create a place for your voices to be heard.

Respectfully,

Jan Jipson
Petra Munro
Susan Victor
Gretchen Freed-Rowland
Karen Froude Jones

# SELECTED REFERENCES

Abu-Lughod, L. (1990). Can there be feminist ethnography? *Women and Performance: A Journal of Feminist Theory, 5*(1), 7–27.

Acker, J., Barry, K., & Esseveld, J. (1983). Objectivity and truth: Problems in doing feminist research. *Women's Studies International Forum, 6*(4), 423–435.

Aisenberg, N., & Harrison, M. (1988). *Women of academe: Outsiders in the sacred grove.* Amherst: University of Massachusetts Press.

Alcoff, L. (1989). Cultural feminism versus poststructuralism: The identity crisis in feminist theory. In M. R. Malson, J. F. O'Barr, S. Westphal-Wihl, & M. Wyer (Eds.), *Feminist theory in practice and process* (pp. 295–327). Chicago: University of Chicago Press.

Allen, P. G. (1987). Bringing home the fact: Tradition and continuity in the imagination. In B. Swann & A. Krupat (Eds.), *Recovering the word: Essays on Native American literature* (pp. 563–579). Berkeley: University of California Press.

Altbach, P., & Lomotey, K. (1991). *The racial crisis in American higher education.* Albany: State University of New York Press.

Anderson, G. (1989). Critical ethnography in education: Origins, current status and new directions. *Review of Educational Research, 59*(3), 249–270.

Anderson, K., Armitage, S., Jack, D., & Wittner, J. (1990). Beginning where we are: Feminist methodology in oral history. In J. Nielson (Ed.), *Feminist research methods* (pp. 94–112). Boulder, CO: Westview Press.

Anzaldua, G. (1990). *Making face, making soul.* San Francisco: An Aunt Lute Foundation Book.

Apple, M. (1978). The new sociology of education: Analyzing cultural and economic reproduction. *Harvard Educational Review, 48*(1), 495–503.

Apple, M. (1979). *Ideology and curriculum.* London: Routledge and Kegan Paul.

Apple, M. (1990, March). Is there a curriculum voice to reclaim? *Phi Delta Kappan, 71*(7), 526–530.

Apple, M., & Beyer, L. (1988). *The curriculum: Problems, politics and possibilities.* Albany: State University of New York Press.

Aptheker, B. (1989). *Tapestries of life.* Amherst: University of Massachusetts Press.

Arendt, H. (1968). *Between past and future: Eight exercises in political thought.* New York: Viking Press.

Arnowitz, S., & Giroux, H. (1991). *Postmodern education.* Minneapolis: University of Minnesota Press.

Bakhtin, M. (1981). *The dialogic imagination* (C. Emerson & M. Holquist, Trans.). Austin: University of Texas Press.

Bannerji, H., Carty, L., Dehli, K., Heald, S., & McKenna, K. (1991). *Unsettling relations: The university as a site of feminist struggles.* Toronto, Canada: Women's Press.

Bateson, G. (1979). *Mind and nature: A necessary unity.* New York: Dutton.

Bateson, M. C. (1989). *Composing a life.* New York: Atlantic Monthly Press.

Belenkey, M. F., Clinchy, B. M., Goldberger, N. R., & Tarule, J. M. (1986). *Women's ways of knowing: The development of self, voice and mind.* New York: Basic Books.

Benhabib, S. (1990). Epistemologies of postmodernism: A rejoinder to Jean-Francois Lyotard. In L. Nicholson (Ed.), *Feminism/postmodernism* (pp. 107–132). New York: Routledge.

Benhabib, S. (1992). *Situating the self.* New York: Routledge.

Berger, P., & Luckmann, T. (1967). *The social construction of reality: A treatise in the sociology of knowledge.* Garden City, NY: Anchor Books.

Berlak, A., & Berlak, H. (1981). *Dilemmas of schooling: Teaching and social change.* New York: Methuen.

Berman, L., Hultgren, F., Lee, D., Rivkin, M., & Roderick, J. (1991). *Toward curriculum for being.* Albany: State University of New York Press.

Bloom, L., & Munro, P. (1995). Conflicts of selves: Non-unitary subjectivity in women administrators' life history narratives. In A. Hatch & R. Wisniewski (Ed.), *Life history and narrative* (pp. 99–112). London: Falmer Press.

Bowers, C. (1993). *Critical essays on education, modernity, and the recovery of the ecological imperative.* New York: Teachers College Press.

Bowers, C. (1993). *Education, cultural myths, and the ecological crisis: Toward deep changes.* Albany: State University of New York Press.

Bowers, C., & Flinders, D. (1990). *Responsive teaching.* New York: Teachers College Press.

Britzman, D. (1991). *Practice makes practice.* Albany: State University of New York Press.

Britzman, D. (1994, April). *On refusing explication: A non-narrative narrativity.* Paper presented at the annual meeting of the American Educational Research Association, New Orleans, LA.

Butler, J. (1990). *Gender trouble: Feminism and the subversion of identity.* London: Routledge.

Cancian, F. (1989). Feminism and participatory research (pp. 29–32). *CSWS Review,* Center for the Study of Women in Society, University of Oregon, Eugene.

Casey, K. (1993). *I answer with my life: Life histories of women teachers working for social change.* New York: Routledge.

Catalano, A. (1992). *Reflective, collegial professional development in pre-service teacher education: A relational perspective.* Unpublished doctoral dissertation, University of Oregon, Eugene.

Chevigny, B. (1984). Daughters writing: Toward a theory of women's biography. In C. Ascher, L. DeSalvo, & S. Ruddick (Eds.), *Between women* (pp. 357–381). Boston: Beacon Press.

Chodorow, N. (1978). *The reproduction of mothering.* Berkeley: University of California Press.

Chodorow, N. (1979). Feminism and difference: Gender, relation and difference in psychoanalytic perspective. *Socialist Review, 9*(14), 51–70.

Christian, B. (1988). The race for theory. *Feminist Studies, 14*(1), 68–79.

Christman, J. (1988). Working the field as female friend. *Anthropology and Education Quarterly, 19*(2), 70–85.

Clifford, J. (1988). *The predicament of culture: Twentieth century ethnography, literature, and art.* Cambridge, MA: Harvard University Press.

Clifford, J., & Marcus, G. (1986). *Writing culture: The poetics and politics of ethnography.* Berkeley: University of California Press.

Comstock, D. (1982). A method for critical research. In E. Bredo & W. Feinberg (Eds.), *Knowledge and values in social and education research* (pp. 370–390). Philadelphia: Temple University Press.

Connelly, F. M., & Clandinin, D. J. (1988). *Teachers as curriculum planners: Narratives of experience.* New York: Teachers College Press.

Connelly, F. M., & Clandinin, D. J. (1990). Stories of experience and narrative inquiry. *Educational Researcher, 19*(4), 2–14.

Cornbleth, C. (1990). *Curriculum in context.* New York: Falmer Press.

Crapanzano, V. (1980). *Tuhami: Portrait of a Moroccan.* Chicago: University of Chicago Press.

Crow Dog, M. (1990). *Lakota woman.* New York: HarperCollins.

DuBois, E., & Ruiz, V. (Eds.). (1990). *Unequal sisters: A multicultural reader in U.S. women's history.* London: Routledge.

Duelli Klein, R. (1983). How to do what we want to do: Thoughts about feminist methodology. In G. Bowles & R. Duelli Klein (Eds.), *Theories of women's studies* (pp. 105–116). London: Routledge and Kegan Paul.

Elkind, D. (1984). *All grown up and no place to go: Teenagers in crisis.* New York: Addison-Wesley.

Ellsworth, E. (1989). Why doesn't this feel empowering?: Working through the repressive myths of critical pedagogy. *Harvard Educational Review, 59*(3), 297–324.

Emecheta, B. (1979). *The joys of motherhood.* New York: George Braziller.

Erdrich, L. (1985). Beet queen. In S. Walker, (Ed.), *The Graywolf annual two: Short stories by women* (pp. 15–31). St. Paul, MN: Graywolf Press.

Erdrich, L. (1987). *The beet queen.* New York: Bantam Books.

Erikson, E. (1968). *Identity, youth and crisis.* New York: W. W. Norton.

Everhart, R. (1977). Between stranger and friend: Some consequences of "long term" field work in schools. *American Educational Research Journal, 14,* 1–15.

Faulconer, T. (1992). *Situating trends in environmental education within the ecological debate.* Unpublished doctoral dissertation, University of Oregon, Eugene.

Felman, S., and Laub, D. (1992). *Testimony: Crises of witnessing in literature, psychoanalysis, and history.* New York: Routledge.

Fine, M. (1988). Sexuality, schooling and adolescent females: The missing discourse of desire. *Harvard Education Review, 58*(1), 29–53.

Fine, M. (1994). Re-inventing the hyphen. In N. Denzin & I. Lincoln (Eds.), *Handbook of Qualitative Research* (pp. 70–82). New York: Sage.

Flax, J. (1989). Postmodernism and gender relations in feminist theory. In M. R. Malson, J. F. O'Barr, S. Westphal-Wihl, & M. Wyer (Eds.), *Feminist theory in practice and process* (pp. 51–74). Chicago: University of Chicago Press.

Flax, J. (1990). *Thinking fragments: Psychoanalysis, feminism and postmodernism in the contemporary west.* Berkeley: University of California Press.

Foucault, M. (1980). *The history of sexuality: Vol. 1. An introduction* (R. Hurley, Trans.). New York: Vintage/Random House.

Fraser, N. (1989). *Unruly practices: Power, discourse and gender in contemporary social theory.* Minneapolis: University of Minnesota Press.

Freed-Rowland, G. (1993). *North American indigenous women of the First Nations: Our own voices, our own songs, our own landscapes.* Unpublished doctoral dissertation, University of Oregon, Eugene.

Freire, P. (1973). *Pedagogy of the oppressed.* New York: Seabury Press.

Fry, K. (1992). *Collaborating on the planning, implementation and evaluation of a multicultural curriculum*. Unpublished doctoral dissertation, University of Oregon, Eugene.

Geiger, S. (1986). Women's life histories: Methods and content. *Signs, 11*(2), 334–351.

Geiger, S. (1990). What's so feminist about women's oral history? *Journal of Women's History, 2*(1), 169–182.

Gilligan, C. (1982). *In a different voice: Psychological theory and women's development.* Cambridge, MA: Harvard University Press.

Gilligan, C., Lyons, N. P., & Hamner, T. J. (Eds.). (1990). *Making connections: The relational world of adolescent girls at Emma Willard School.* Cambridge, MA: Harvard University Press.

Gilmore, L. (1994). *Autobiographics: A feminist theory of women's self-representation.* Ithaca, NY: Cornell University Press.

Giroux, H. (1986). Curriculum, teaching and the resisting intellectual. *Curriculum and Teaching, 1*(1 & 2), pp. 33–42.

Giroux, H. A., Penna, A. N., & Pinar, W. F. (Eds.). (1981). *Curriculum and instruction: Alternatives in education.* Berkeley, CA: McCutchan.

Gitlin, A. D. (1990). Educative research, voice and school change. *Harvard Educational Review, 60*(4), 443–466.

Gluck, S., & Patai, D. (1991). *Women's words, women's words, women's words: The feminist practice of oral history.* New York: Routledge.

Golde, P. (1970). *Women in the field: Anthropological experiences.* Chicago: Aldine.

Gore, J. (1993). *The struggle for pedagogies.* New York: Routledge.

Gramsci, A. (1971). *Selections from the prison notebooks.* New York: International.

Greene, M. (1975). Curriculum and cultural transformation: A humanistic view. *Cross Currents, 25*(2), 175–186.

Greene, M. (1994). The lived world. In L. Stone (Ed.), *The education feminism reader* (pp. 17–25). New York: Routledge.

Gross, E. (1986). What is feminist theory? In C. Pateman & E. Gross (Eds.), *Feminist challenges: Social and political theory* (pp. 190–204). Boston: Northeastern University Press.

Grumet, M. (1988). *Bitter milk: Women and teaching.* Amherst, MA: University of Massachusetts Press.

Grumet, M. (1990). On daffodils that come before the swallow dares. In E. Eisner & A. Peshkin (Eds.), *Qualitative inquiry in education* (pp. 101–120). New York: Teachers College Press.

Gunn Allen, P. (1989). *The sacred hoop: Recovering the feminine in American Indian traditions.* Boston: Beacon Press.

Harding, S. (Ed.). (1987). *Feminism and methodology.* Bloomington: Indiana University Press.

Harding, S. (1989). Is there a feminist method? In N. Tuana (Ed.), *Feminism and science* (pp. 17–32). Bloomington: Indiana University Press.

Harding, S. (1989). The instability of the analytical categories of feminist theory. In M. R. Malson, J. F. O'Barr, S. Westphal-Wihl, & M. Wyer (Eds.), *Feminist theory in practice and process* (pp. 15–34). Chicago: University of Chicago Press.

Harding, S. (1992). *Whose science/whose knowledge?* Ithaca, NY: Cornell University Press.

Hawkesworth, M. (1989). Knowers, knowing, know: Feminist theory and claims or truth. In M. R. Malson, J. F. O'Barr, S. Westphal-Wihl, & M. Wyer (Eds.), *Feminist theory in practice and process* (pp. 327–353). Chicago: University of Chicago Press.

Heilbrun, C. G. (1988). *Writing a woman's life.* New York: Ballantine Books.

Hertzberg, H. (1966). *The great tree and the longhouse: The culture of the Iroquois.* New York: Macmillan.

Heslip, R. (1991). *As the curriculum turns: Reconstructing for relational education through reflection and resistance.* Unpublished doctoral dissertation, University of Oregon, Eugene.

Hirsch, M. (1989). *The mother/daughter plot: Narrative, psychoanalysis, feminism.* Bloomington: Indiana University Press.

Hollingsworth, S. (1994). *Teacher research and urban literacy education.* New York: Teachers College Press.

hooks, b. (1989). *Talking back: Thinking feminist, thinking black.* Boston: South End Press.

hooks, b. (1990). *Yearning: Race, gender and cultural politics.* Boston: South End Press.

hooks, b. (1994). *Teaching to transgress: Education as the practice of freedom.* New York: Routledge.

Hurston, Z. N. (1984). *Dust tracks on a road: An autobiography* (R. Hemingway, Ed.). Chicago: University of Illinois Press.

Huyssen, A. (1990). Mapping the postmodern. In L. Nicholson (Ed.), *Feminism/postmodernism* (pp. 234–280). New York: Routledge.

Irigaray, L. (1985). *Speculum of the other woman* (G. Gill, Trans.). Paris: Editions de Minuit. (Original work published 1974)

Jipson, J. (1989, October). *The emergent curriculum: Contextualizing a feminist perspective.* Paper presented at the Bergamo Conference, Dayton, OH.

Jipson, J. (1992). Midwife and mother: Multiple reflections on curriculum, connections, and change. *Journal of Curriculum Theorizing, 10*(1), 89–116.

Jipson, J. (1992). What's feminist pedagogy got to do with early childhood practice? In S. Kessler & B. Swadener, (Eds.), *Reconceptualizing early childhood education* (pp. 149–161). New York: Teachers College Press.

Jipson, J., & Munro, P. (1992). What's real: Fictions of the maternal. *Journal of Curriculum Theorizing, 10*(2), 7–28.

Jipson, J. A., & Proudfoot, R. C. (1990, March). *The challenge and promise of educational reform.* Paper presented at Northwest Holmes Group, Seattle, WA.

Johnson, M. (1988). *Strong mothers, weak wives.* Berkeley: University of California Press.

Jones, K. (1990, April). *Curriculum development in a cross cultural context.* Paper presented at the American Educational Research Association, Boston, MA.

Kingston, M. (1989). *The woman warrior.* New York: Vintage Books.

Kluckhohn, C. (1962). *Culture and behavior: Collected essays.* New York: Free Press of Glencoe.

Kozol, J. (1980). *The night is dark and I am far from home.* New York: Continuum.

Kozol, J. (1991). *Savage inequalities: Children in America's schools.* New York: Crown.

Krieger, S. (1991). *Social science and the self: Personal essays on an art form.* New Brunswick, NJ: Rutgers University Press.

La Croix, D. (1993). *Indian boarding school daughters coming home: Survival stories as oral history of Native American women.* Unpublished doctoral dissertation, University of Oregon, Eugene.

Langness, L. L., & Frank, G. (1981). *Lives: Anthropological approach to biography.* Novato, CA: Chandler and Sharp.

Lather, P. (1986). Research as praxis. *Harvard Educational Review, 56*(3), 257–277.

Lather, P. (1988). Feminist perspectives on empowering research methodologies. *Women's Studies International Forum, 11*(6), 568–581.

Lather, P. (1989, March). *Deconstructing/deconstructive inquiry: The politics of knowing and being known.* Paper presented at the American Educational Research Association, San Francisco, CA.

Lather, P. (1991). *Getting smart: Feminist research and pedagogy with/in the postmodern.* New York: Routledge.

Lather, P. (1993). Fertile obsession: Validity after poststructuralism. *Sociological Quarterly, 34*(4), 673–693.

LeCompte, M. (1993). A framework for hearing silence: What does telling stories mean when we are supposed to be doing science? In D. McLaughlin & W. G. Tierney (Eds.), *Naming silenced lives* (pp. 9–28). New York: Routledge.

Lerner, G. (1986). *Creation of patriarchy.* New York: Oxford University Press.

Lesko, N. (1990). *Social context and the "problem" of teenage pregnancy.* Paper presented at the American Educational Research Association, Boston, MA.

Lessing, D. (1988). *The fifth child.* New York: Random House.

Levesque-Lopman, J. (1990). *Claiming reality: Phenomenology and women's experience.* New York: Rowman & Littlefield.

Lewis, M. (1993). *Without a word: Teaching beyond women's silence.* New York: Routledge.

Lorde, A. (1985). *I am your sister: Black women organizing across sexualities.* New York: Kitchen Table, Women of Color Press.

Lugones, M., & Spelman, E. (1983). Have we got a theory for you!: Feminist theory, cultural imperialism and the demand for "The woman's voice." *Women's Studies International Forum, 6*(6), 573–581.

Luire, N. (1966). *Mountain Wolf Woman, sister of Crashing Thunder: The autobiography of a Winnebago Indian.* Ann Arbor: University of Michigan Press.

Luke, C., & Gore, J. (1992). Women in the academy: Strategy, struggle, survival. In C. Luke & J. Gore (Eds.), *Feminism and critical pedagogy* (pp. 192–210). New York: Routledge.

Maher, F., & Tetreault, M. (1994). *The feminist classroom.* New York: Basic Books.

Mandelbaum, D. (1973). The study of life history: Gandhi. *Current Anthropology, 14*(3), 177–206.

Manganaro, M. (Ed.). (1990). *Modernist anthropology.* Princeton, NJ: Princeton University Press.

Marcus, G., & Fischer, M. (1986). *Anthropology as cultural critique.* Chicago: University of Chicago Press.

Marcus, J. (1984). Invisible mending. In C. Ascher, L. DeSalvo, & S. Ruddick (Eds.), *Between women* (pp. 381–397). Boston: Beacon Press.

Martin, B., & Moharity, C. J. (1986). Feminist politics: What's home got to do with it? In T. G. Lauretis (Ed.), *Feminist study/critical studies* (pp. 191–212). Bloomington: Indiana University Press.

Martin, J. R. (1994). Methodological essentialism, false difference, and other dangerous traps. *Signs, 19*(3), 630–657.

Martin, T. P. (1987). *The sound of our own voices: Women's study clubs, 1860–1910.* Boston: Beacon Press.

Martusewicz, R. (1992). Mapping the post-modern subject: Post-structuralism and the educated woman. In W. Pinar & W. Reynolds (Eds.), *Understanding curriculum as phenomenological and deconstructed text* (pp. 131–158). New York: Teachers College Press.

Mascia-Lees, F. E., Sharpe, P., & Cohen, C. (1989). The postmodernist turn in anthropology: Cautions from a feminist perspective. *Signs, 15*(1), 7–33.

McClaren, P. (1989). *Life in schools.* New York: Longman.

McLaughlin, D., & Tierney, W. (1993). *Naming silenced lives: Personal narratives and processes of educational change.* New York: Routledge.

McRobbie, A. (1982). The politics of feminist research: Between text, talk and action. *Feminist Review, 12,* 46–57.

McRobbie, A. (1991). The culture of working class girls. In A. McRobbie (Ed.), *Feminism and youth culture: From Jackie to just seventeen* (pp. 35–61). Boston: Unwin Myman.

McRobbie, A., & Nava, M. (1984). *Gender and generation.* London: Macmillan.

Merleau-Ponty, M. (Ed.). (1988). *Consciousness and the acquisition of language* (H. Silverman, Trans.). Evanston, IL: Northwestern University Press.

Middleton, S. (1993). *Educating feminists: Life histories and pedagogy.* New York: Teachers College Press.

Mies, M. (1983). Towards a methodology for feminist research. In G. Bowles & R. Duelli Klein (Eds.), *Theories of women studies* (pp. 117–125). London: Routledge and Kegan Paul.

Miller, J. (1987). Women as teachers/researchers: Gaining a sense of ourselves. *Teacher Education Quarterly, 14*, 52–58.

Miller, J. (1989, April). *Critical issues in curriculum.* Paper presented at the annual meeting of the American Educational Research Association, San Francisco, CA.

Miller, J. (1990). *Creating spaces and finding voices.* Albany: State University of New York Press.

Miller, J. (1990). Teachers as curriculum creators. In J. T. Sears & J. D. Marshall (Eds.), *Teaching and thinking about curriculum: Critical inquiries* (pp. 85–96). New York: Teachers College Press.

Minh-ha, T. (1987). Difference: A special third world women issue. *Feminist Review, 25*(1), 5–22.

Minh-ha, T. (1988). Not you/like you: Post colonial women and the interlocking questions of identity and difference. *Inscriptions, 3/4,* 71–77.

Minh-ha, T. (1989). *Woman, native, other.* Bloomington: Indiana University Press.

Mohanty, C., Russo, A., & Lourdes, L. (Eds.). (1990). *Third world women and the politics of feminism.* Bloomington: Indiana University Press.

Moi, T. (1985). *Sexual/textual politics: Feminist literary theory.* New York: Methuen.

Moore, H. L. (1988). *Feminism and anthropology.* Minneapolis: University of Minnesota Press.

Moraga, C., & Anzaldua, G. (1983). *This bridge called my back: Writings by radical women of color.* New York: Kitchen Table, Women of Color Press.

Morrison, T. (1987). *Beloved.* New York: New American Library.

Munro, P. (1990, April). *Common differences: Curriculum decision making and feminist pedagogy.* Paper presented at the American Educational Research Association, Boston, MA.

Munro, P. (1991). *A life of work: Stories women teachers tell.* Unpublished doctoral dissertation, University of Oregon, Eugene.

Munro, P. (1991). Supervision: What's imposition got to do with it? *Journal of Curriculum and Supervision, 7*(1), 77–89.

Munro, P. (1992, April). *Teaching as women's work: A century of resistant voices.* Paper presented at the annual meeting of the American Educational Research Association, San Francisco, CA.

Munro, P. (1993). Continuing dilemmas of life history research: A reflexive account of feminist qualitative inquiry. In D. Flinders & G. Mills (Eds.), *Theory and concepts in qualitative research: Perspectives from the field* (pp. 163–177). New York: Teachers College Press.

Munro, P., and Elliot, J. (1987). Instructional growth through peer coaching. *Journal of Staff Development, 8*(1), 25–28.

Narayan, U. (1988). Working together across difference: Some considerations on emotions and political practice. *Hypatia, 3,* 31–47.

Nicholson, L. (1990). *Feminism/postmodernism.* New York: Routledge.

Noddings, N. (1984). *Caring: A feminist approach to ethics and moral education.* Berkeley: University of California Press.

Noddings, N. (1990). Foreword. In J. T. Sears & J. D. Marshall (Eds.), *Teaching and thinking about curriculum: Critical inquiries* (pp. ix–xi). New York: Teachers College Press.

Olsen, T. (1980). As I stand there ironing. In J. Mazow, (Ed.), *The woman who lost her names.* (pp. 29–37). San Francisco: Harper & Row.

On, B.-A. B. (1993). Marginality and epistemic privilege. In L. Alcoff & E. Potter (Eds.), *Feminist epistemologies* (pp. 83–100). New York: Routledge.

Ong, A. (1988). Colonialism and modernity: Feminist re-presentations of women in non-western societies. *Inscriptions: Feminism and the Critique of Colonial Discourse, 3/4,* 79–93.

Pagano, J. (1990). *Exiles and communities: Teaching in the patriarchal wilderness.* Albany: State University of New York Press.

Patai, D. (1989). *Brazilian women speak: Contemporary life stories.* New Brunswick, NJ: Rutgers University Press.

Paz, O. (1985). *The labyrinth of solitude and other writings* (L. Kemp, Y. Milos, & R. Belash, Trans.). New York: Grove Weidenfield.

Personal Narratives Group. (1989). *Interpreting women's lives: Feminist theory and personal narratives.* Bloomington: Indiana University Press.

Peshkin, A. (1988). In search of subjectivity—one's own. *Educational Researcher, 17*(7), 17–21.

Philips, S. (1983). *The invisible cultures: Communication in classroom and community on the Warm Springs Indian reservation.* New York: Longman. (Original work published 1979)

Pinar, W. F. (1994). *Autobiography, politics and sexuality: Essays in curriculum theory, 1972–1992.* New York: Peter Lang.

Plummer, K. (1983). *Documents of life: An introduction to the problems and literature of a humanistic method.* London: Allen & Unwin.

Pogrebin, L. C. (1991). *Deborah, Golda and me: Being female and Jewish in America.* New York: Crown Books.

Powdermaker, H. (1966). *Stranger and friend: The way of an anthropologist.* New York: W. W. Norton.

Proudfoot, R. (1986). *Model for the synergy of relational education: The dynamics of cultural interaction and connection.* Unpublished manuscript, University of Oregon, Eugene.

Proudfoot, R. (1990). *Even the birds don't sound the same here: The Laotian refugees' search for heart in American culture.* New York: Peter Lang.

Rabinow, P. (1977). *Reflections on fieldwork in Morocco.* Berkeley: University of California Press.

Reinharz, S. (1979). *On becoming a social scientist: From survey research and participant observation to experiential analysis.* San Francisco: Jossey-Bass.

Reynolds, U. (1991). *Teachers' perceptions of kids and the systems: Inclusion, cultures and curriculum.* Unpublished doctoral dissertation, University of Oregon, Eugene.

Rich, A. (1979). *On lies, secrets, and silence.* New York: W. W. Norton.

Richardson, M. (1975). Anthropologist—the myth teller. *American Ethnologist, 2*(3), 517–533.

Richardson, M. (1991). Point of view in anthropological discourse: The ethnographer as Gilgamesh. In I. Brady (Ed.). *Anthroplogical poetics* (pp. 207–214). Savage, MD: Rowman & Littlefield.

Ricoeur, P. (1974). *The conflict of interpretations.* Evanston, IL: Northwestern University Press.

Robertson, C. (1983). In pursuit of life histories: The problem of bias. *Frontiers, 7*(2), 63–69.

Roman, L. G. (1989, April). *Double exposure: The politics of feminist materialist ethnography.* Paper presented at the American Educational Research Association, San Francisco, CA.

Roman, L. G., & Apple, M. W. (1990). Is naturalism a move away from positivism?: Materialist and feminist approaches to subjectivity in ethnographic research. In A. Peshkin & E. Eisner (Eds.), *Qualitative inquiry in education: The continuing debate* (pp. 38–74). New York: Teachers College Press.

Romero, M. (1991, April). *The maid's daughter: A modern version of upstairs/downstairs.* Paper presented to the Center for the Study of Women in Society, University of Oregon, Eugene.

Rosaldo, M., & Lamphere, L. (1974). *Women, Culture and Society.* Stanford, CA: Stanford University Press.

Roy, P., & Schen, M. (1987). Feminist pedagogy: Transforming the high school classroom. *Women's Studies Quarterly, 15*(3 & 4), 110–115.

Ruby, J. (1982). *A crack in the mirror: Reflexive perspectives in anthropology.* Philadelphia: University of Pennsylvania Press.

Ruddick, S. (1989). *Maternal thinking: Toward a politics of peace*. Boston: Beacon Press.

Said, E. (1989). Representing the colonized: Anthropology's interlocutors. *Critical Inquiry, 15,* 205–225.

Said, E. (1993). *Culture and imperialism*. New York: Alfred A. Knopf.

Said, E. (1993). *Orientalism*. New York: Random House. (Original work published 1978)

Salzman, J. P. (1990). Save the world, save myself: Responses to problematic attachment. In C. Gilligan, N. P. Lyons, & T. J. Hamner (Ed.), *Making connections: The relational worlds of adolescent girls at Emma Willard School* (pp. 110–146). Cambridge, MA: Harvard University Press.

Schniedewind, N. (1987). Teaching feminist process. *Women's Studies Quarterly, 15*(3 & 4), 15–31.

Shrewsbury, C. (1987). What is feminist pedagogy? *Women's Studies Quarterly, 15*(3 & 4), 6–14.

Sidel, R. (1990). *On her own: Growing up in the shadow of the American dream*. New York: Penguin.

Silko, L. M. (1977). *Ceremony*. New York: Penguin Books.

Sleeter, C. E., & Grant, C. A. (1987). An analysis of multicultural education in the United States. *Harvard Educational Review, 57*(4), 421–444.

Smith, D. (1989). *The conceptual practices of power: A feminist sociology of knowledge*. Boston: Northeastern University Press.

Smith, S. (1987). *A poetics of women's autobiography*. Bloomington: Indiana University Press.

Smith, S. (1993). *Subjectivity, identity and the body: Women's autobiographical practices in the twentieth century*. Bloomington: Indiana University Press.

Smith, S. (1993). Who's talking/who's talking back?: The subject of personal narrative. *Signs, 18*(2), 392–407.

Souers, T. (1993). *Circles of power: Life histories of native American Indian women elders in education*. Unpublished doctoral dissertation, University of Oregon, Eugene.

Sparkes, A. (1994). Life histories and the issue of voice: Reflection on an emerging relationship. *Qualitative Studies in Education, 7*(2), 165–183.

Spelman, E. (1988). *Inessential women*. Boston: Beacon Press.

Spindler, G. (Ed.). (1982). *Doing the ethnography of schooling: Educational anthropology in action*. Prospect Heights, IL: Waveland Press.

Spivak, G. (1987). *In other worlds: Essays in cultural politics*. New York: Methuen.

Stacey, J. (1988). Can there be a feminist ethnography? *Women's Studies International Forum, 11*(1), 21–27.

Stern, L. (1990). Conceptions of separation and connection in female adolescents. In C. Gilligan, N. P. Lyons, & T. J. Hamner, (Eds.), *Making connections: The relational worlds of adolescent girls at Emma Willard School* (pp. 73–87). Cambridge, MA: Harvard University Press.

Strathern, M. (1987). An acquired relationship: The case of feminism and anthropology. *Signs, 12*(2), 276–292.

Swann, B., & Krupat, A. (Eds.). (1987). *I tell you now: Autobiographical essays by Native American writers*. Lincoln: University of Nebraska Press.

Swann, B., & Krupat, A. (Eds.). (1987). *Recovering the word: Essays on Native American literature*. Los Angeles: University of California Press.

Tokarczyk, M., & Fay, E. (1993). *Working-class women in the academy: Laborers in the knowledge factory*. Amherst: University of Massachusetts Press.

Tolkien, J. R. (1966). *The lord of the rings*. Boston: Houghton Mifflin.

Turner, F. (1986). *Beyond geography: The western spirit against the wilderness*. New Brunswick, NJ: Rutgers University Press.

Van Maanen, J. (1988). *Tales of the field*. Chicago: University of Chicago Press.

Victor, S. (1990). The emerging concerns of adolescent mothers. *Oregon Counseling Association Journal, 12*(2), 25–29.

Victor, S. (1992). Days of their lives: Reflections on adolescent girls and adolescent mothers. *School of Education Review, 4,* 72–81.

Villanueva, A. (1992). *Case studies of Chicano educators who have successfully transisted the public school system and who have not lost their primary cultural identity.* Unpublished doctoral dissertation, University of Oregon, Eugene.

Visweswaran, K. (1988). Defining feminist ethnography. *Inscriptions,* (3 & 4), 27–44.

Visweswaran, K. (1994). *Fictions of feminist ethnography.* Minneapolis: University of Minnesota Press.

Vizenor, G. (1989). *Narrative chance: Postmodern discourse on Native American Indian literatures.* Albuquerque: University of New Mexico Press.

Waite, D. (1993). Teachers in conference: A qualitative study of teacher-supervisor face-to-face interactions. *American Educational Research Journal, 30*(4), 675–702.

Walkerdine, V. (1990). *Schoolgirl fictions.* London: Verso.

Walkerdine, V. (1994). Femininity as performance. In L. Stone (Ed.), *The education feminism reader* (pp. 57–72). New York: Routledge.

Warner, G. (1950). *The box car children.* Chicago: Albert Whitman.

Watson, L., & Watson-Sparks, F. (1985). *Interpreting life histories: An anthropological inquiry.* New Brunswick, NJ: Rutgers University Press.

Weedon, C. (1987). *Feminist practice and poststructuralist theory.* Oxford, England: Basil Blackwell.

Weiler, K. (1988). *Women teaching for change: Gender, class & power.* South Hadley, MA: Bergin & Garvey.

Whitson, J. A. (1991). Poststructuralist pedagogy as counter-hegemonic discourse. *Education and Society, 9*(1), 73–86.

Whorf, B. (1964). A linguistic consideration of thinking in primitive communities. In J. Carroll (Ed.), *Language, culture and society: Selected writings of Benjamin Lee Whorf.* Cambridge, MA: MIT Press.

Wolcott, H. (1990). On seeking—and rejecting—validity in qualitative research. In A. Peshkin & E. Eisner (Eds.), *Qualitative inquiry in education: The continuing debate* (pp. 121–153). New York: Teachers College Press.

Wolcott, H. (1990). *Writing up qualitative research.* Newbury Park, CA: Sage.

# INDEX

# ABOUT THE AUTHORS

GRETCHEN FREED-ROWLAND is an Ojibwa-Winnebago artist, poet, writer, and practitioner whose poetry has been published in *Talking Leaves: The Journal of Deep Ecology and Spiritual Activism*. She currently teaches in the Department of Education at Pacific University in Oregon, is a research associate at the Center for the Study of Women in Society (CSWS) at the University of Oregon, and is and executive member of the Native American Research Committee affiliated with CSWS.

KAREN FROUDE JONES is a research associate at the Institute for a Sustainable Environment at the University of Oregon and Professor of Education at Pacific University. Her work as a practitioner and an advocate for self-sufficiency has been documented in *Akwesasne Notes* (1986), *Talking Leaves: The Journal of Deep Ecology and Spiritual Activism* (1993), and on the "Discovery" channel.

JANICE JIPSON is Associate Professor of Education at Carroll College in Wisconsin, where she teaches in the Graduate Studies Program. Her recent publications have included writings on feminist pedagogy, developmentally appropriate and culturally appropriate practice in early childhood education, and the selective tradition in teacher education. She is co-author with Peter Lang of *Daredevil Research: Recreating Analytic Practice* (forthcoming).

PETRA MUNRO is Assistant Professor in the Department of Curriculum and Instruction and Women's and Gender Studies at Louisiana State University. She has published several book chapters in the area of feminist life history narrative research as well as articles in the *Journal of Curriculum and Supervision, Journal of Curriculum Theorizing,* and *Qualitative Inquiry.* She is currently completing a book, *Rereading "Women's True Profession": Life History Narratives and the Cultural Politics of Teaching.*

SUSAN VICTOR is a lecturer in Secondary Education at San Francisco State University. She is currently involved in a collaborative curriculum development project to integrate the Holocaust into the multicultural curriculum in secondary schools in Oakland. She has published in the *School of Education Review* and *Oregon Counseling Association Journal.*

ISBN 0-89789-436-7

90000>

EAN

9 780897 894364

HARDCOVER BAR CODE